WRITER: **DUANE SWIERCZYNSKI**

ARTIST: **ARIEL OLIVETTI**

LETTERS: **VIRTUAL CALLIGRAPHY'S JOE CARAMAGNA**

ASSISTANT EDITOR: **WILL PANZO**

EDITOR: **AXEL ALONSO**

AND A VERY SPECIAL THANKS TO **SGT. JEFF GUERIN,**
A CABLE FAN AND A REAL HERO.

COLLECTION EDITOR: **JENNIFER GRÜNWALD**
EDITORIAL ASSISTANT: **ALEX STARBUCK**
ASSISTANT EDITORS: **CORY LEVINE** & **JOHN DENNING**
EDITOR, SPECIAL PROJECTS: **MARK D. BEAZLEY**
SENIOR EDITOR, SPECIAL PROJECTS: **JEFF YOUNGQUIST**
SENIOR VICE PRESIDENT OF SALES: **DAVID GABRIEL**
PRODUCTION: **JERRY KALINOWSKI**
BOOK DESIGNER: **RODOLFO MURAGUCHI**

EDITOR IN CHIEF: **JOE QUESADA**
PUBLISHER: **DAN BUCKLEY**

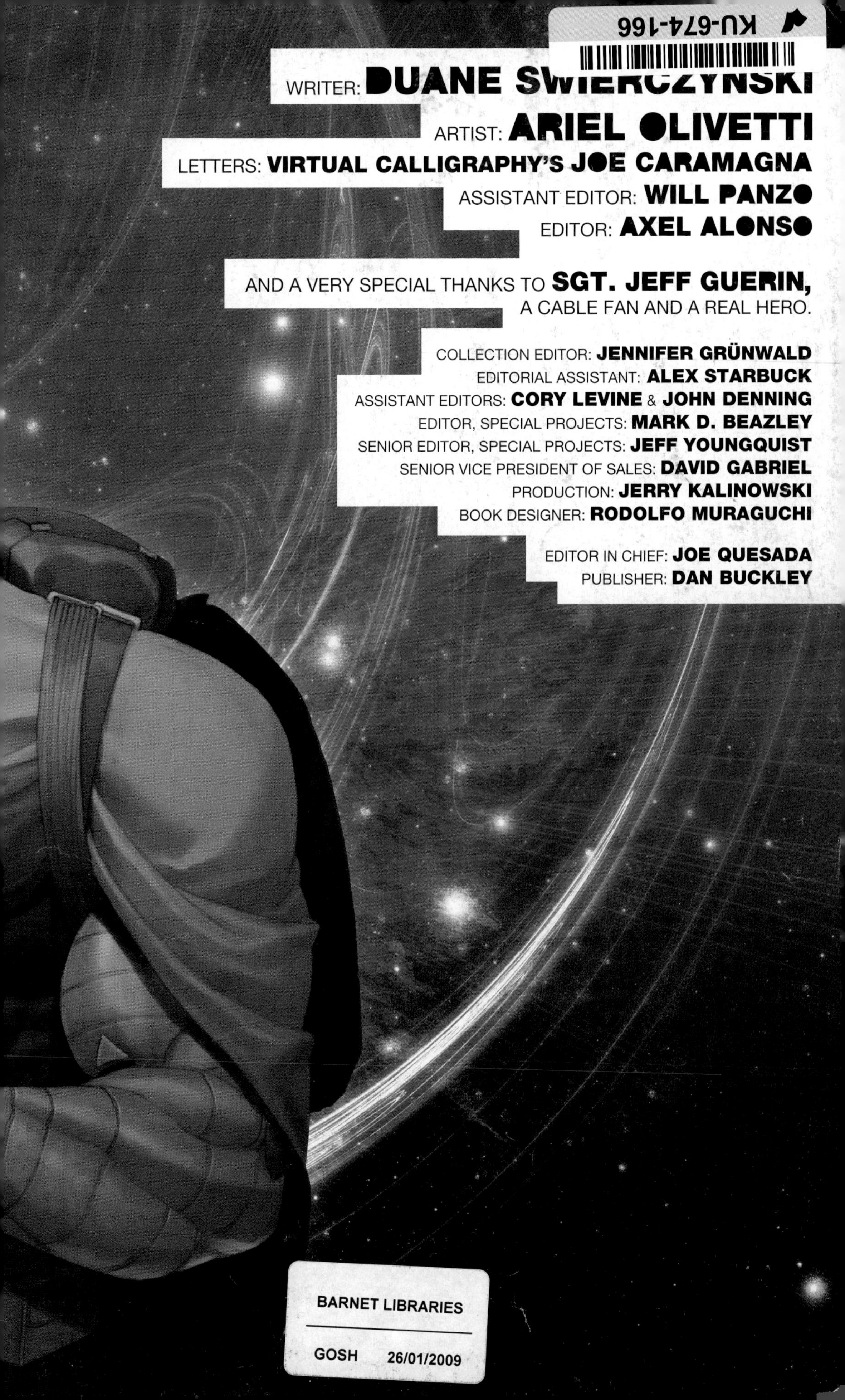

CABLE

Soldier. Hero. X-Man. Nathan Summers, the former mercenary known as Cable, is many things to many people, but above all he is a mutant. Born with special abilities that distinguish him from normal humans, he has fought to prevent his dwindling race's extinction.

Now charged with protecting the first mutant born since M -Day, the day when all but one percent of mutantkind lost their powers, he has escaped with the "messiah baby" into the timestream.

Abandoning his world and his allies, Cable knows that wherever he lands he'll have to fight for survival.

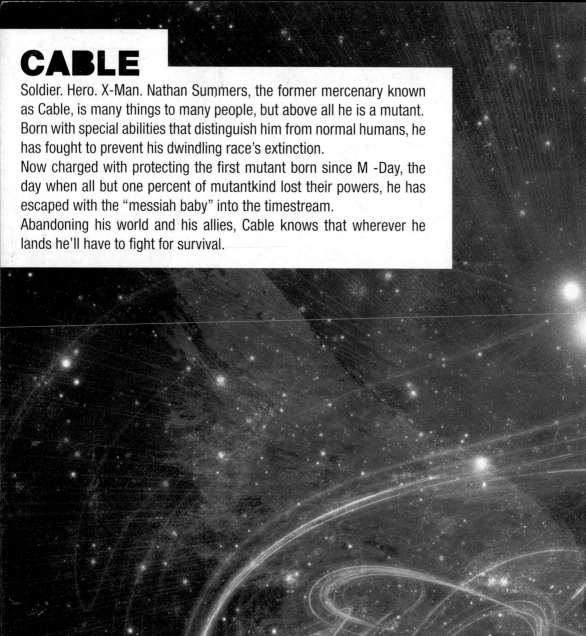

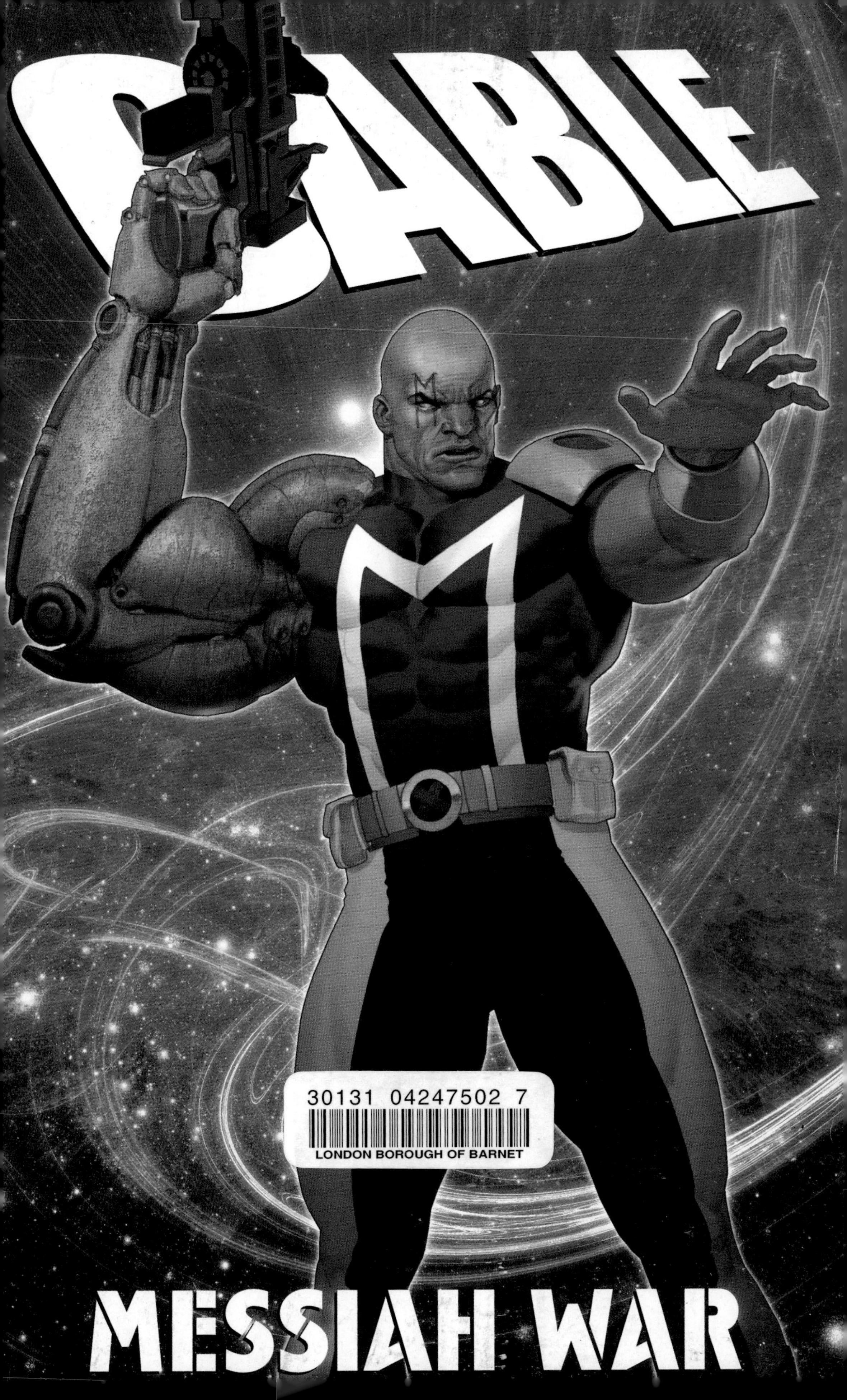
CABLE
MESSIAH WAR

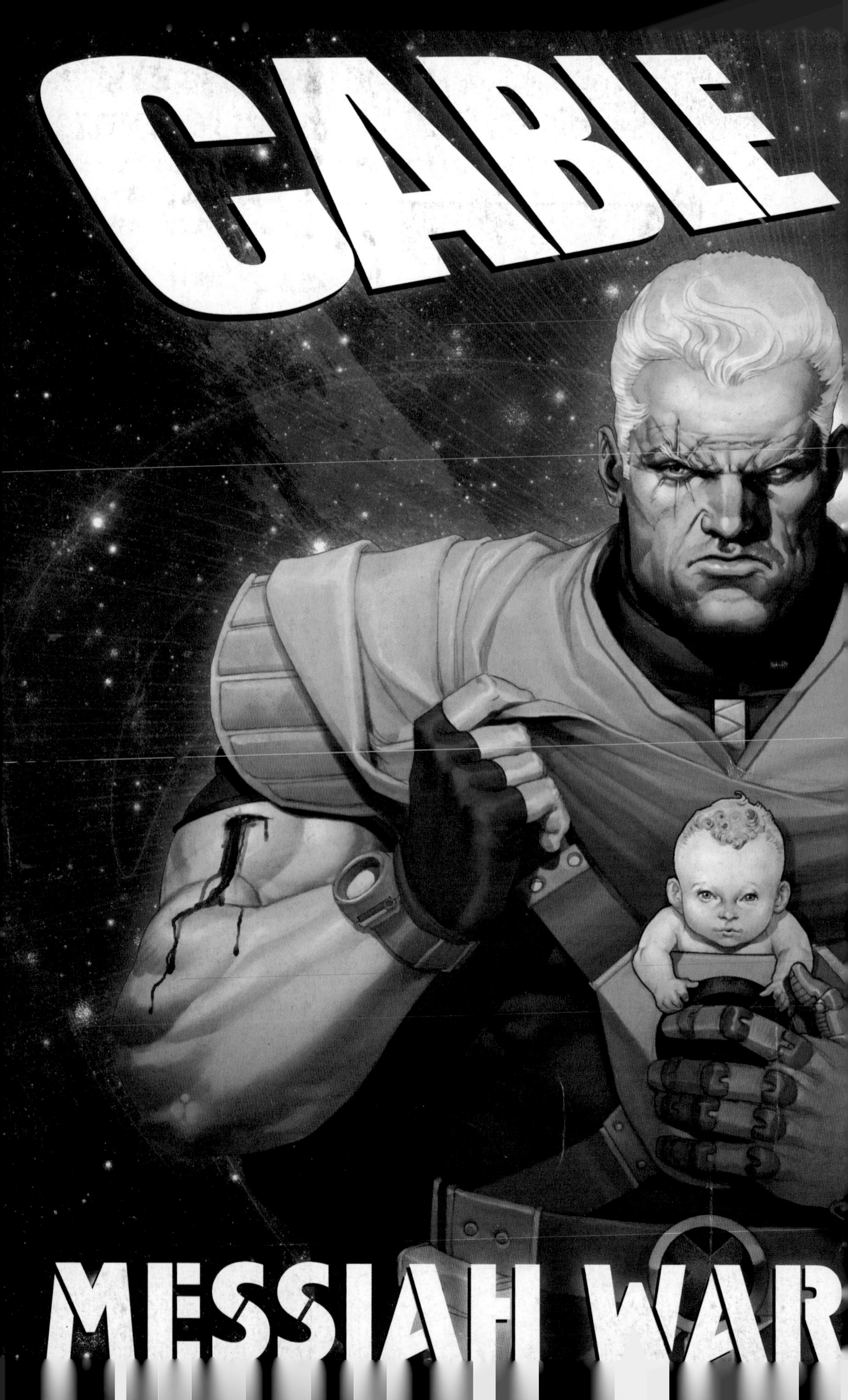
CABLE
MESSIAH WAR

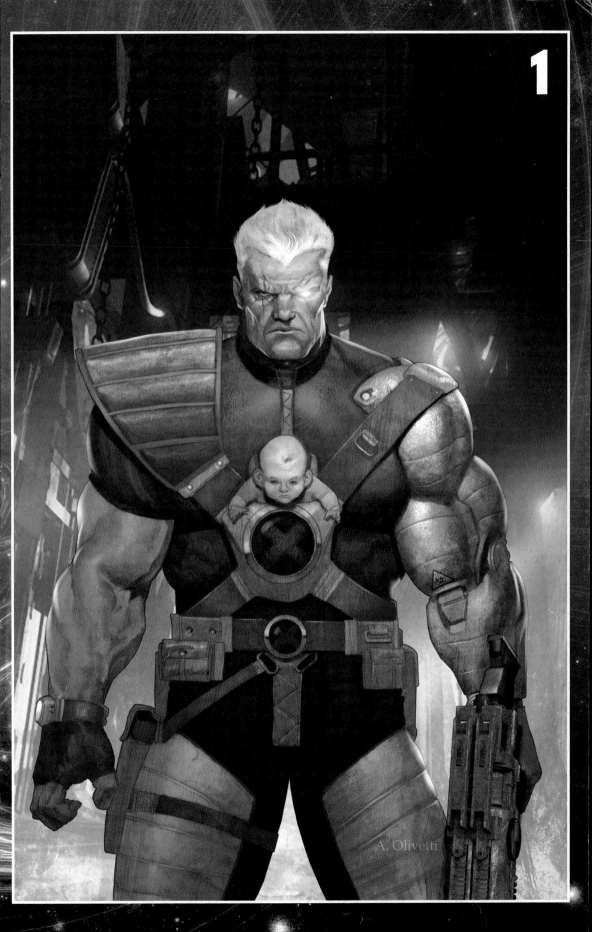

A. Olivetti

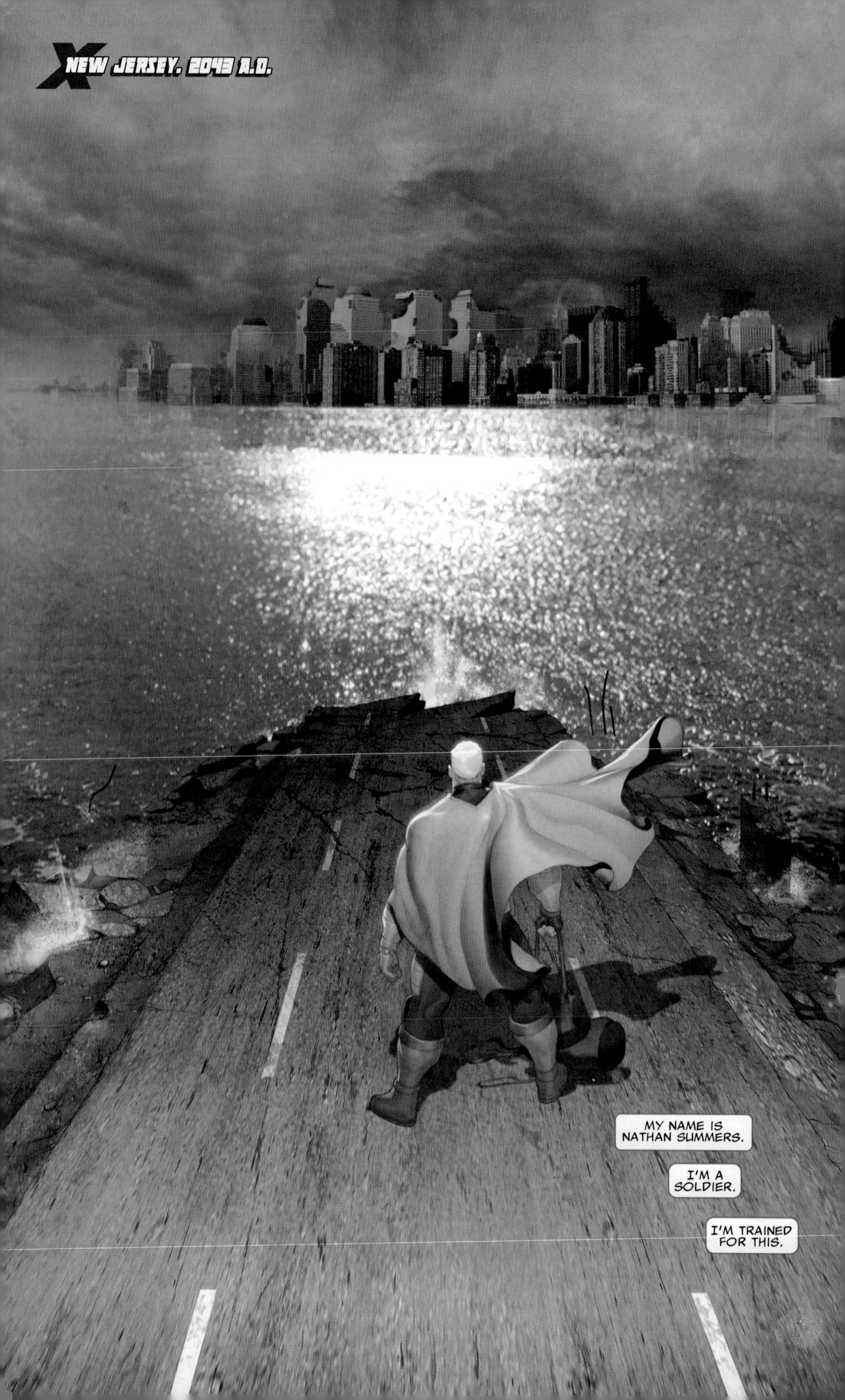
NEW JERSEY. 2043 A.D.
MY NAME IS NATHAN SUMMERS.
I'M A SOLDIER.
I'M TRAINED FOR THIS.

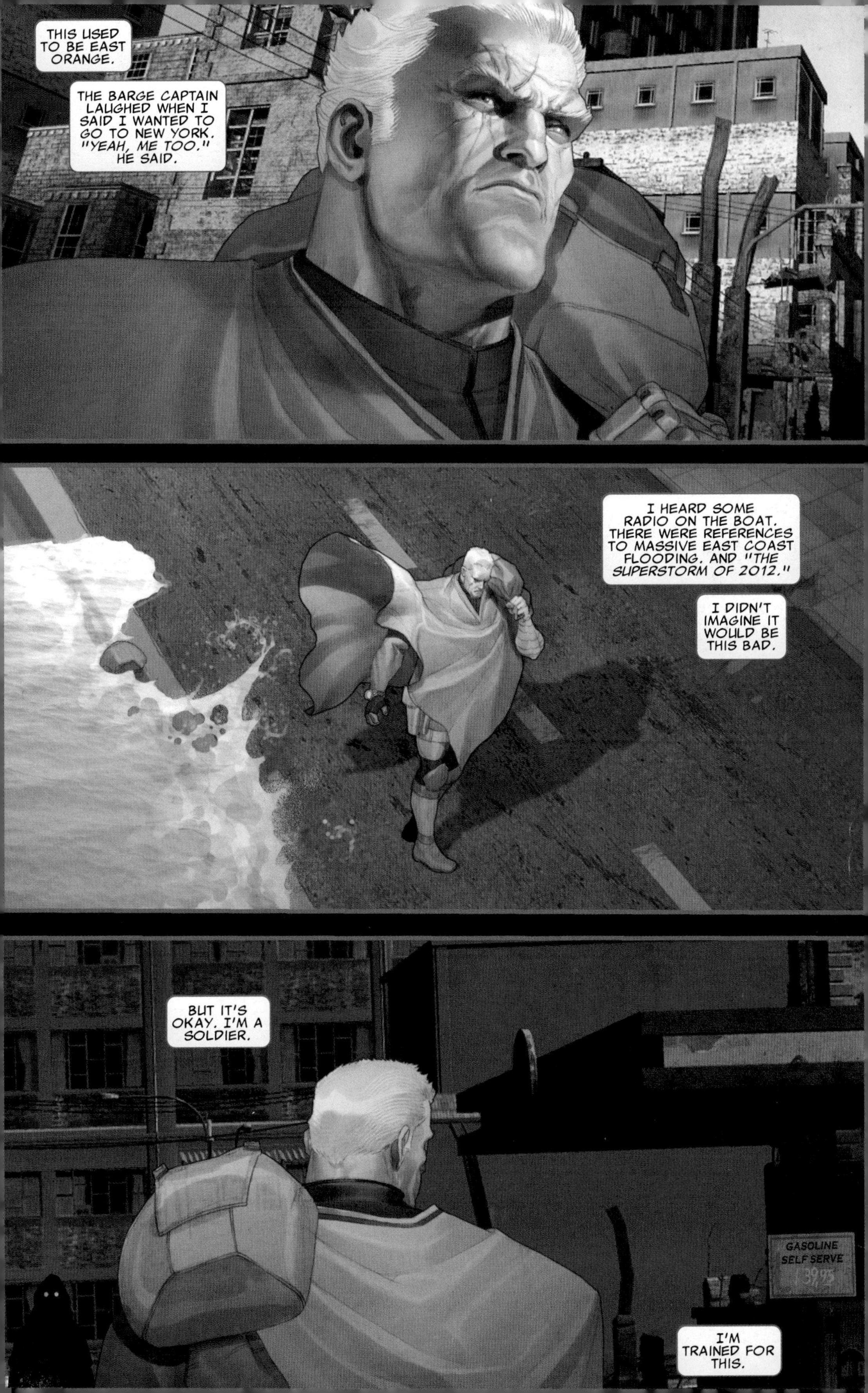
THIS USED TO BE EAST ORANGE.
THE BARGE CAPTAIN LAUGHED WHEN I SAID I WANTED TO GO TO NEW YORK. "YEAH, ME TOO." HE SAID.
I HEARD SOME RADIO ON THE BOAT. THERE WERE REFERENCES TO MASSIVE EAST COAST FLOODING. AND "THE SUPERSTORM OF 2012."
I DIDN'T IMAGINE IT WOULD BE THIS BAD.
BUT IT'S OKAY. I'M A SOLDIER.
GASOLINE
SELF SERVE
I'M TRAINED FOR THIS.

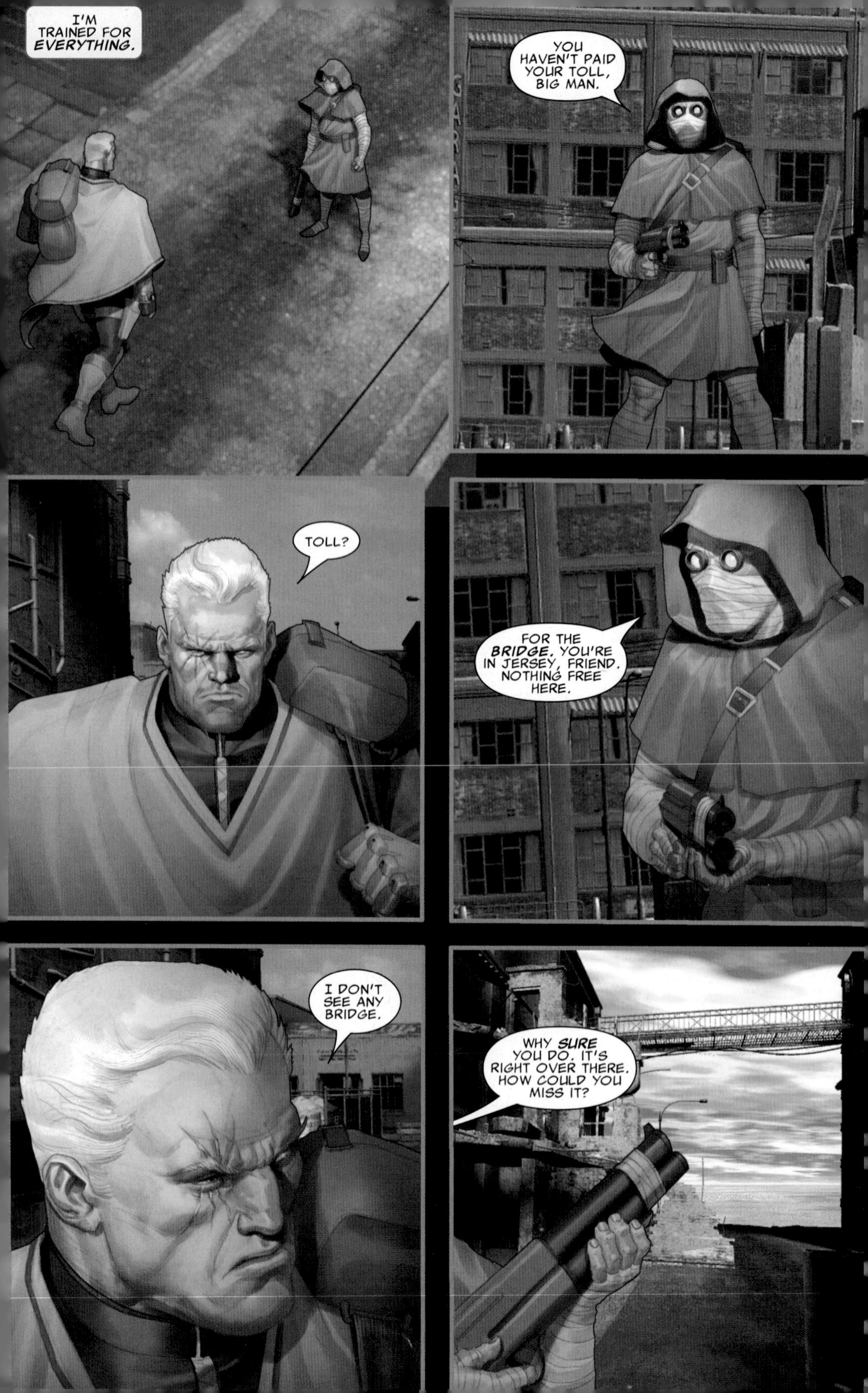

I'M TRAINED FOR *EVERYTHING.*
YOU HAVEN'T PAID YOUR TOLL, BIG MAN.
TOLL?
FOR THE *BRIDGE.* YOU'RE IN JERSEY, FRIEND. NOTHING FREE HERE.
I DON'T SEE ANY BRIDGE.
WHY *SURE* YOU DO. IT'S RIGHT OVER THERE. HOW COULD YOU MISS IT?

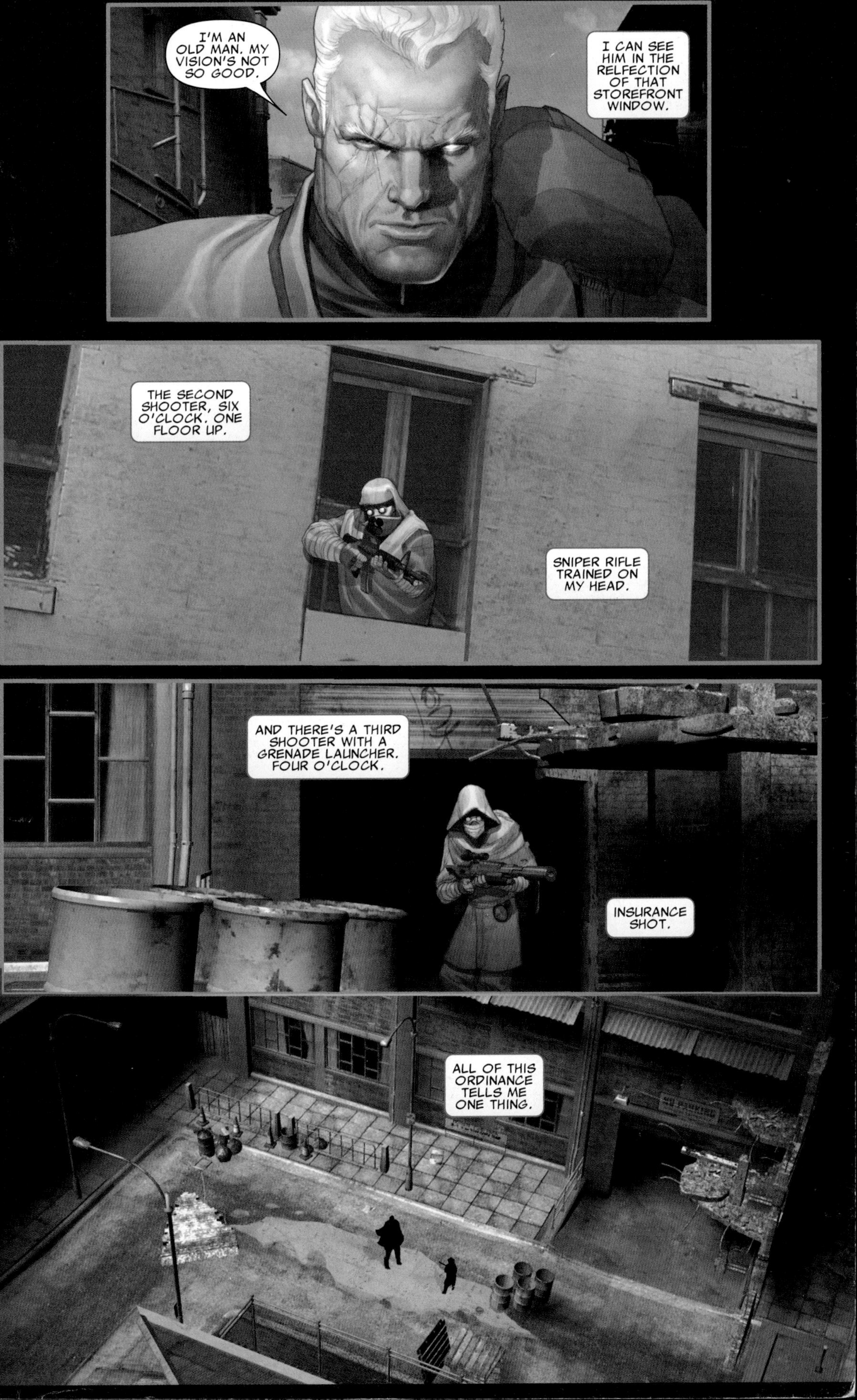

I'M AN OLD MAN. MY VISION'S NOT SO GOOD.
I CAN SEE HIM IN THE RELFECTION OF THAT STOREFRONT WINDOW.
THE SECOND SHOOTER, SIX O'CLOCK. ONE FLOOR UP.
SNIPER RIFLE TRAINED ON MY HEAD.
AND THERE'S A THIRD SHOOTER WITH A GRENADE LAUNCHER. FOUR O'CLOCK.
INSURANCE SHOT.
ALL OF THIS ORDINANCE TELLS ME ONE THING.

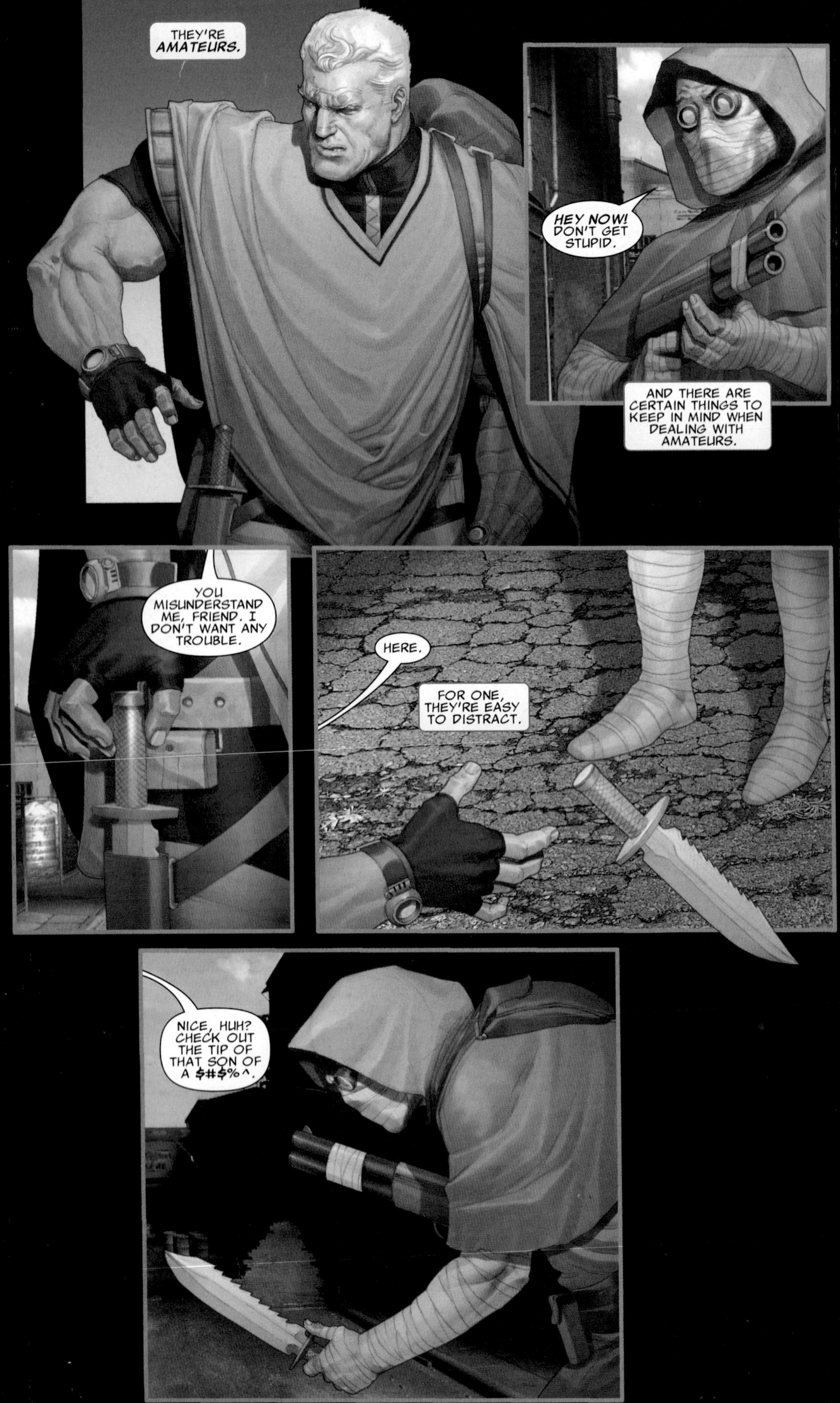
THEY'RE AMATEURS.
HEY NOW! DON'T GET STUPID.
AND THERE ARE CERTAIN THINGS TO KEEP IN MIND WHEN DEALING WITH AMATEURS.
YOU MISUNDERSTAND ME, FRIEND. I DON'T WANT ANY TROUBLE.
HERE.
FOR ONE, THEY'RE EASY TO DISTRACT.
NICE, HUH? CHECK OUT THE TIP OF THAT SON OF A $#$%^.

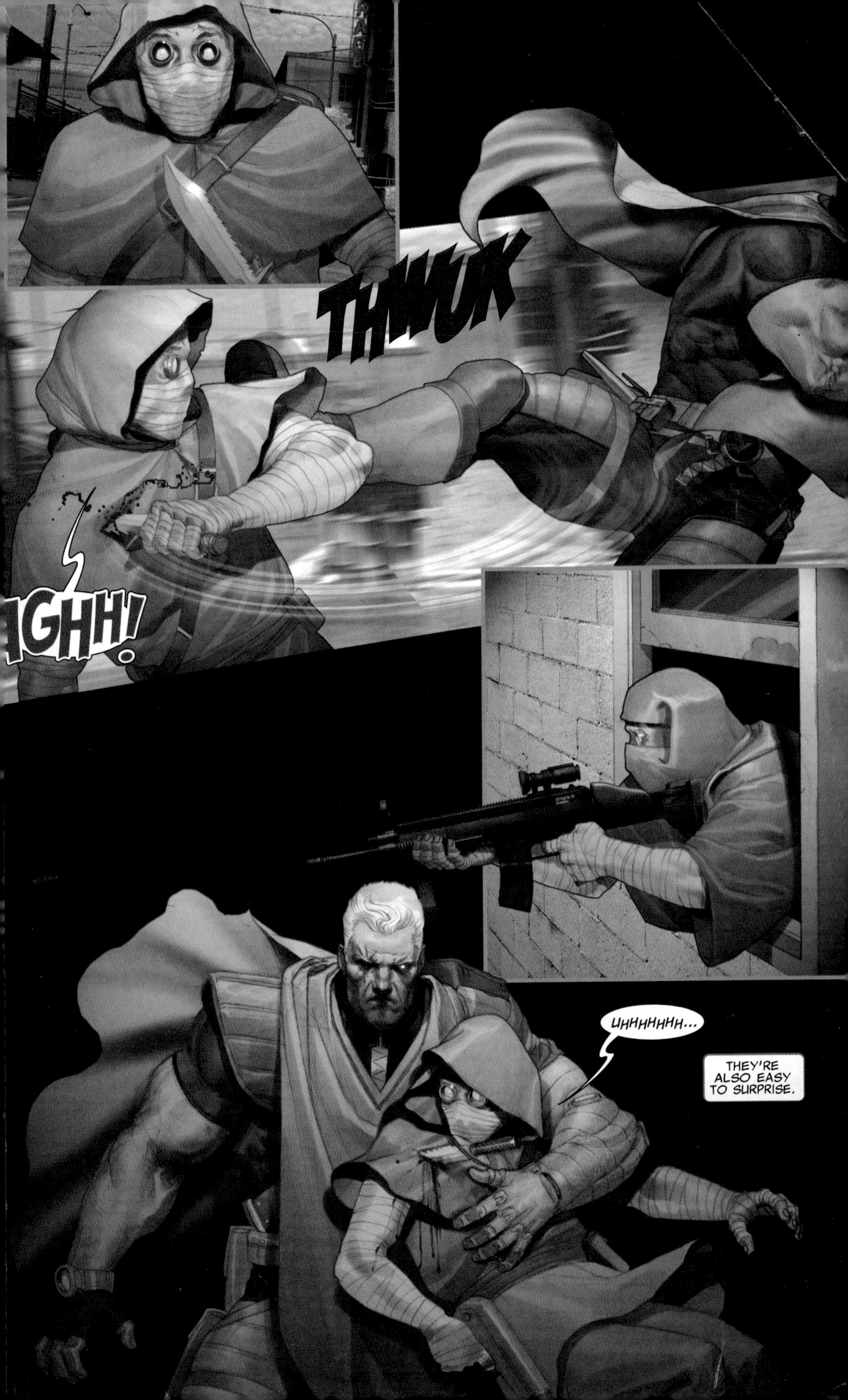
THWUK
IGHH!
UHHHHHHH...
THEY'RE ALSO EASY TO SURPRISE.

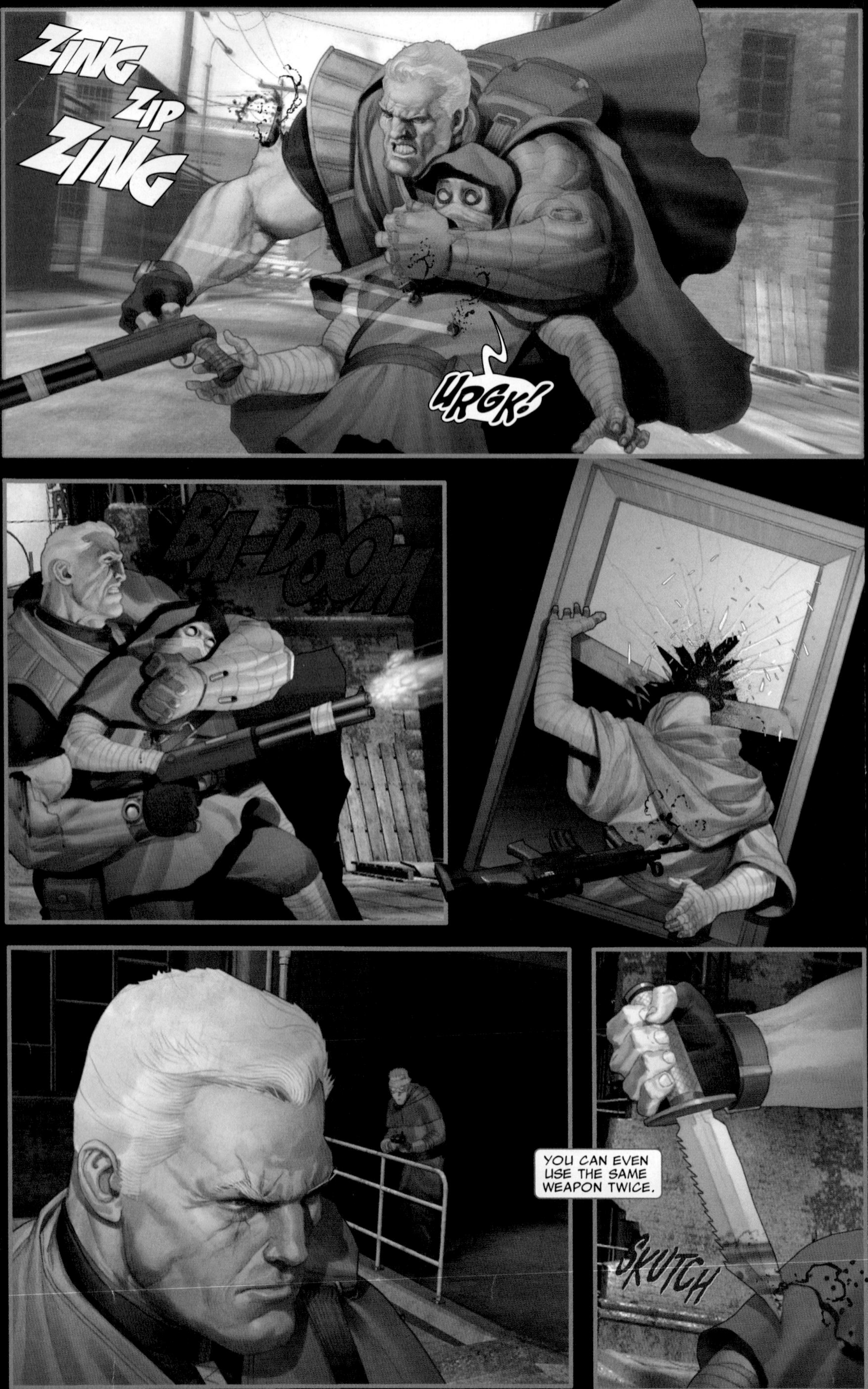
ZING
ZIP
ZING
URGK!
BI-DOOM
YOU CAN EVEN USE THE SAME WEAPON TWICE.
SKUTCH

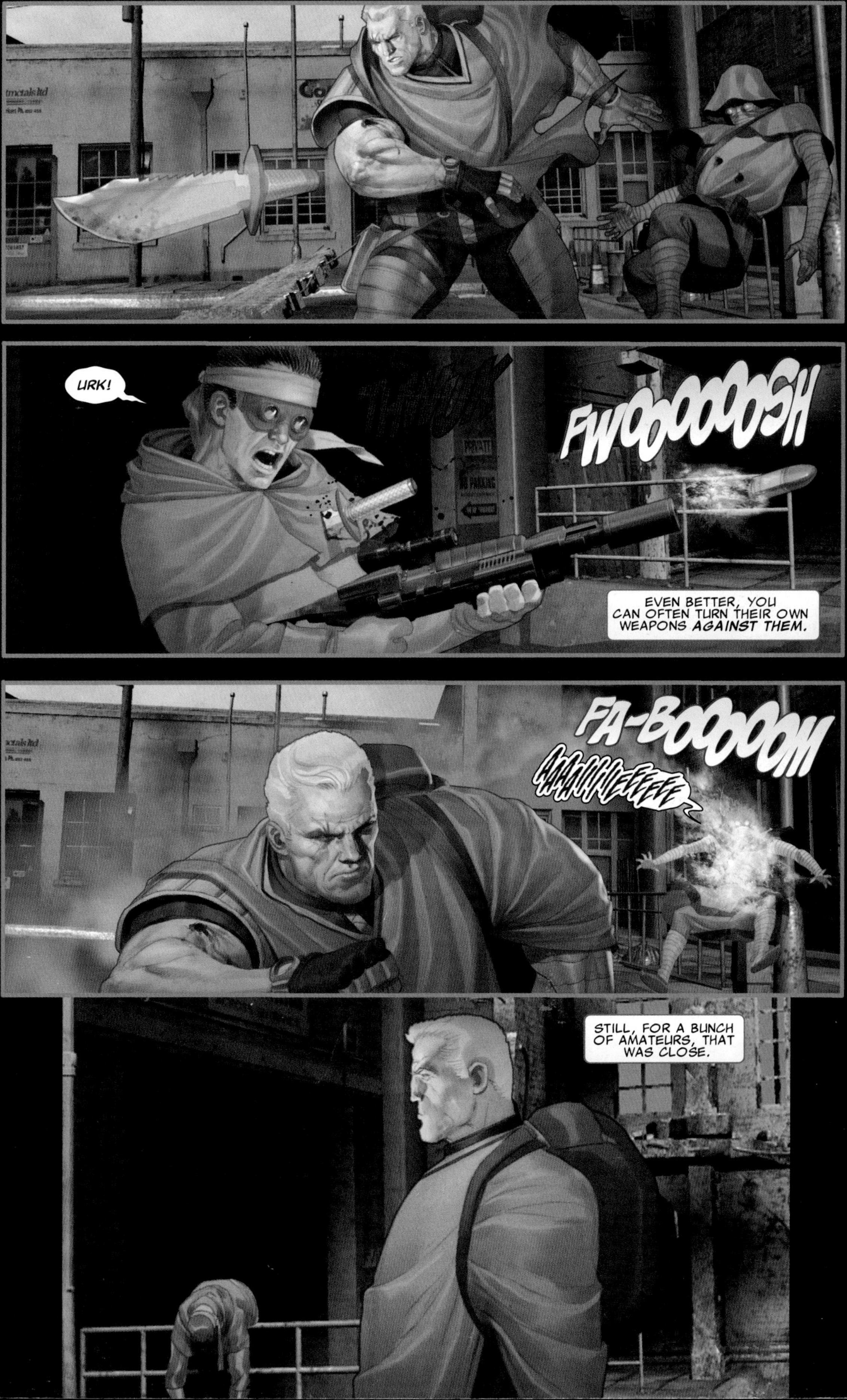
URK!
FWOOOOOOSH
EVEN BETTER, YOU CAN OFTEN TURN THEIR OWN WEAPONS AGAINST THEM.
FA-BOOOOOM
STILL, FOR A BUNCH OF AMATEURS, THAT WAS CLOSE.

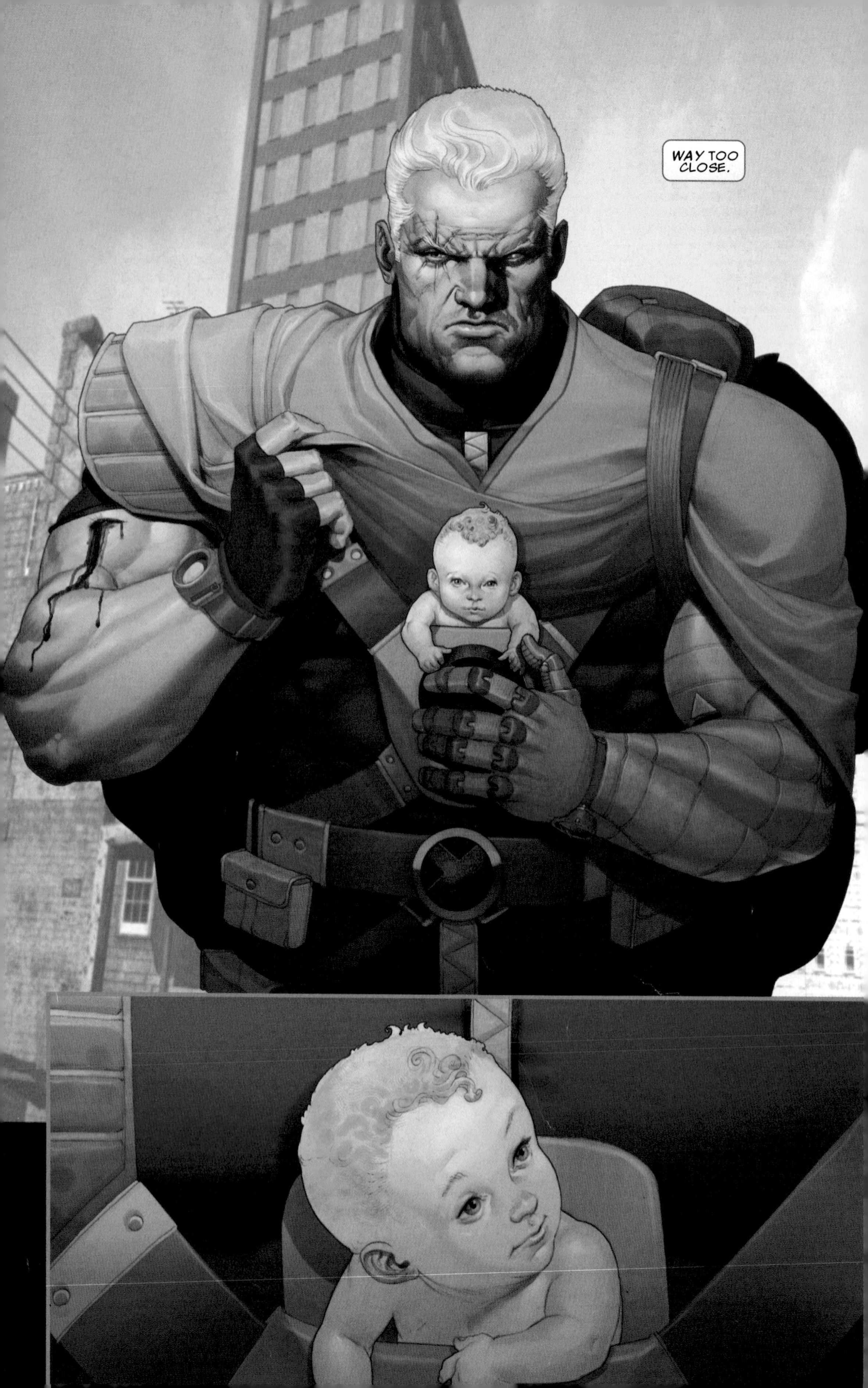
WAY TOO CLOSE.

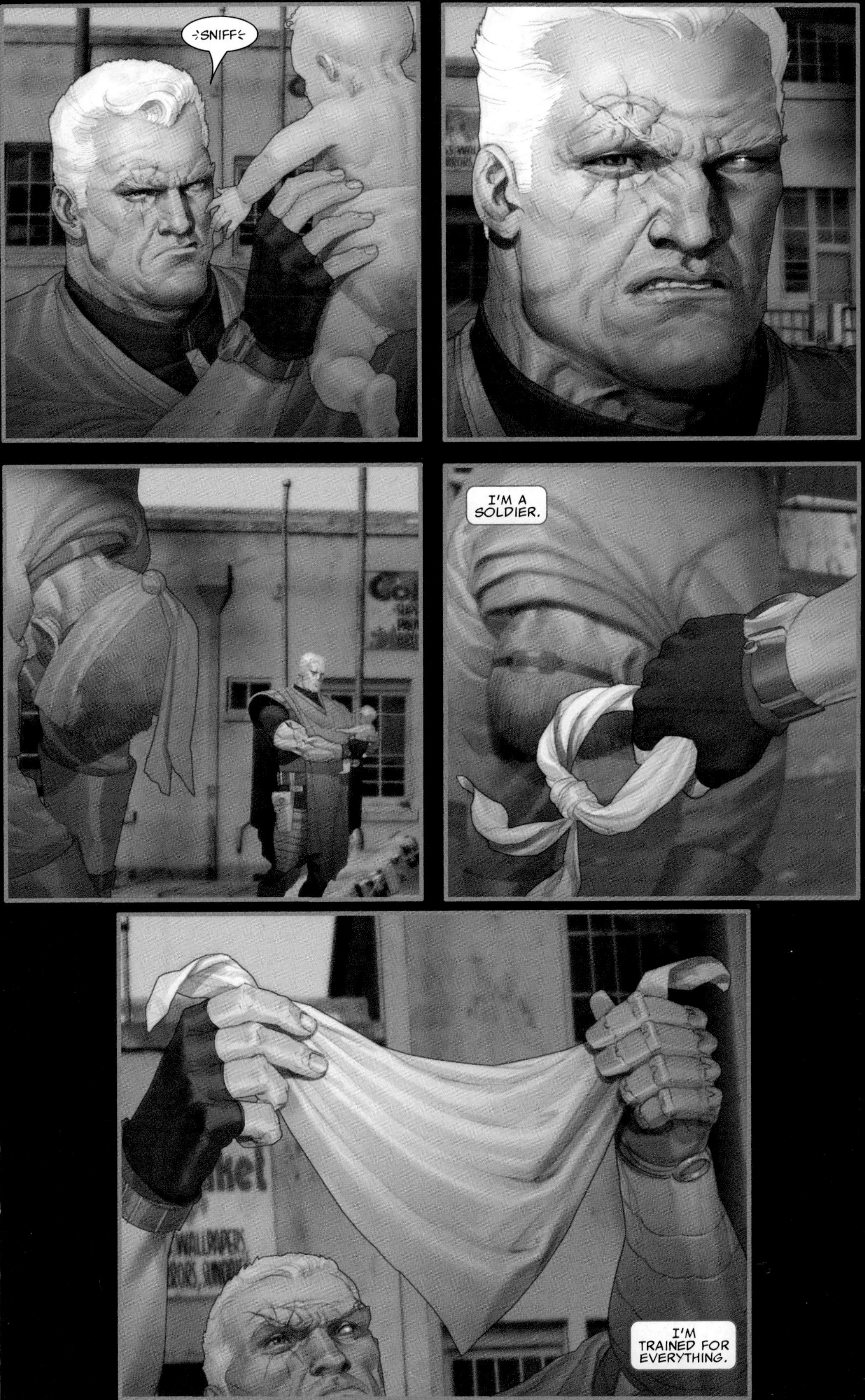

-SNIFF-
I'M A SOLDIER.
I'M TRAINED FOR EVERYTHING.

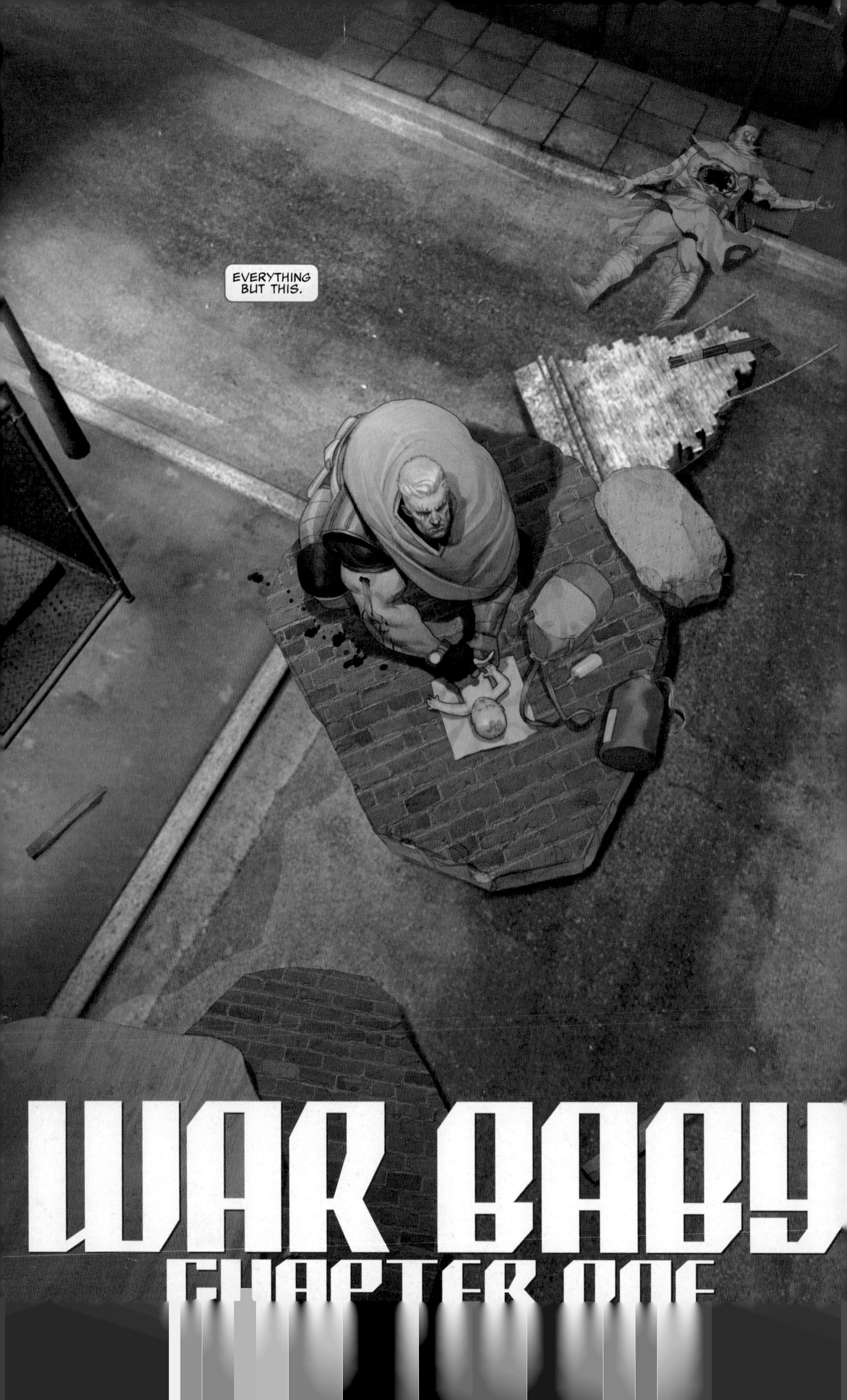
EVERYTHING BUT THIS.
WAR BABY
CHAPTER ONE

WAAAHHHHH!

WE'VE BEEN TRAVELING FIVE MONTHS. MUCH OF IT ON A BOAT, FROM THE COAST OF SCOTLAND TO HERE.

THE BEACH TOWN OF EAST ORANGE, NEW JERSEY.

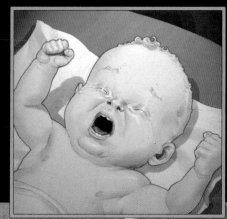

MUCH OF IT LISTENING TO THE BABY CRY.

AHHHHHHH!

COME ON, LITTLE GIRL. IT'S OKAY.

WHICH IS STRANGE, BECAUSE FIVE MONTHS AGO SHE RARELY CRIED.

NOT WHEN I TOOK HER FROM THE INCUBATOR.

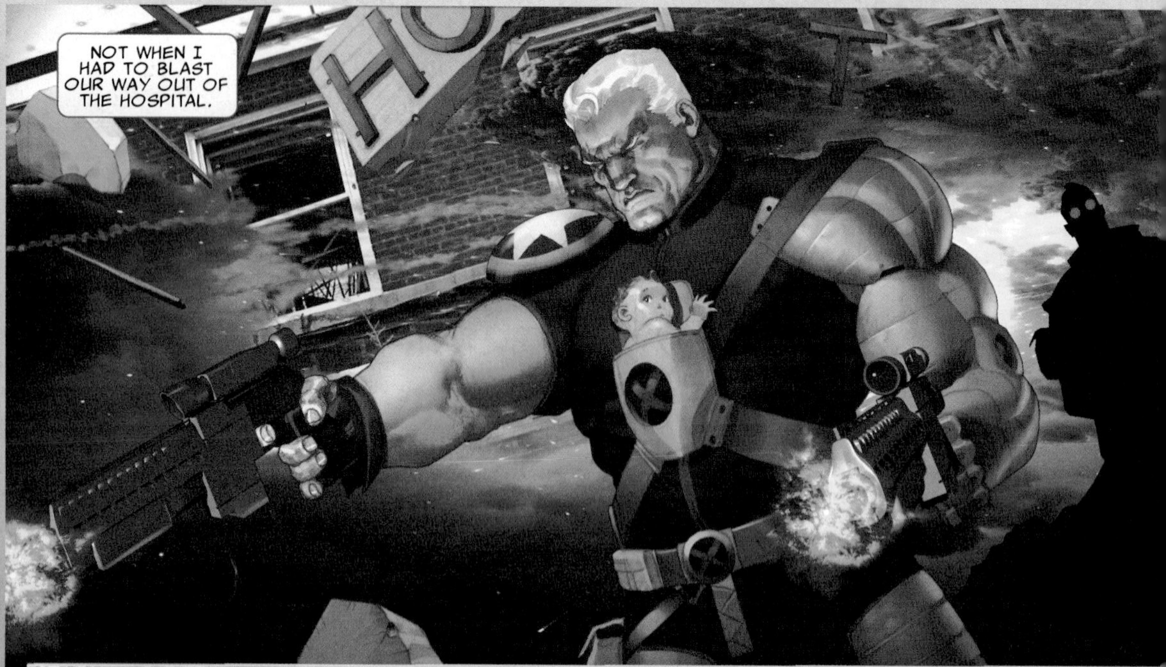
NOT WHEN I HAD TO BLAST OUR WAY OUT OF THE HOSPITAL.
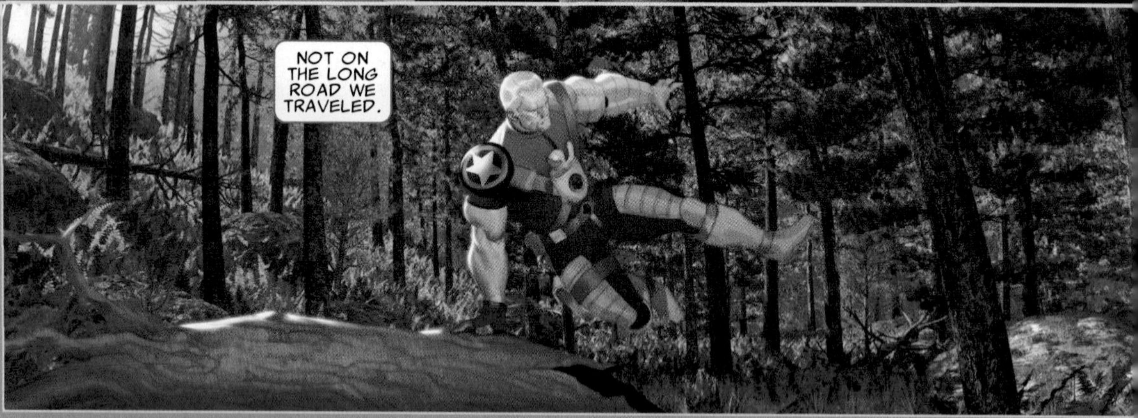
NOT ON THE LONG ROAD WE TRAVELED.
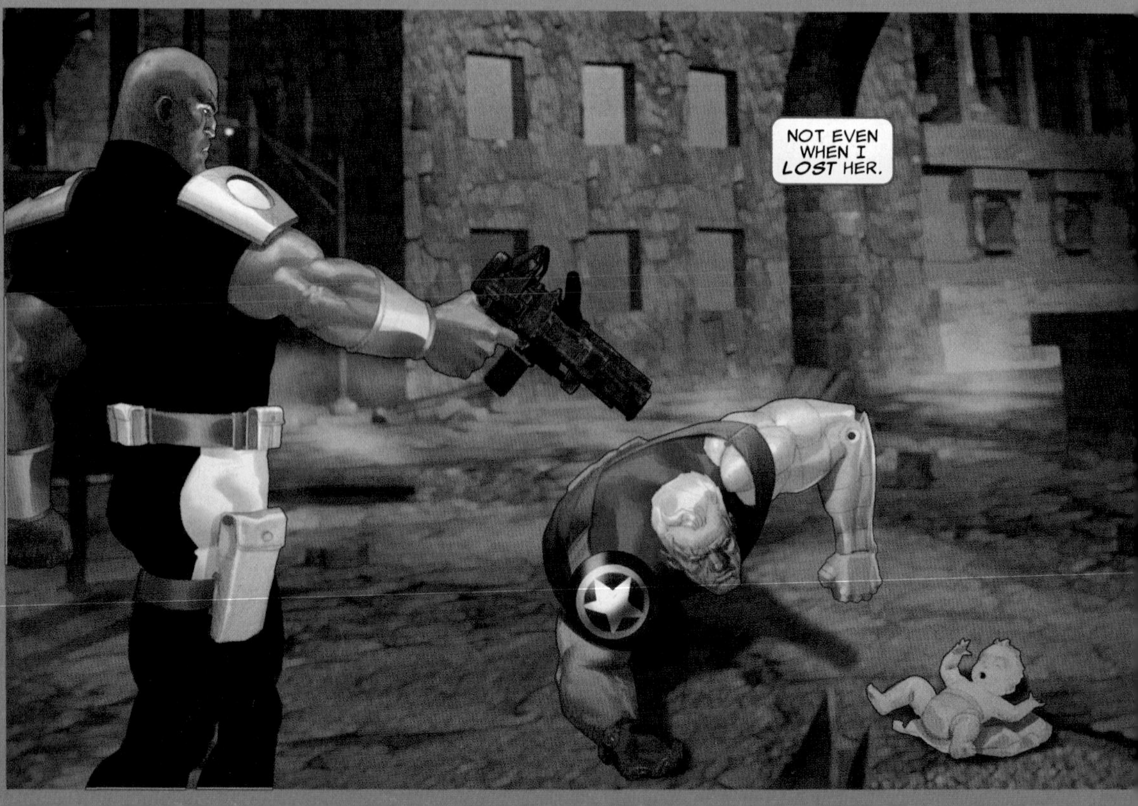
NOT EVEN WHEN I *LOST* HER.

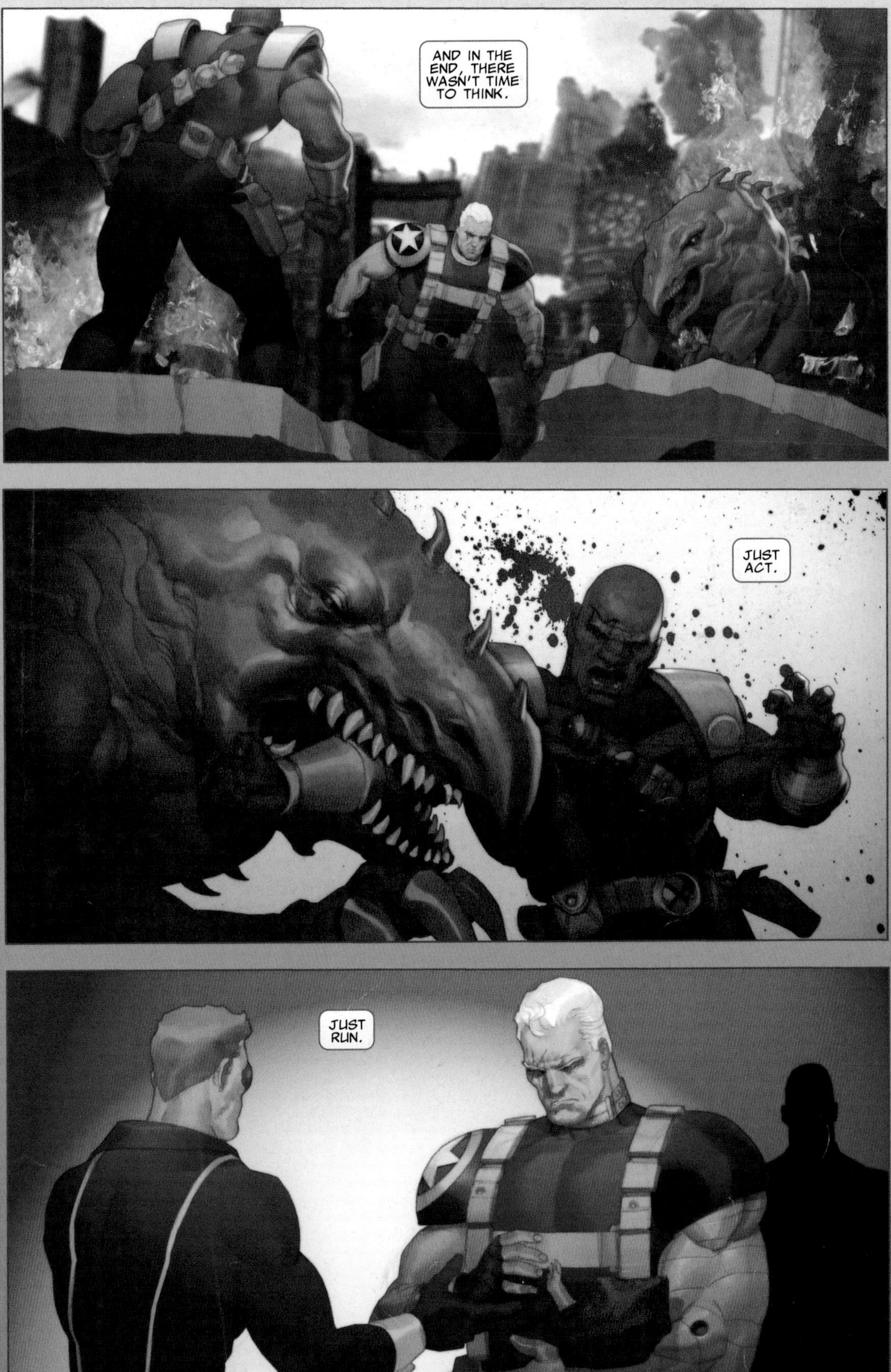
AND IN THE END, THERE WASN'T TIME TO THINK.
JUST ACT.
JUST RUN.

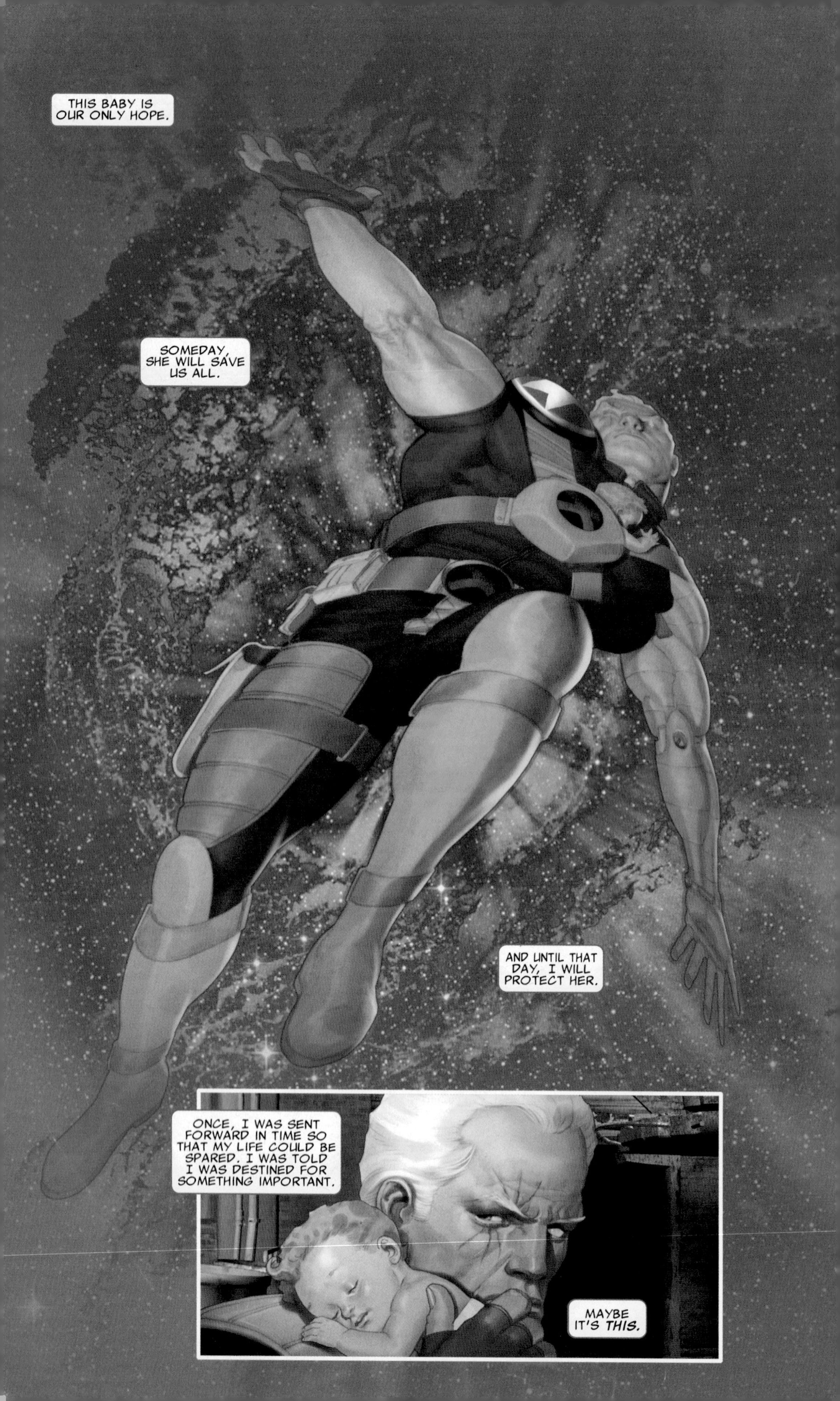
THIS BABY IS OUR ONLY HOPE.
SOMEDAY, SHE WILL SAVE US ALL.
AND UNTIL THAT DAY, I WILL PROTECT HER.
ONCE, I WAS SENT FORWARD IN TIME SO THAT MY LIFE COULD BE SPARED. I WAS TOLD I WAS DESTINED FOR SOMETHING IMPORTANT.
MAYBE IT'S *THIS*.

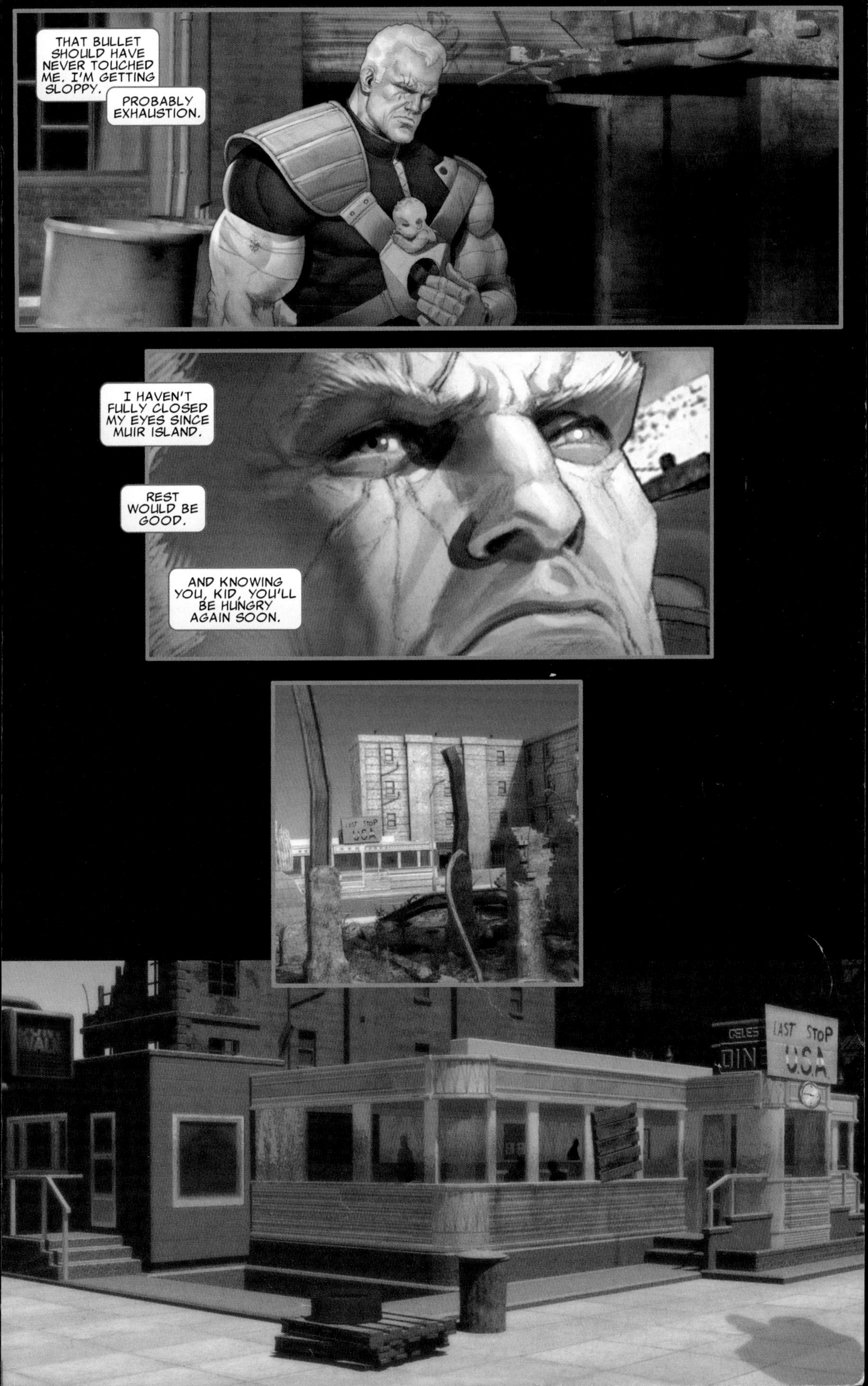
THAT BULLET SHOULD HAVE NEVER TOUCHED ME. I'M GETTING SLOPPY.
PROBABLY EXHAUSTION.
I HAVEN'T FULLY CLOSED MY EYES SINCE MUIR ISLAND.
REST WOULD BE GOOD.
AND KNOWING YOU, KID, YOU'LL BE HUNGRY AGAIN SOON.
LAST STOP U.S.A
LAST STOP U.S.A

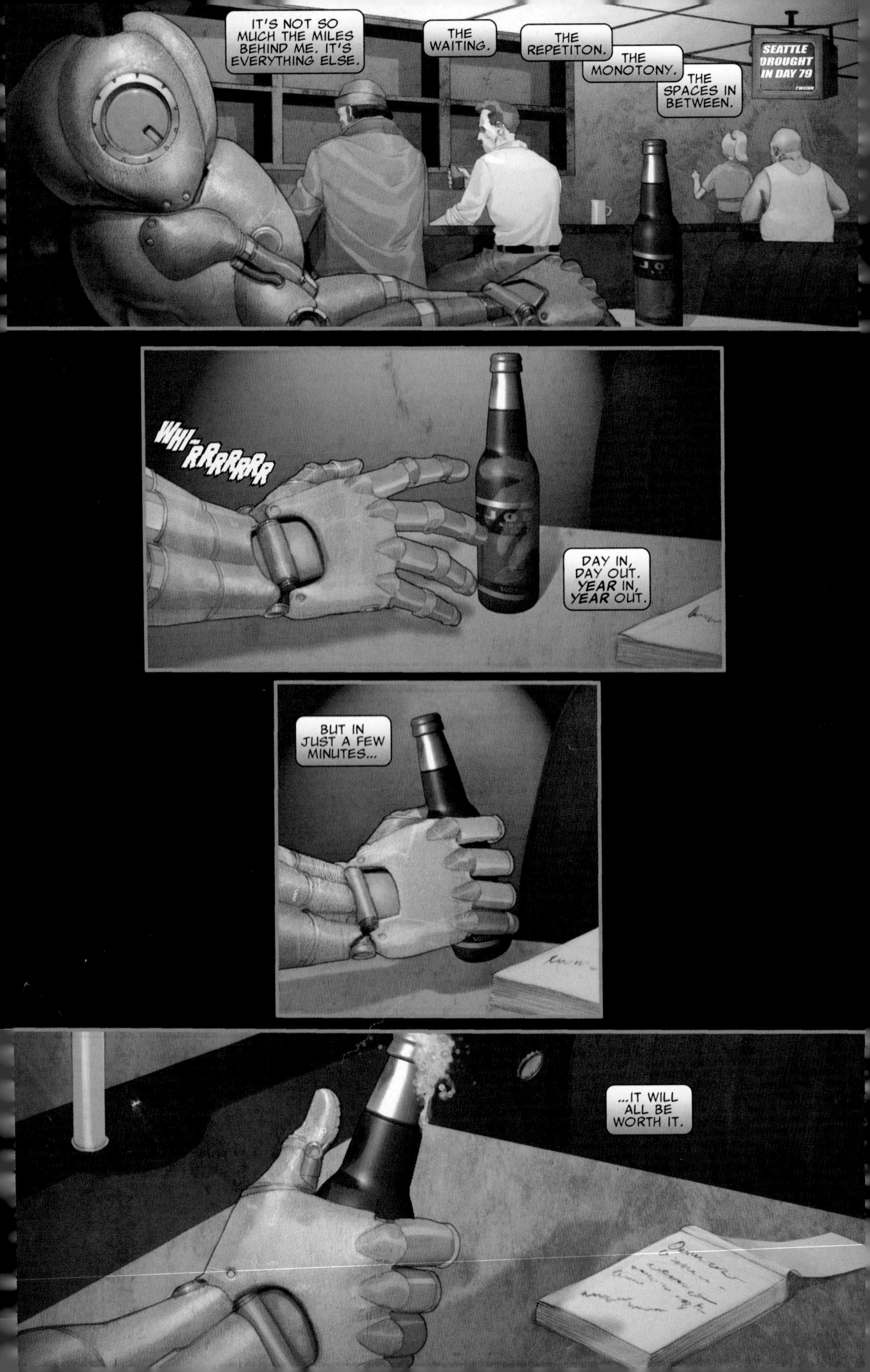
IT'S NOT SO MUCH THE MILES BEHIND ME. IT'S EVERYTHING ELSE.
THE WAITING.
THE REPETITON.
THE MONOTONY.
THE SPACES IN BETWEEN.
SEATTLE DROUGHT IN DAY 79
TWCNN
WHI-RRRRRRR
DAY IN, DAY OUT. YEAR IN, YEAR OUT.
BUT IN JUST A FEW MINUTES...
...IT WILL ALL BE WORTH IT.

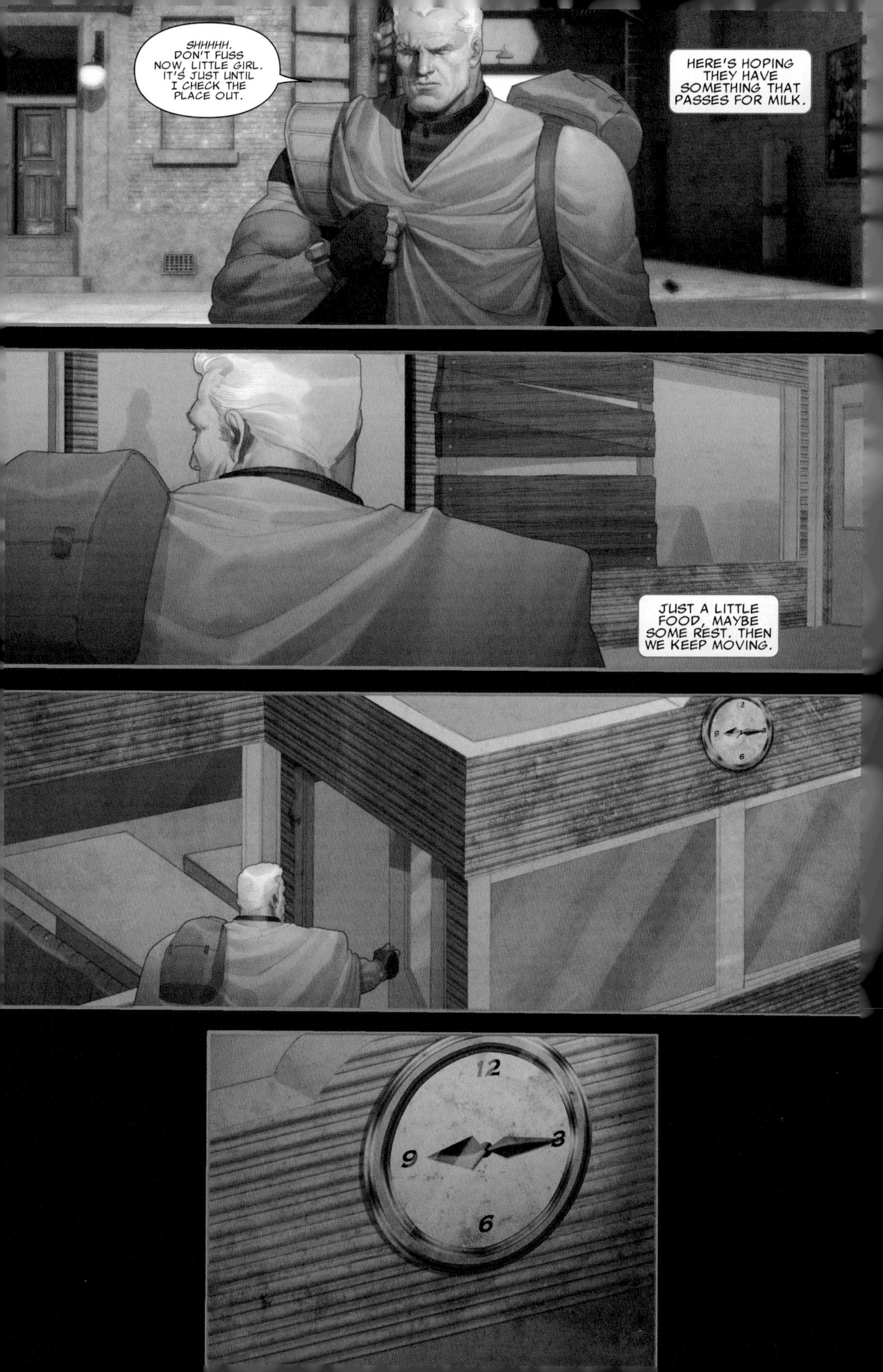
SHHHHH. DON'T FUSS NOW, LITTLE GIRL. IT'S JUST UNTIL I CHECK THE PLACE OUT.
HERE'S HOPING THEY HAVE SOMETHING THAT PASSES FOR MILK.
JUST A LITTLE FOOD, MAYBE SOME REST. THEN WE KEEP MOVING.

JUST SECONDS AWAY NOW.

OH YEAH.

I CAN FEEL THEM.

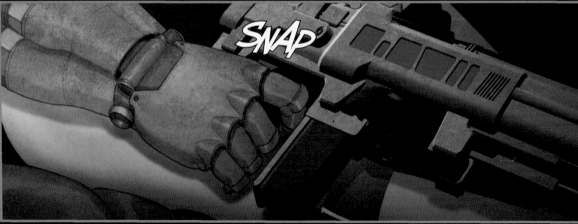

SNAP

NO HESITATION THIS TIME.

NOT *THIS* TIME.

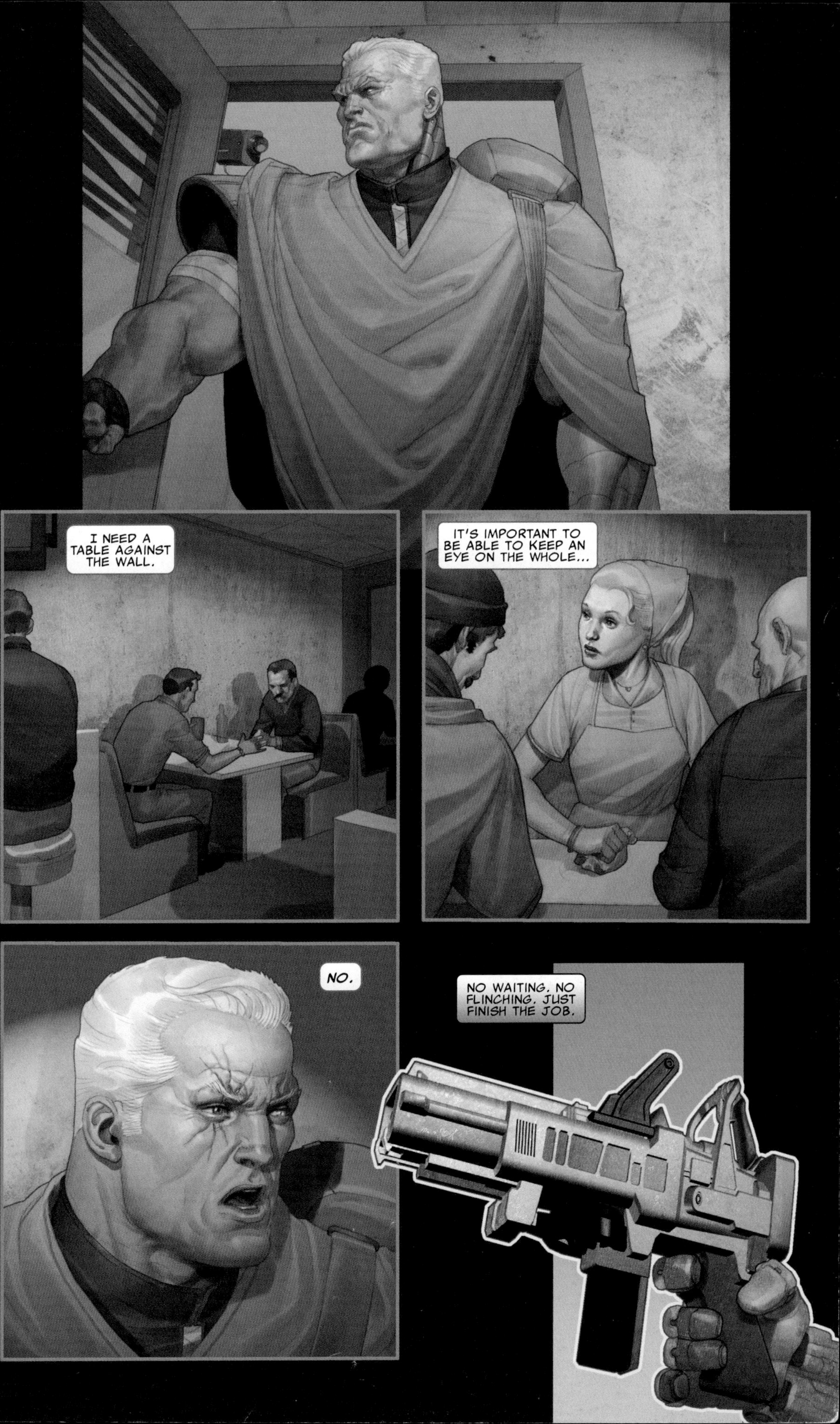

I NEED A TABLE AGAINST THE WALL.
IT'S IMPORTANT TO BE ABLE TO KEEP AN EYE ON THE WHOLE...
NO.
NO WAITING. NO FLINCHING. JUST FINISH THE JOB.

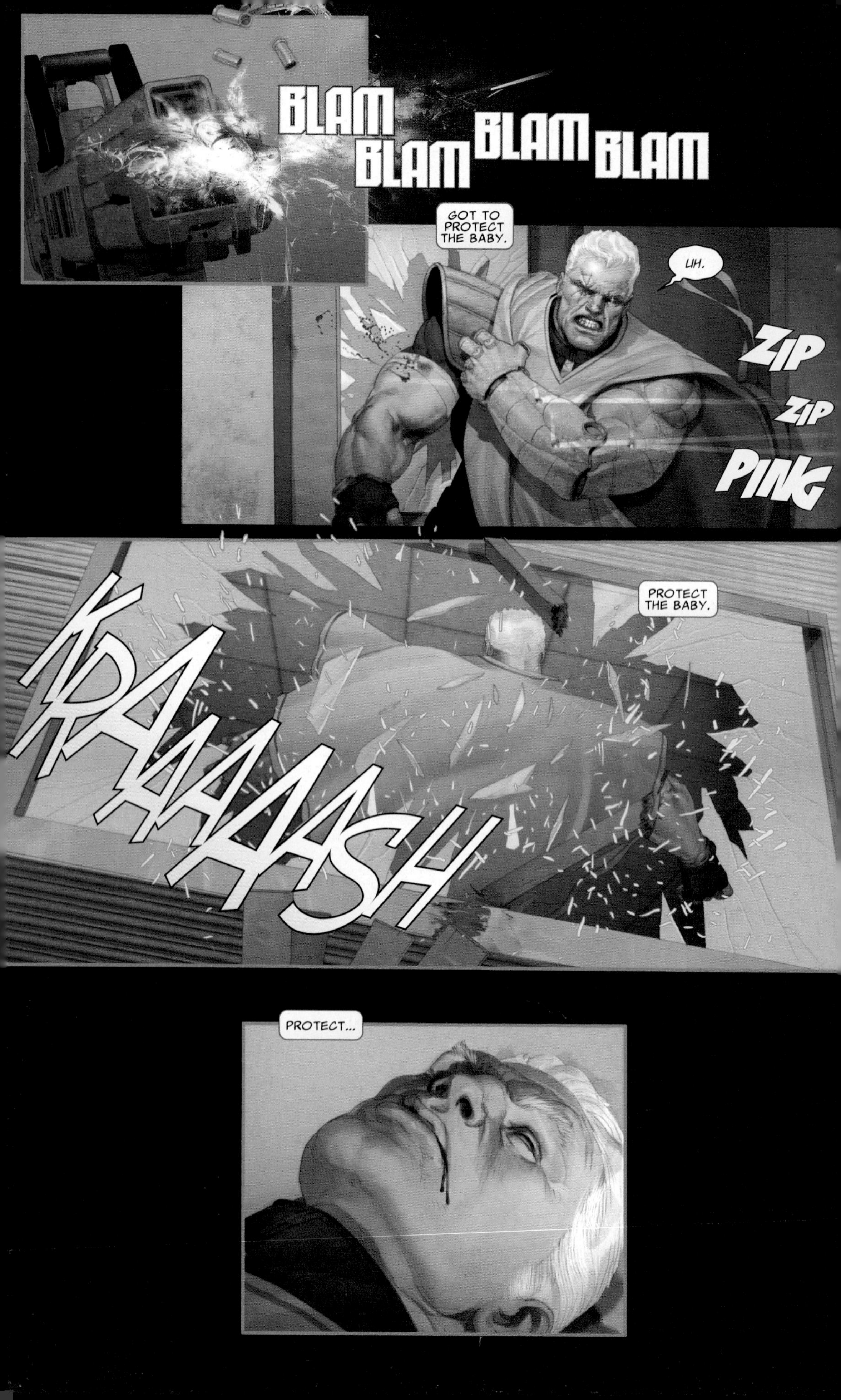

BLAM
BLAM
BLAM
BLAM
GOT TO PROTECT THE BABY.
UH.
ZIP
ZIP
PING
KRAAAAASH
PROTECT THE BABY.
PROTECT...

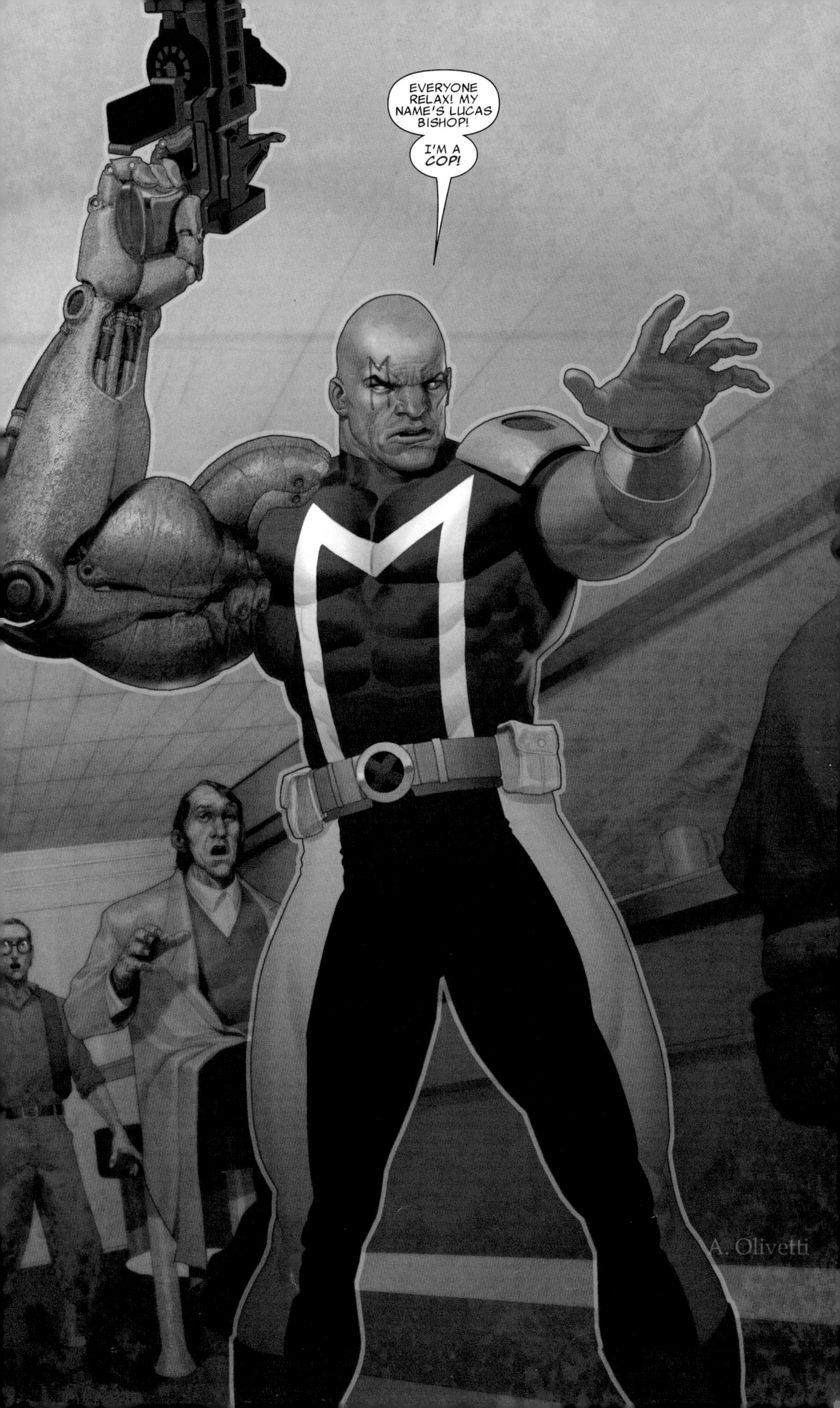
EVERYONE RELAX! MY NAME'S LUCAS BISHOP!
I'M A COP!
A. Olivetti

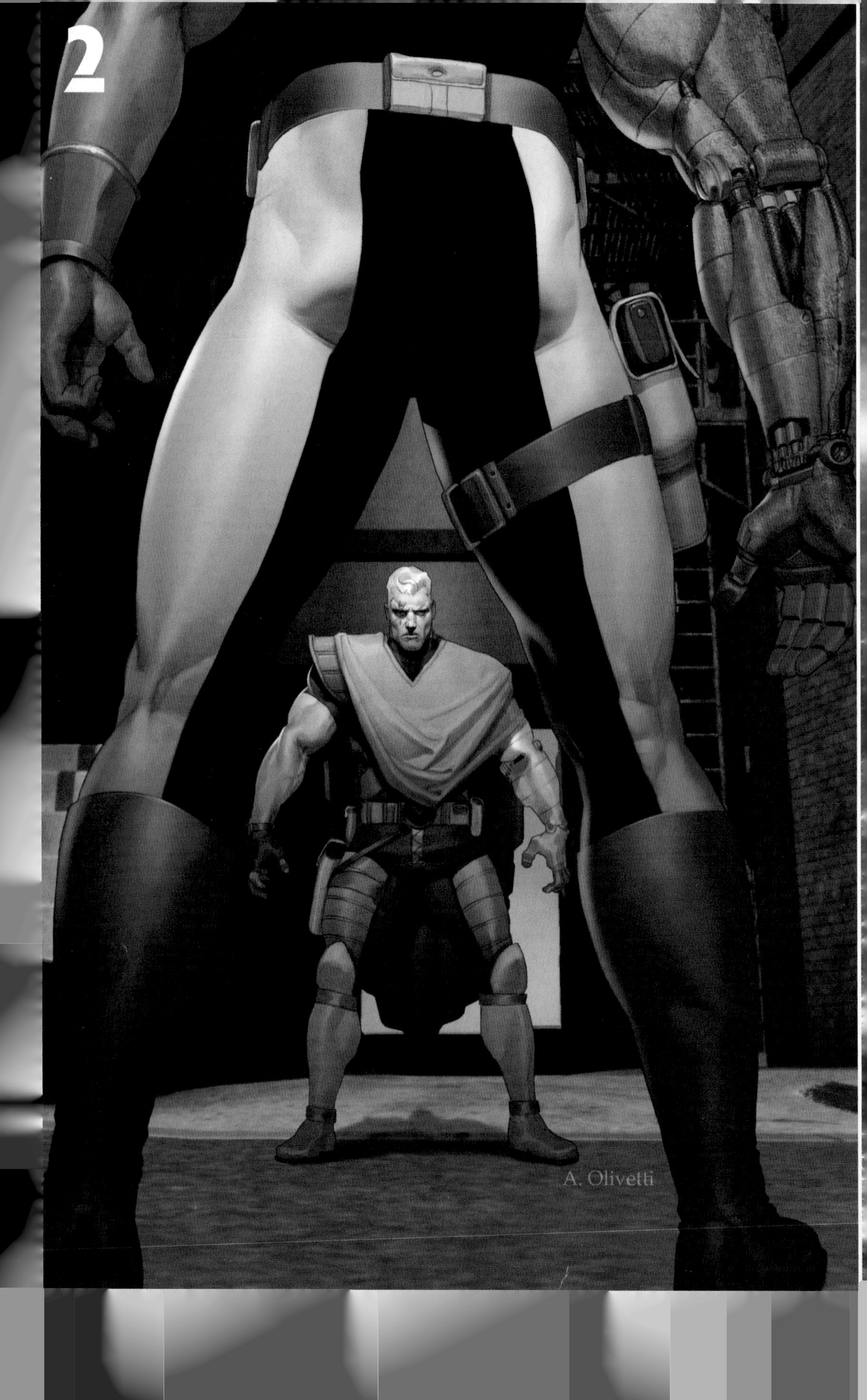
2
A. Olivetti

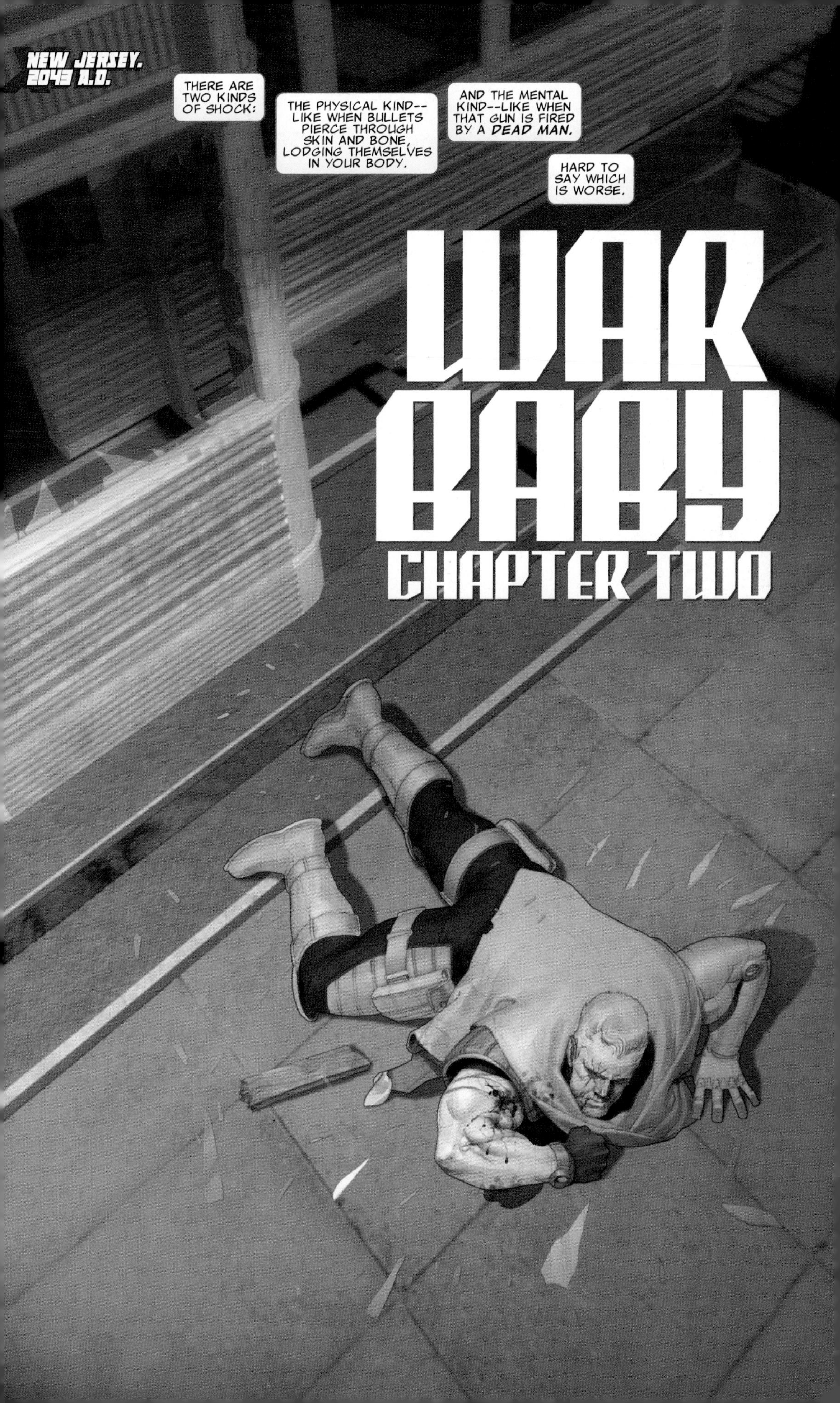
NEW JERSEY. 2043 A.D.
THERE ARE TWO KINDS OF SHOCK:
THE PHYSICAL KIND--LIKE WHEN BULLETS PIERCE THROUGH SKIN AND BONE, LODGING THEMSELVES IN YOUR BODY.
AND THE MENTAL KIND--LIKE WHEN THAT GUN IS FIRED BY A *DEAD MAN*.
HARD TO SAY WHICH IS WORSE.
WAR BABY
CHAPTER TWO

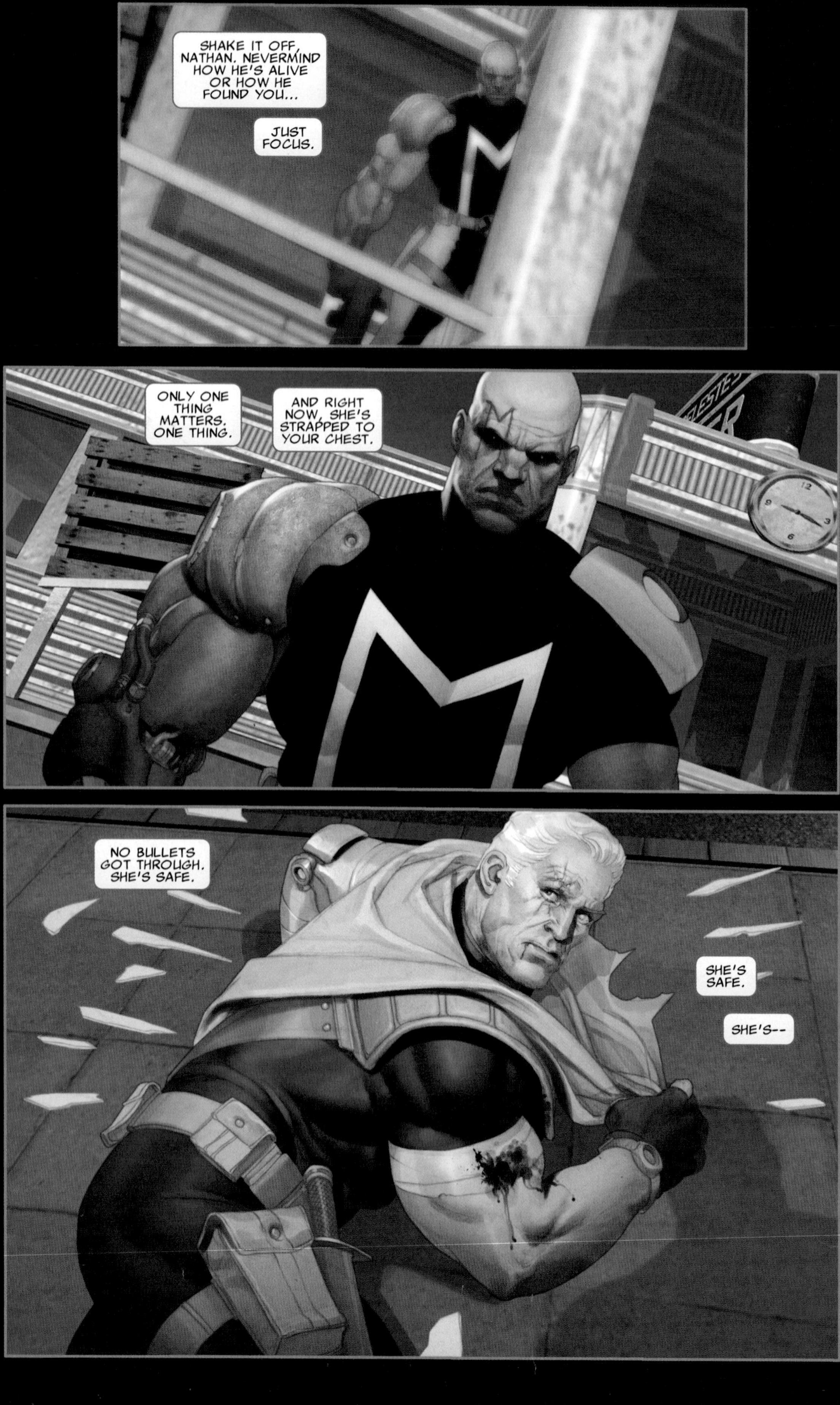
SHAKE IT OFF, NATHAN. NEVERMIND HOW HE'S ALIVE OR HOW HE FOUND YOU...
JUST FOCUS.
ONLY ONE THING MATTERS. ONE THING.
AND RIGHT NOW, SHE'S STRAPPED TO YOUR CHEST.
NO BULLETS GOT THROUGH. SHE'S SAFE.
SHE'S SAFE.
SHE'S--

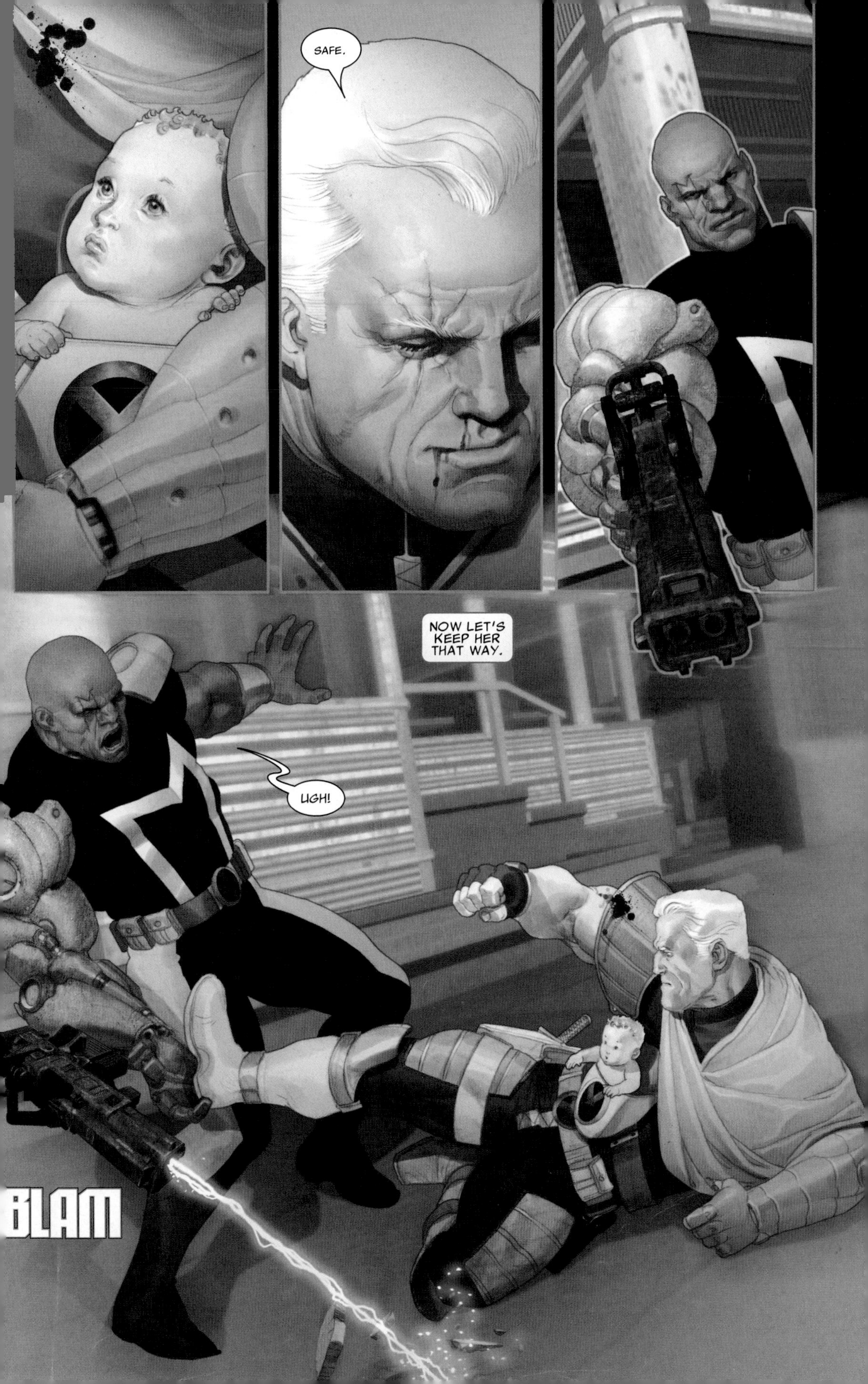
SAFE.
NOW LET'S KEEP HER THAT WAY.
UGH!
BLAM

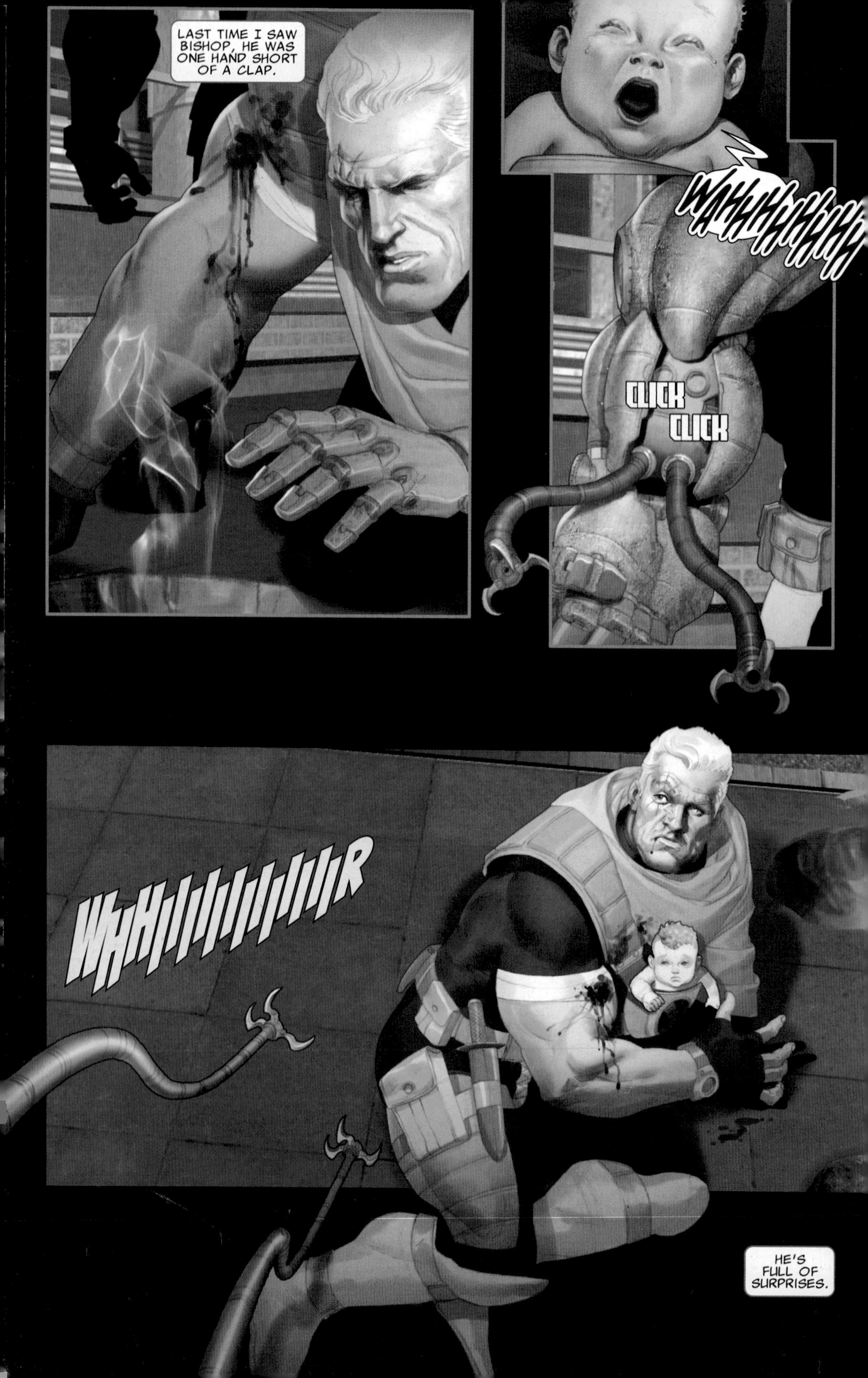
LAST TIME I SAW BISHOP, HE WAS ONE HAND SHORT OF A CLAP.
WAHHHHHHHH
CLICK
CLICK
WHHIIIIIIIIIIIR
HE'S FULL OF SURPRISES.

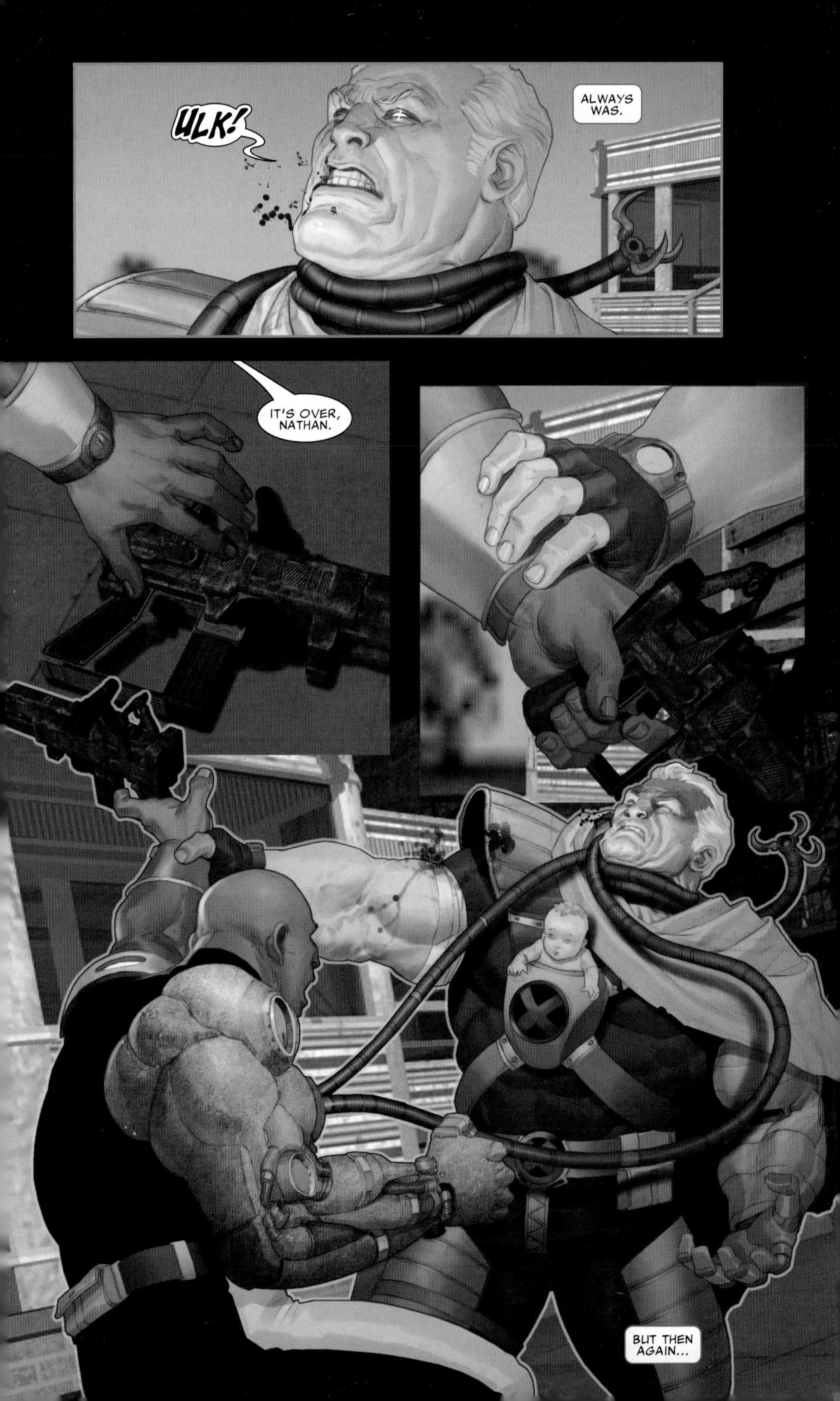
ULK!
ALWAYS WAS.
IT'S OVER, NATHAN.
BUT THEN AGAIN...

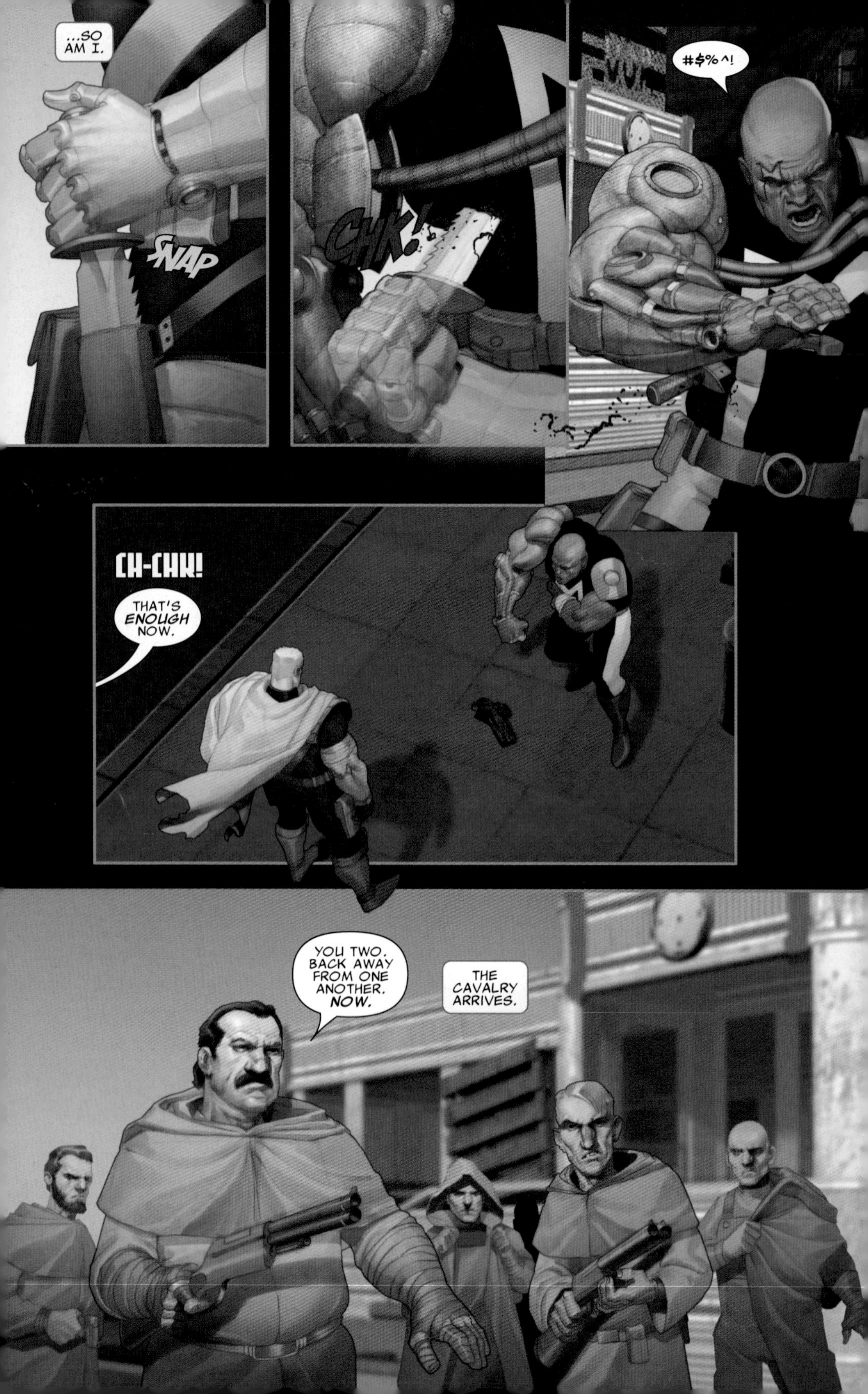
...SO AM I.
SNAP
CHK!
#$%^!
CH-CHK!
THAT'S *ENOUGH* NOW.
YOU TWO. BACK AWAY FROM ONE ANOTHER. *NOW.*
THE CAVALRY ARRIVES.

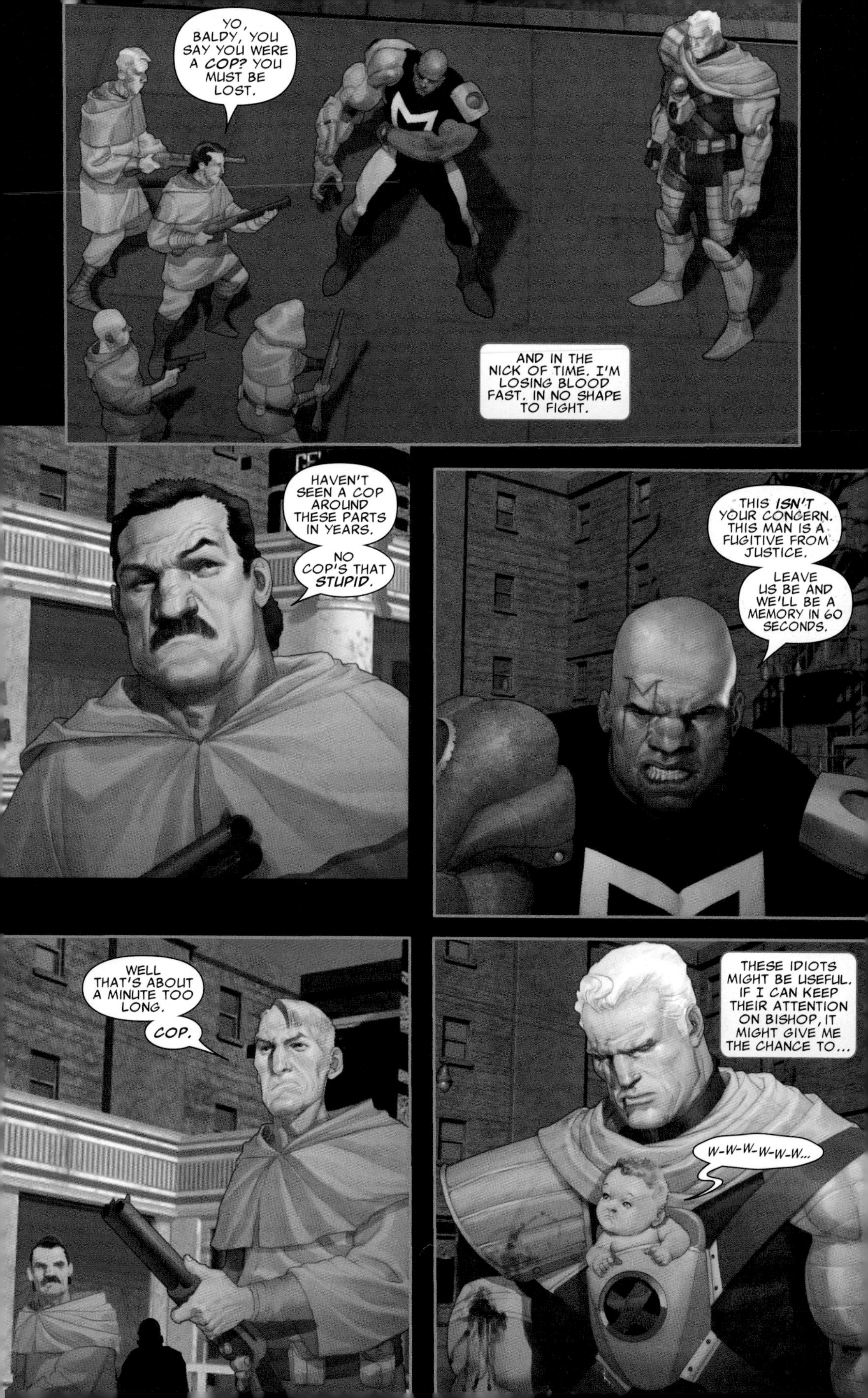
YO, BALDY, YOU SAY YOU WERE A COP? YOU MUST BE LOST.
AND IN THE NICK OF TIME. I'M LOSING BLOOD FAST. IN NO SHAPE TO FIGHT.
HAVEN'T SEEN A COP AROUND THESE PARTS IN YEARS.
NO COP'S THAT STUPID.
THIS ISN'T YOUR CONCERN. THIS MAN IS A FUGITIVE FROM JUSTICE.
LEAVE US BE AND WE'LL BE A MEMORY IN 60 SECONDS.
WELL THAT'S ABOUT A MINUTE TOO LONG.
COP.
THESE IDIOTS MIGHT BE USEFUL. IF I CAN KEEP THEIR ATTENTION ON BISHOP, IT MIGHT GIVE ME THE CHANCE TO...
W-W-W-W-W-W...

WELL, LOOKÉE HERE...

WAAAAAAAAAAAWAAAAAAAAAA

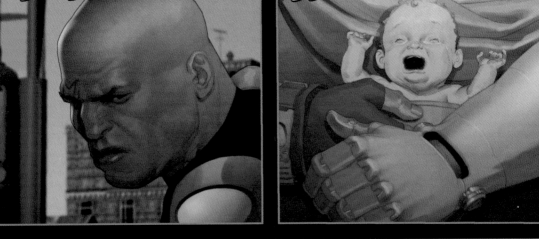

IT ALL COMES DOWN TO LUCK.

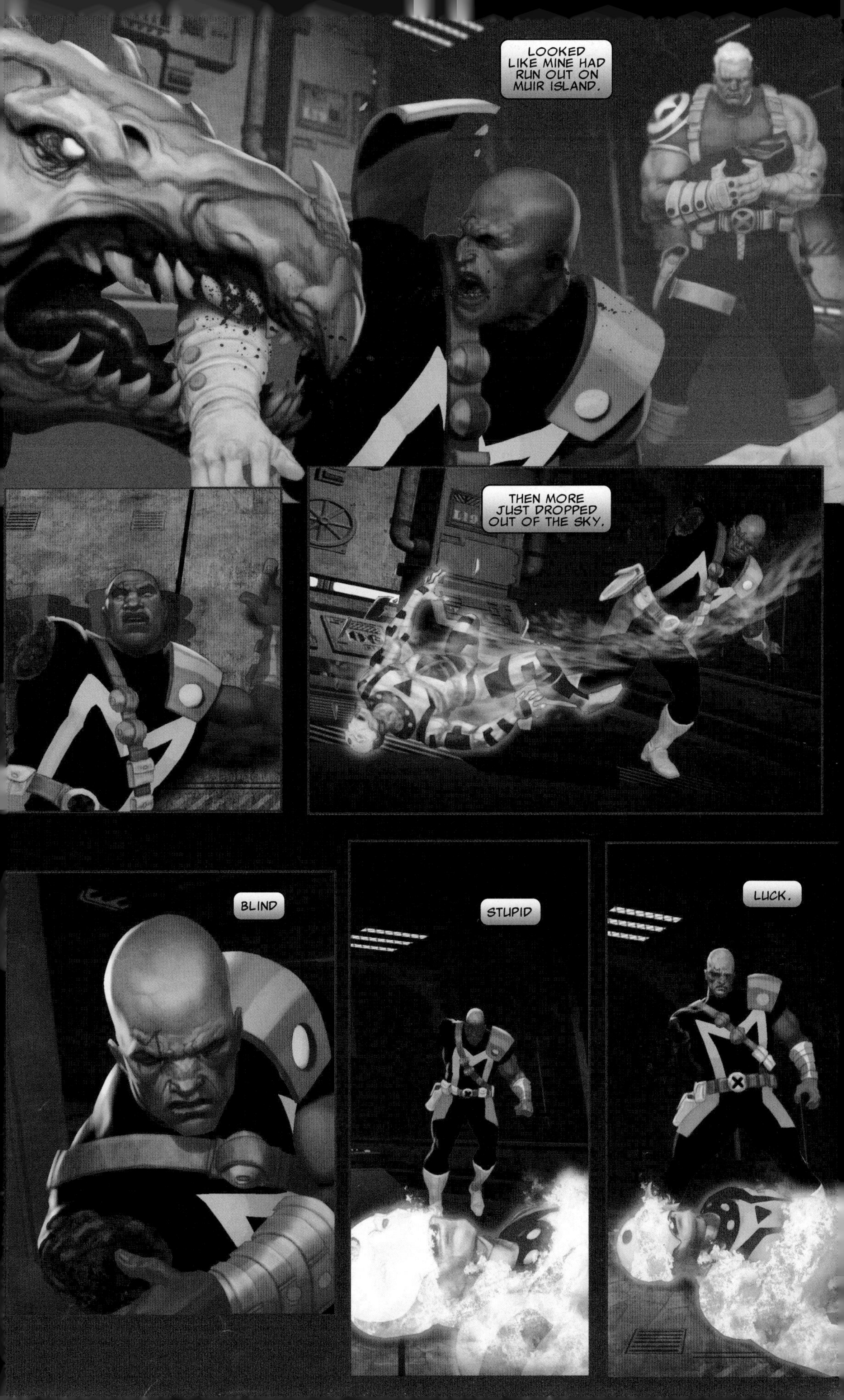
LOOKED LIKE MINE HAD RUN OUT ON MUIR ISLAND.
THEN MORE JUST DROPPED OUT OF THE SKY.
BLIND
STUPID
LUCK.

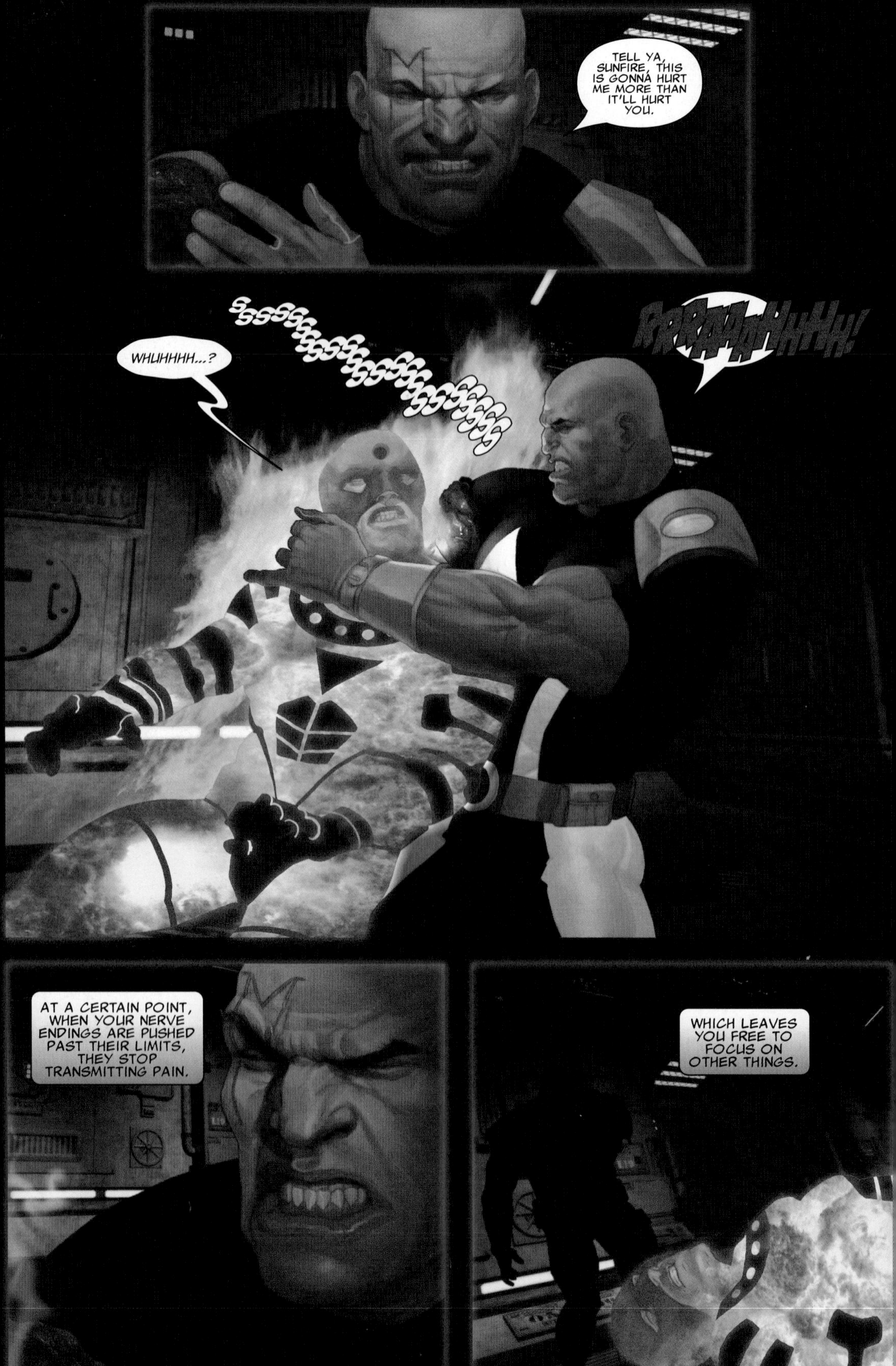

TELL YA, SUNFIRE, THIS IS GONNA HURT ME MORE THAN IT'LL HURT YOU.
WHUHHHH...?
SSSSSSSSSSSSSSSSSSSSSSSSSSSSSSSSS
RRRAAAHHHHH!
AT A CERTAIN POINT, WHEN YOUR NERVE ENDINGS ARE PUSHED PAST THEIR LIMITS, THEY STOP TRANSMITTING PAIN.
WHICH LEAVES YOU FREE TO FOCUS ON OTHER THINGS.

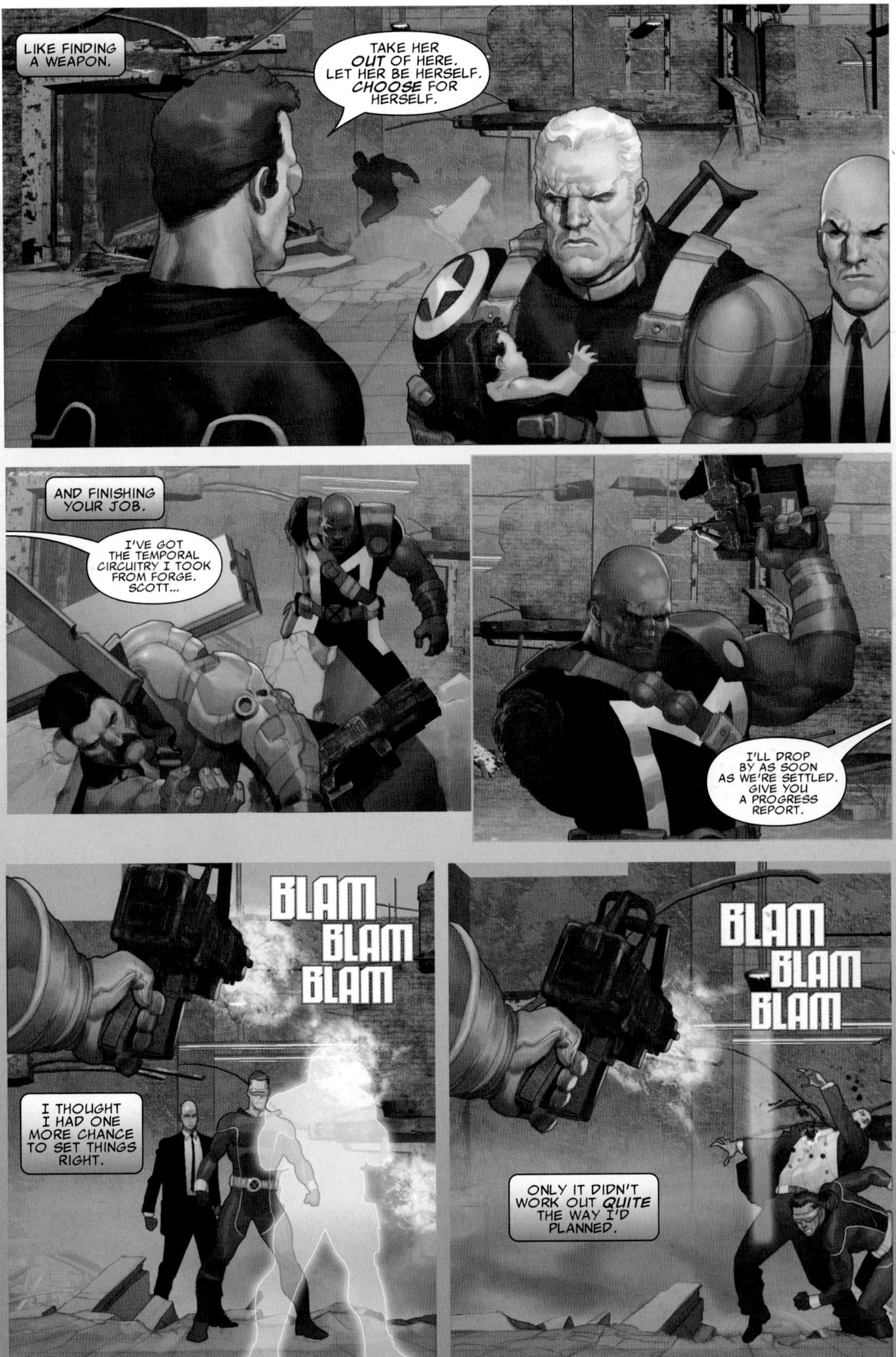

LIKE FINDING A WEAPON.
TAKE HER OUT OF HERE. LET HER BE HERSELF. CHOOSE FOR HERSELF.
AND FINISHING YOUR JOB.
I'VE GOT THE TEMPORAL CIRCUITRY I TOOK FROM FORGE. SCOTT...
I'LL DROP BY AS SOON AS WE'RE SETTLED. GIVE YOU A PROGRESS REPORT.
BLAM BLAM BLAM
I THOUGHT I HAD ONE MORE CHANCE TO SET THINGS RIGHT.
BLAM BLAM BLAM
ONLY IT DIDN'T WORK OUT QUITE THE WAY I'D PLANNED.

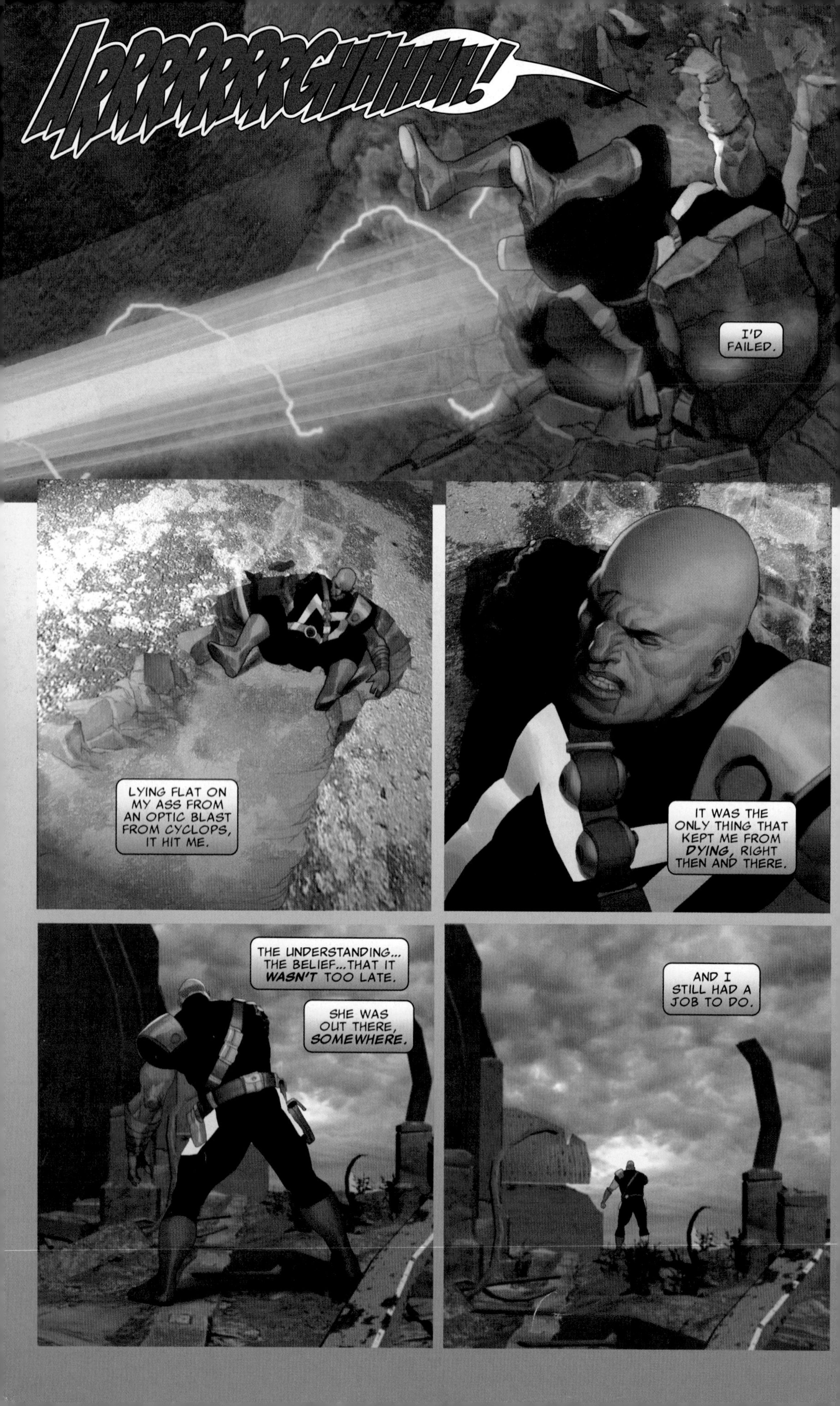
AHRRRRRRRGHHHHH!
I'D FAILED.
LYING FLAT ON MY ASS FROM AN OPTIC BLAST FROM CYCLOPS, IT HIT ME.
IT WAS THE ONLY THING THAT KEPT ME FROM DYING, RIGHT THEN AND THERE.
THE UNDERSTANDING... THE BELIEF...THAT IT WASN'T TOO LATE.
SHE WAS OUT THERE, SOMEWHERE.
AND I STILL HAD A JOB TO DO.

I KNEW EXACTLY WHERE TO FIND THE RIGHT TOOLS.

BEEP-BEEP

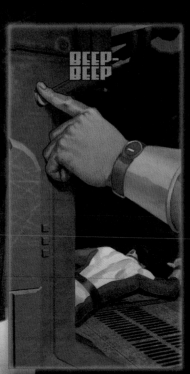

FWOOOOOSHHHHH

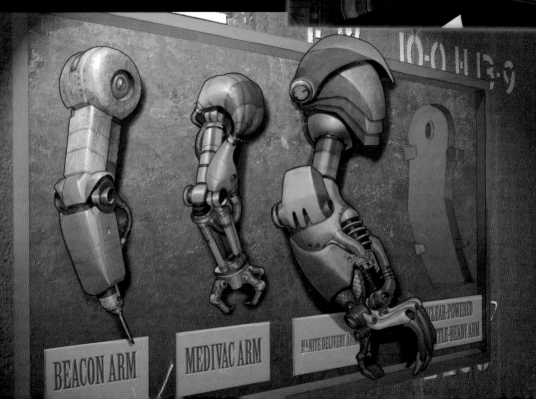

BEACON ARM

MEDIVAC ARM

N'ANITE DELIVERY ARM

NUCLEAR-POWERED BATTLE-READY ARM

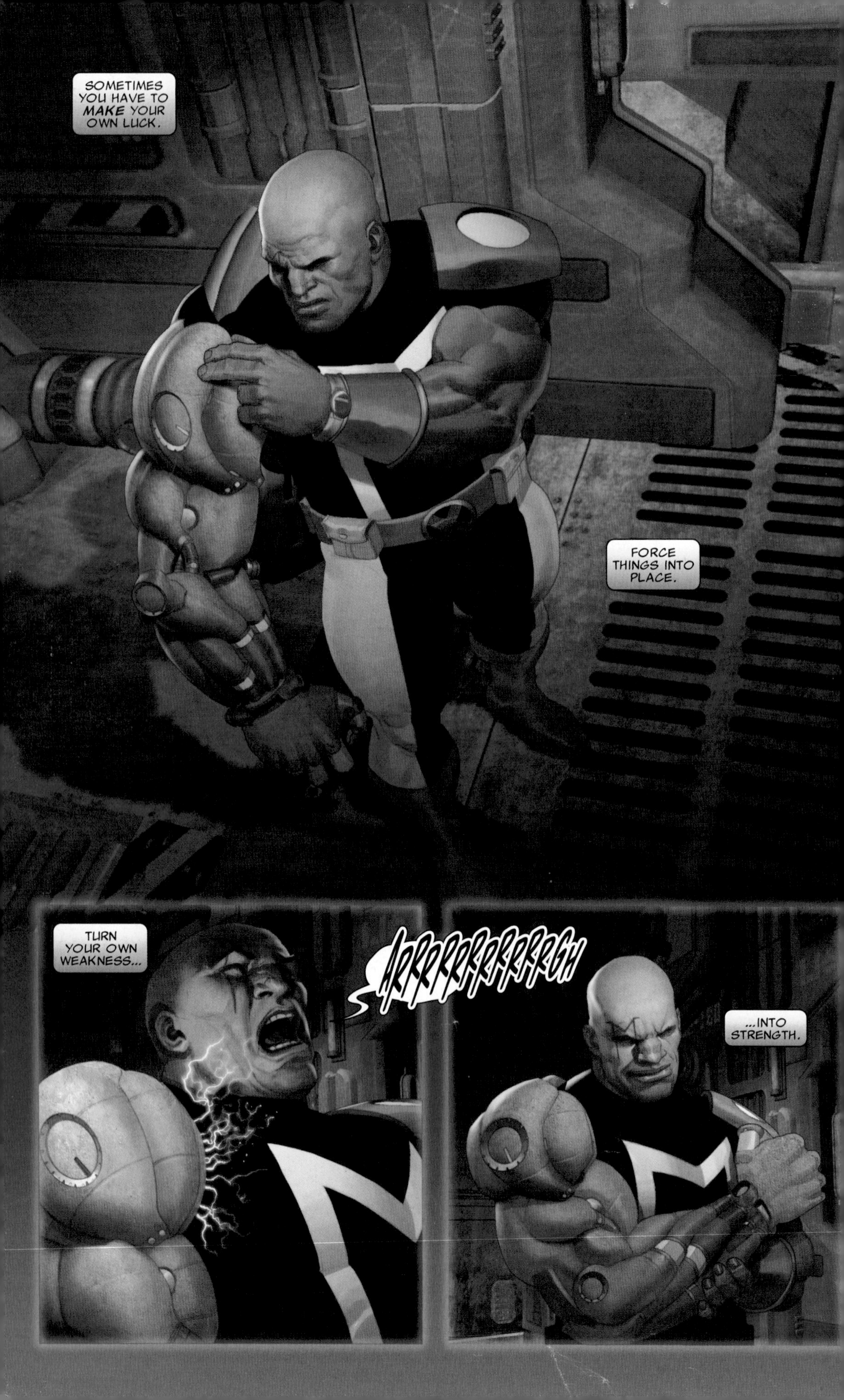
SOMETIMES YOU HAVE TO MAKE YOUR OWN LUCK.
FORCE THINGS INTO PLACE.
TURN YOUR OWN WEAKNESS...
ARRRRRRRRRRRGH
...INTO STRENGTH.

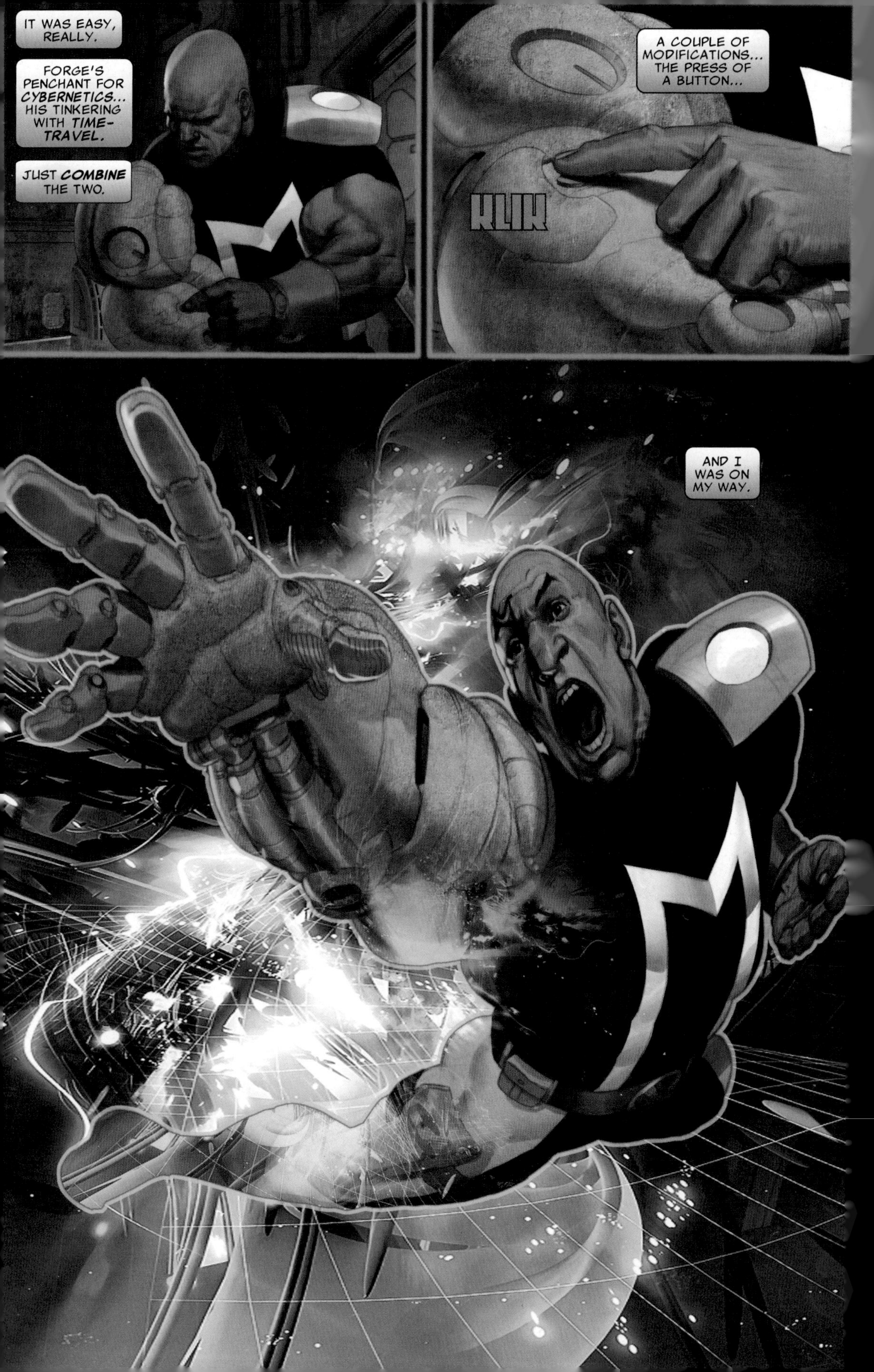
IT WAS EASY, REALLY.
FORGE'S PENCHANT FOR CYBERNETICS... HIS TINKERING WITH TIME-TRAVEL.
JUST COMBINE THE TWO.
A COUPLE OF MODIFICATIONS... THE PRESS OF A BUTTON...
KLIK
AND I WAS ON MY WAY.

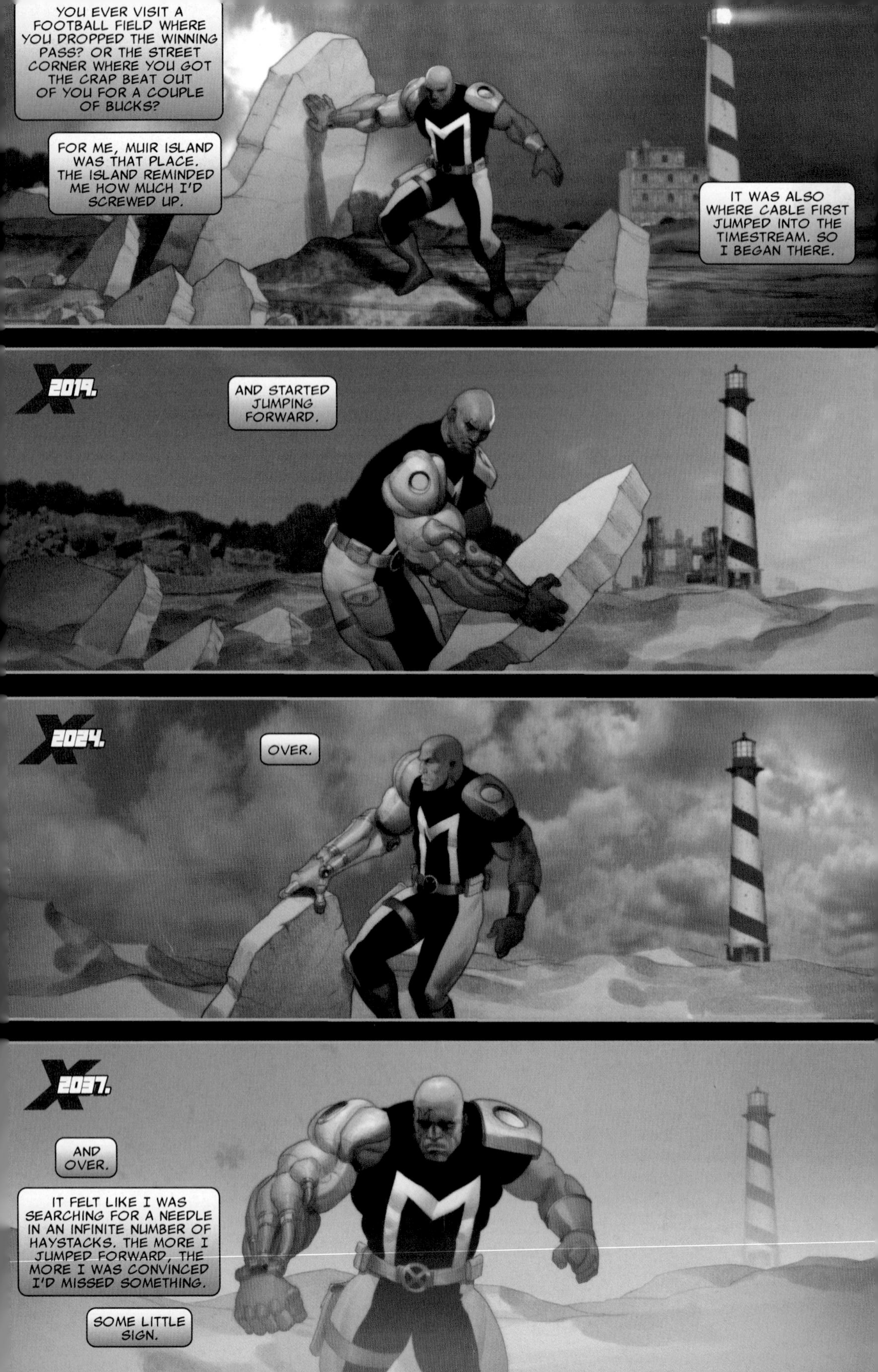
YOU EVER VISIT A FOOTBALL FIELD WHERE YOU DROPPED THE WINNING PASS? OR THE STREET CORNER WHERE YOU GOT THE CRAP BEAT OUT OF YOU FOR A COUPLE OF BUCKS?
FOR ME, MUIR ISLAND WAS THAT PLACE. THE ISLAND REMINDED ME HOW MUCH I'D SCREWED UP.
IT WAS ALSO WHERE CABLE FIRST JUMPED INTO THE TIMESTREAM. SO I BEGAN THERE.
2019.
AND STARTED JUMPING FORWARD.
2024.
OVER.
2037.
AND OVER.
IT FELT LIKE I WAS SEARCHING FOR A NEEDLE IN AN INFINITE NUMBER OF HAYSTACKS. THE MORE I JUMPED FORWARD, THE MORE I WAS CONVINCED I'D MISSED SOMETHING.
SOME LITTLE SIGN.

SOME LITTLE BIT OF LUCK.

HAD TO BE FOR THE BABY.

TOO MUCH OF A COINCIDENCE OTHERWISE.

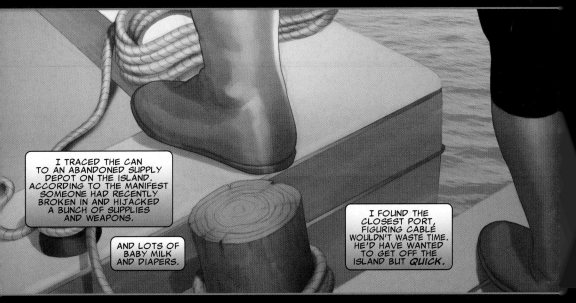

I TRACED THE CAN TO AN ABANDONED SUPPLY DEPOT ON THE ISLAND. ACCORDING TO THE MANIFEST SOMEONE HAD RECENTLY BROKEN IN AND HIJACKED A BUNCH OF SUPPLIES AND WEAPONS.

AND LOTS OF BABY MILK AND DIAPERS.

I FOUND THE CLOSEST PORT, FIGURING CABLE WOULDN'T WASTE TIME. HE'D HAVE WANTED TO GET OFF THE ISLAND BUT *QUICK*.

A QUICK CHAT WITH AN OLD BARGE CAPTAIN NAMED AL BUCHANAN CONFIRMED IT.

AH, THAT WAS A MONTH AGO, MATE.

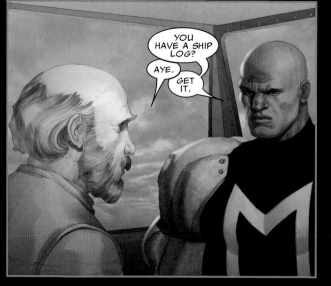

YOU HAVE A SHIP LOG?

AYE. GET IT.

THE LOG TOLD ME THE BARGE UNLOADED ITS SOLE PASSENGERS--A "BIG GUY WHO CALLED HIMSELF CAMPBELL AND HIS INFANT DAUGHTER"--NEAR THE SUNKEN RUINS OF NEWARK.

"BUT LIKE I SAID, THAT WAS MONTHS AGO," BUCHANAN TOLD ME. "THEY WOULD HAVE SKEDADDLED BY NOW."

I TOLD HIM THAT WOULDN'T BE A PROBLEM.

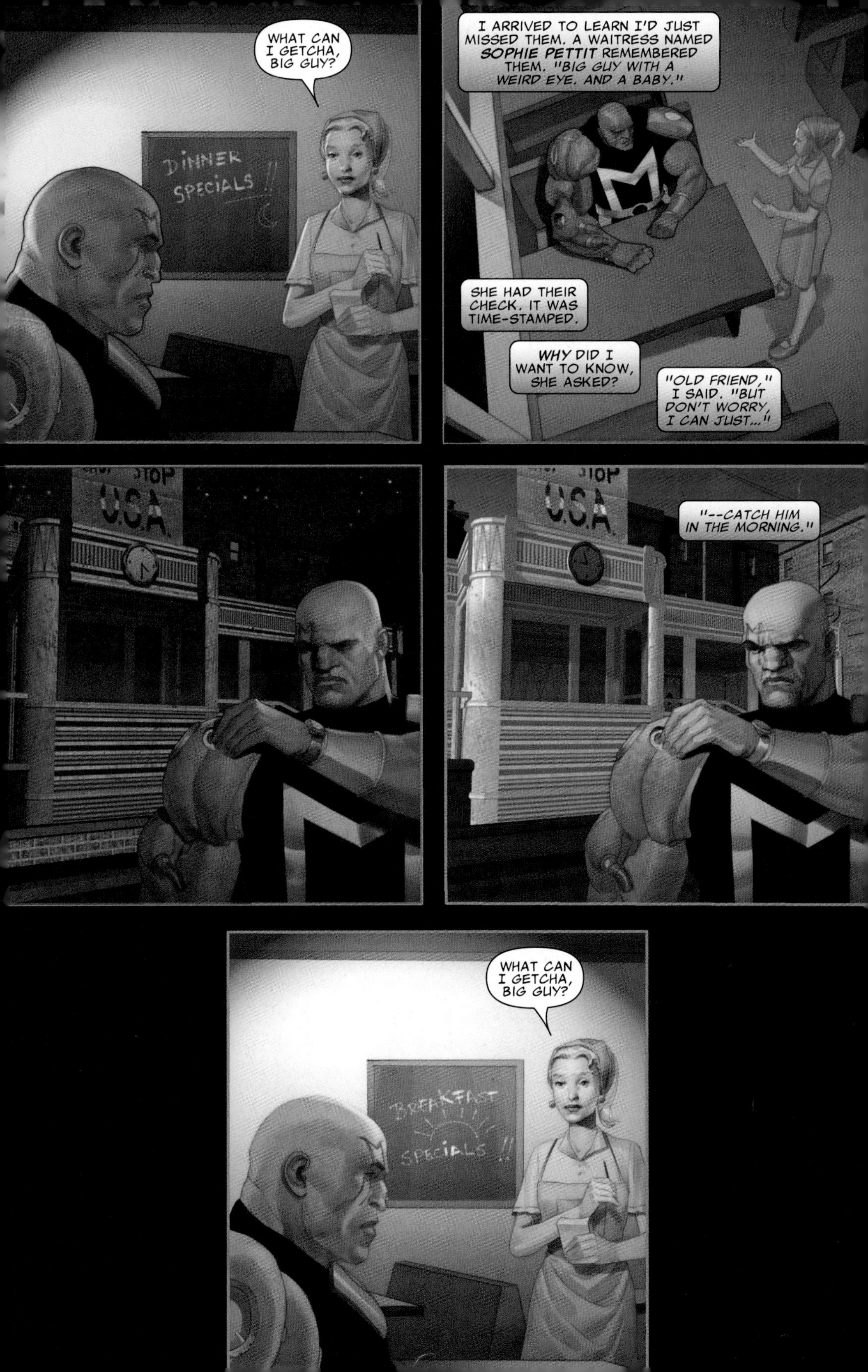
WHAT CAN I GETCHA, BIG GUY?
DINNER SPECIALS !!
I ARRIVED TO LEARN I'D JUST MISSED THEM. A WAITRESS NAMED SOPHIE PETTIT REMEMBERED THEM. "BIG GUY WITH A WEIRD EYE. AND A BABY."
SHE HAD THEIR CHECK. IT WAS TIME-STAMPED.
WHY DID I WANT TO KNOW, SHE ASKED?
"OLD FRIEND," I SAID. "BUT DON'T WORRY, I CAN JUST..."
U.S.A
"--CATCH HIM IN THE MORNING."
WHAT CAN I GETCHA, BIG GUY?
BREAKFAST SPECIALS !!

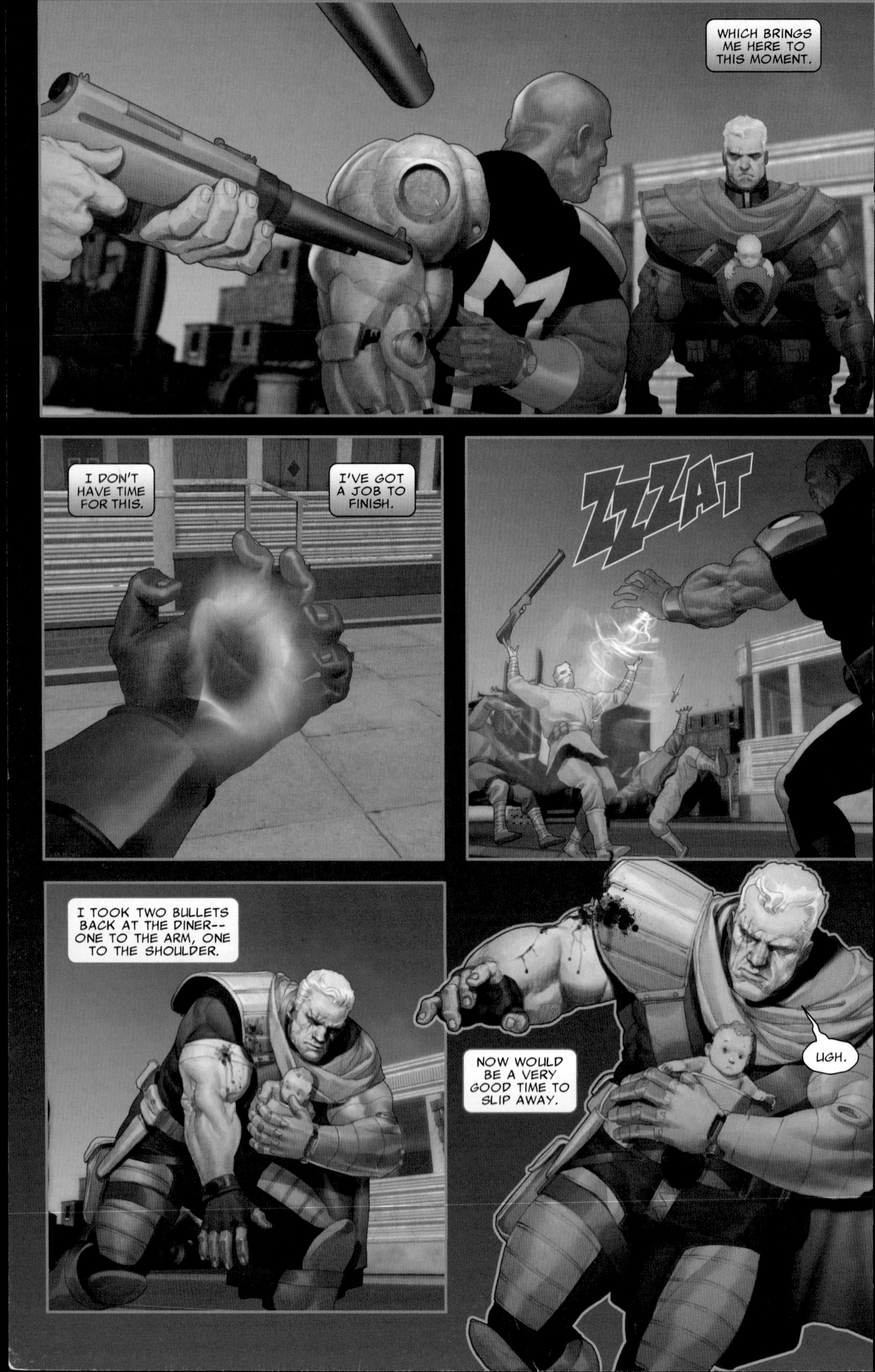
WHICH BRINGS ME HERE TO THIS MOMENT.
I DON'T HAVE TIME FOR THIS.
I'VE GOT A JOB TO FINISH.
ZZZAT
I TOOK TWO BULLETS BACK AT THE DINER-- ONE TO THE ARM, ONE TO THE SHOULDER.
NOW WOULD BE A VERY GOOD TIME TO SLIP AWAY.
UGH.

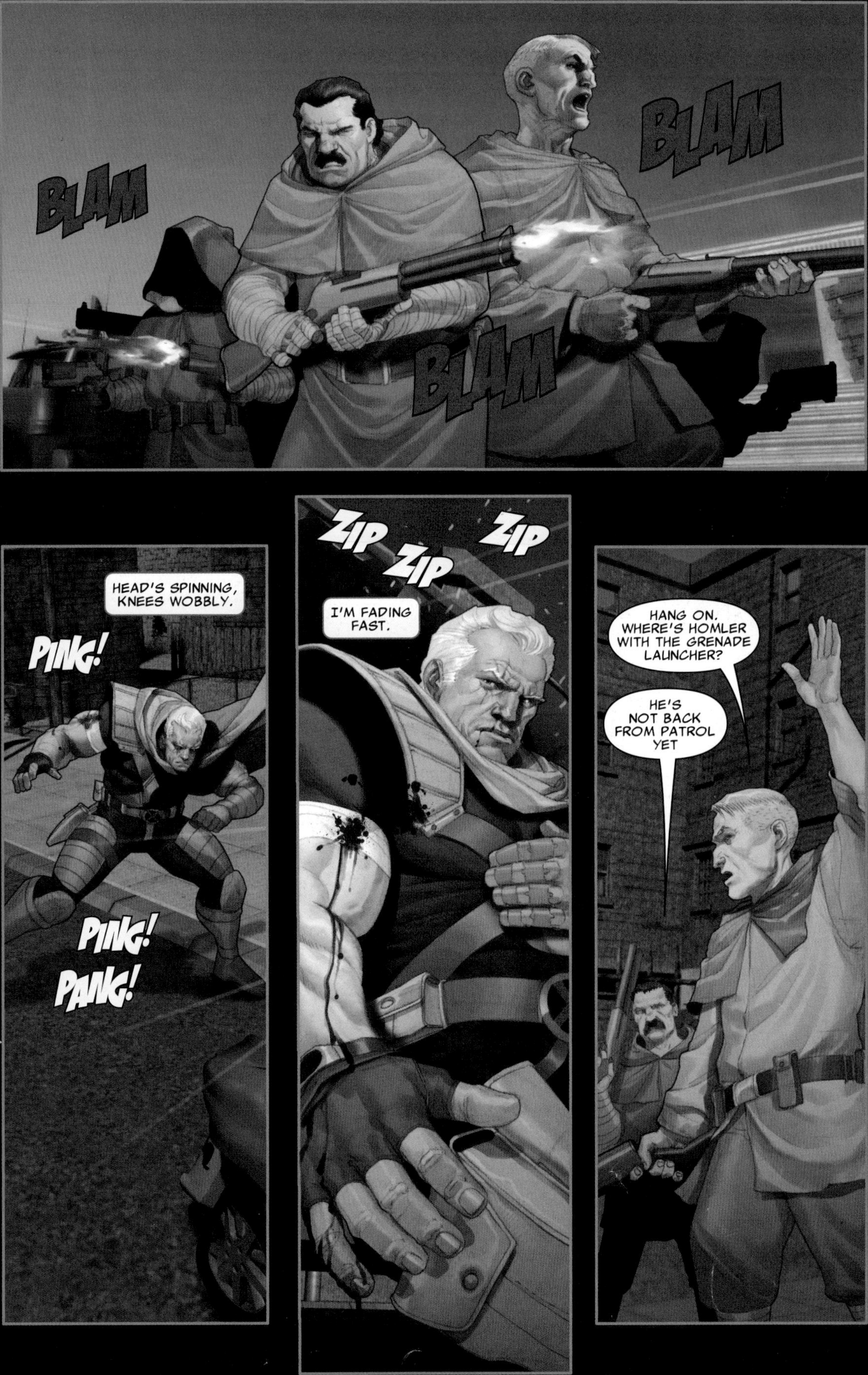
BLAM
BLAM
BLAM
HEAD'S SPINNING, KNEES WOBBLY.
PING!
PING!
PANG!
ZIP
ZIP
ZIP
I'M FADING FAST.
HANG ON. WHERE'S HOMLER WITH THE GRENADE LAUNCHER?
HE'S NOT BACK FROM PATROL YET

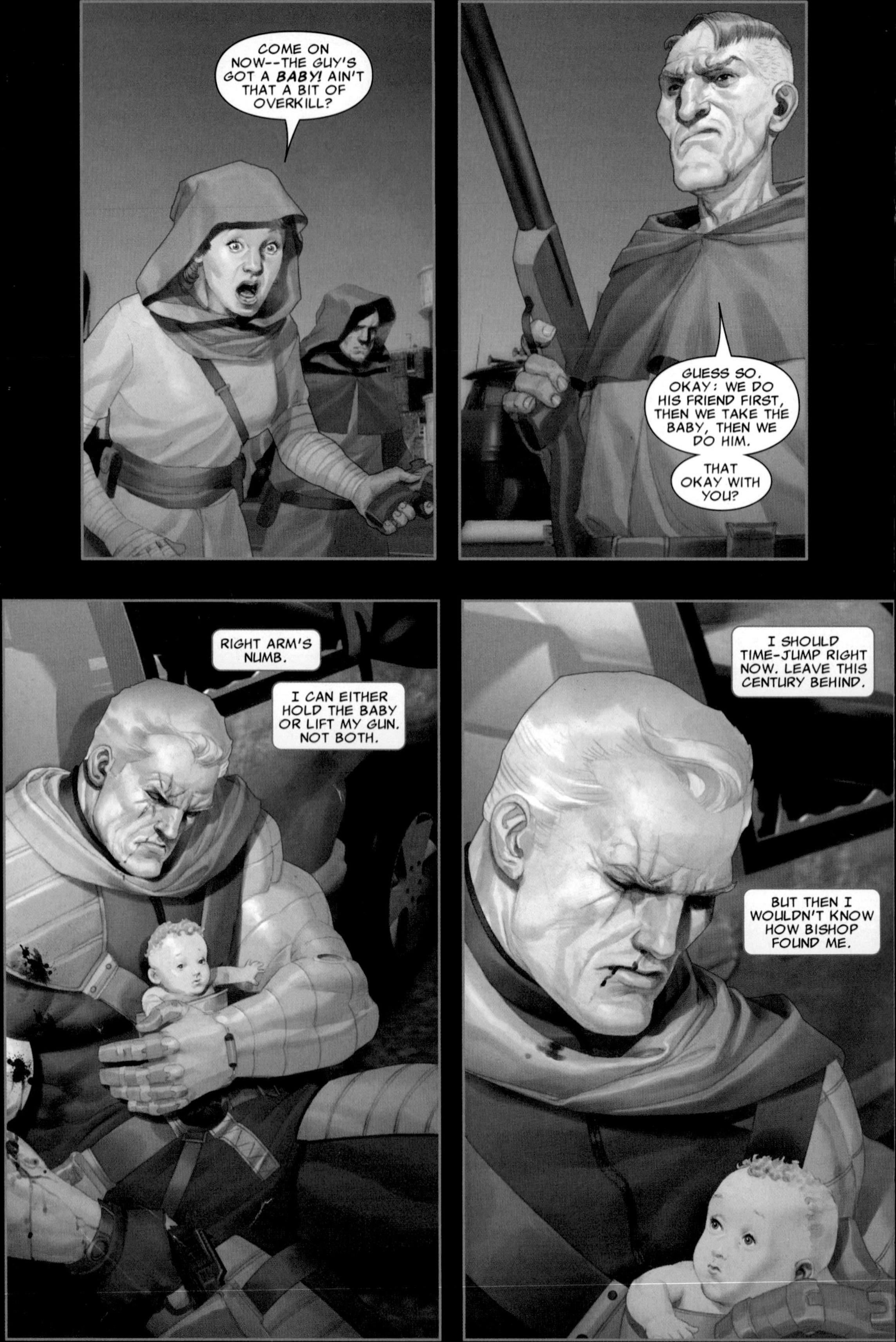

COME ON NOW--THE GUY'S GOT A BABY! AIN'T THAT A BIT OF OVERKILL?
GUESS SO. OKAY: WE DO HIS FRIEND FIRST, THEN WE TAKE THE BABY, THEN WE DO HIM.
THAT OKAY WITH YOU?
RIGHT ARM'S NUMB.
I CAN EITHER HOLD THE BABY OR LIFT MY GUN. NOT BOTH.
I SHOULD TIME-JUMP RIGHT NOW. LEAVE THIS CENTURY BEHIND.
BUT THEN I WOULDN'T KNOW HOW BISHOP FOUND ME.

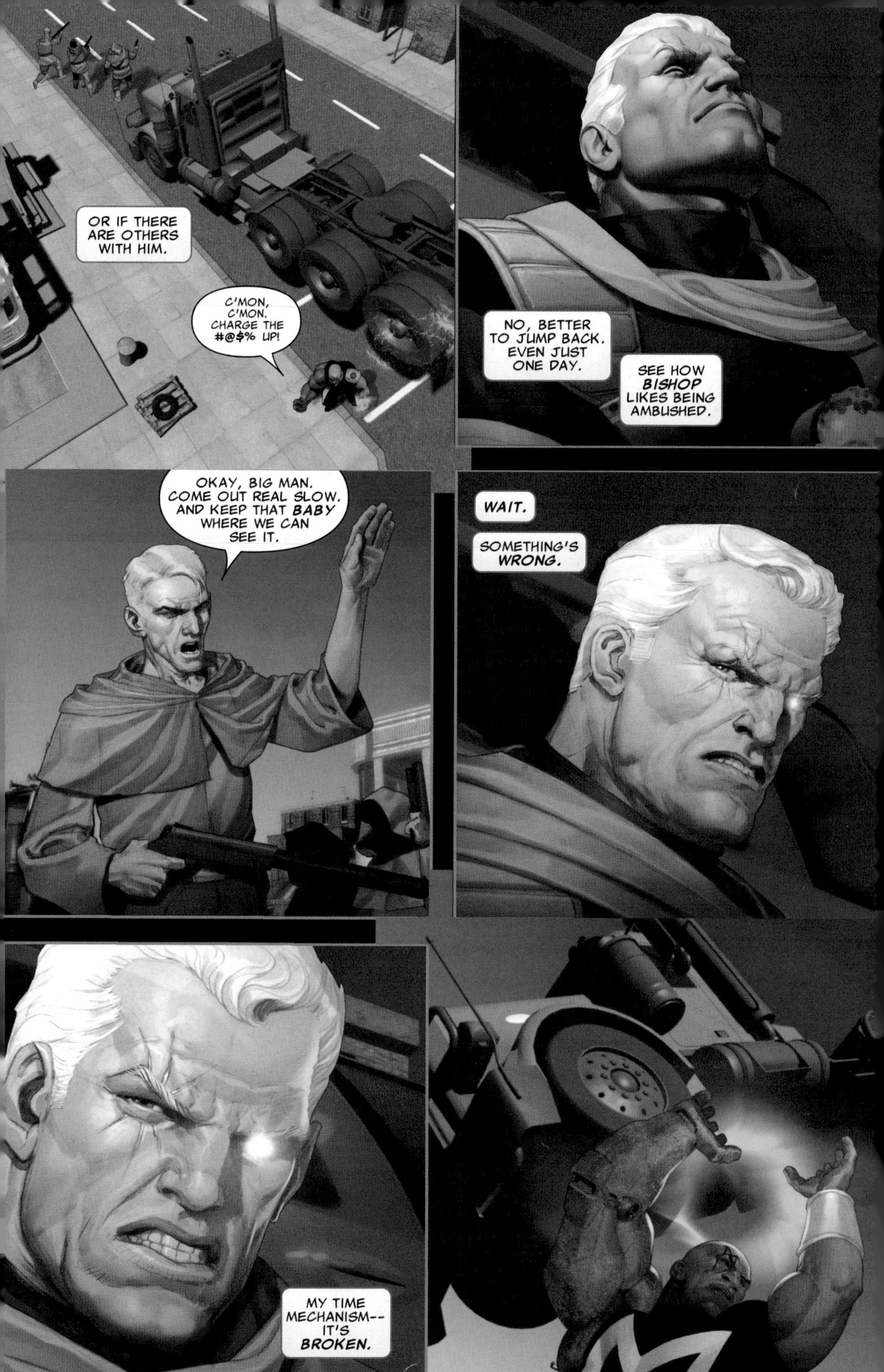
OR IF THERE ARE OTHERS WITH HIM.
C'MON, C'MON. CHARGE THE #@$% UP!
NO, BETTER TO JUMP BACK. EVEN JUST ONE DAY.
SEE HOW BISHOP LIKES BEING AMBUSHED.
OKAY, BIG MAN. COME OUT REAL SLOW. AND KEEP THAT BABY WHERE WE CAN SEE IT.
WAIT.
SOMETHING'S WRONG.
MY TIME MECHANISM-- IT'S BROKEN.

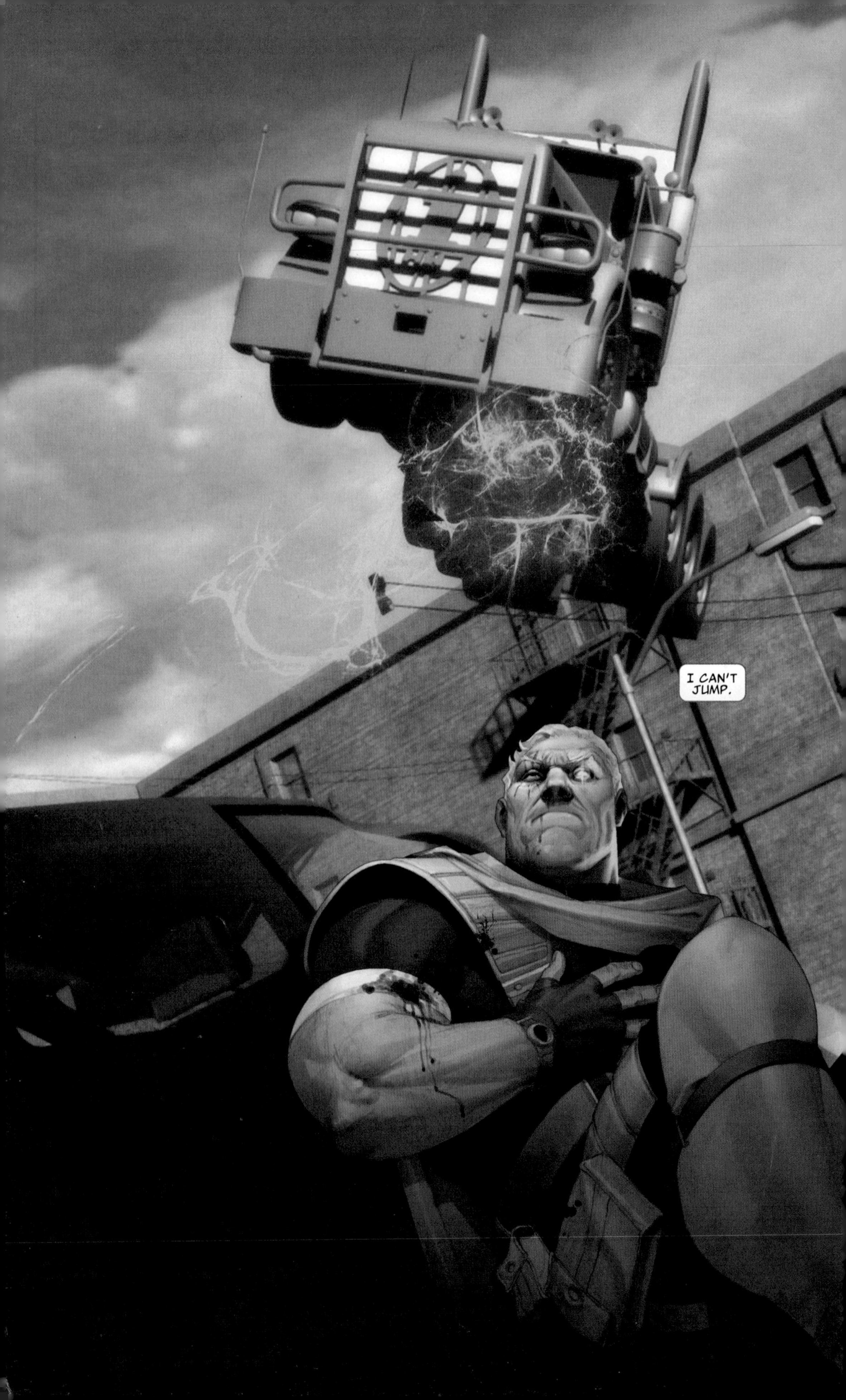
I CAN'T JUMP.

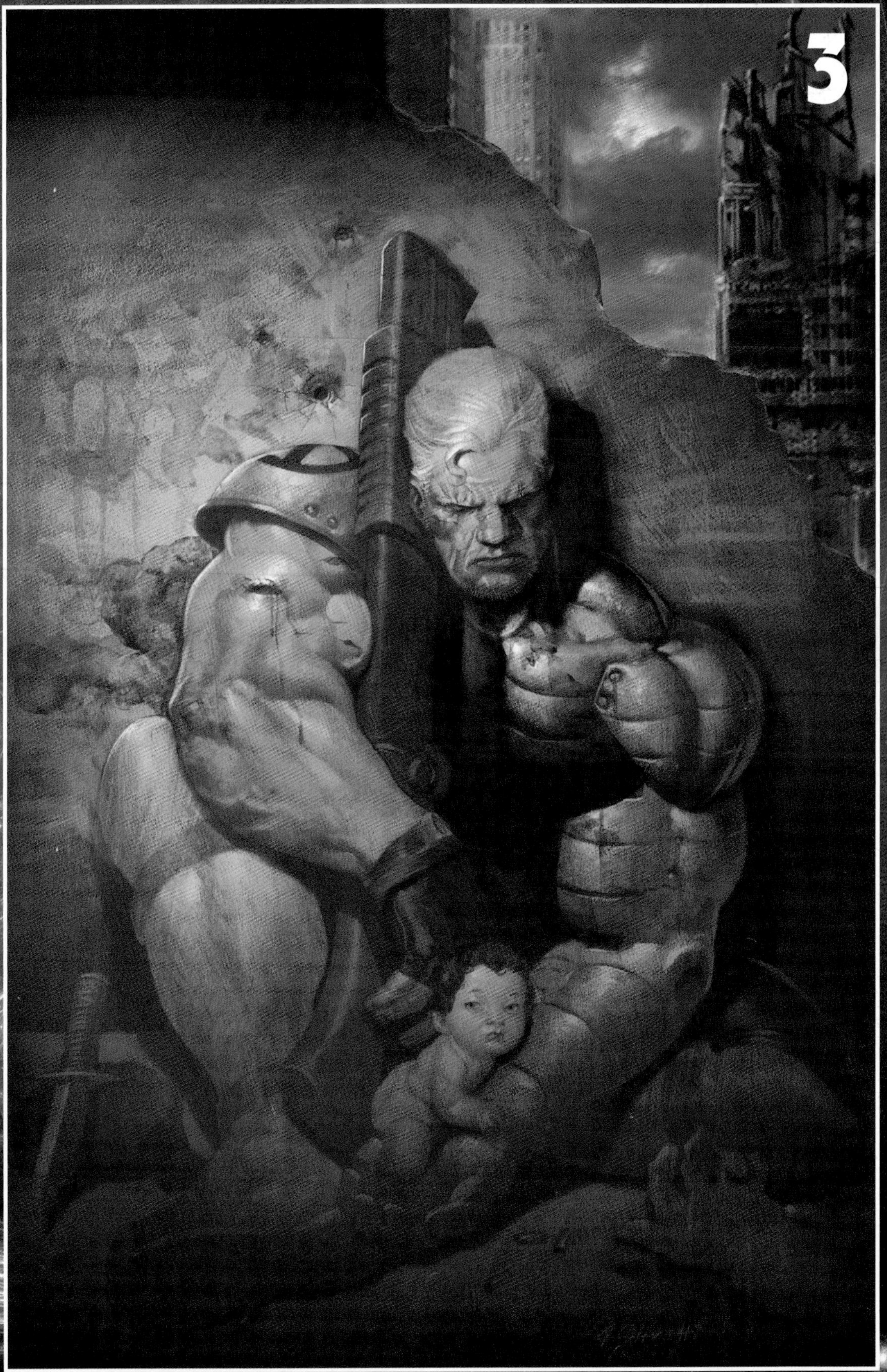
3

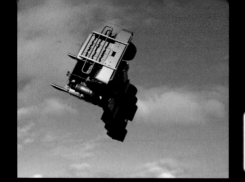

FIVE MINUTES AGO, A DEAD MAN FIRED A GUN AT ME, TRYING TO KILL THE BABY STRAPPED TO MY CHEST.

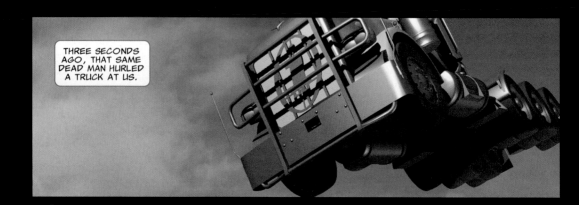

THREE SECONDS AGO, THAT SAME DEAD MAN HURLED A TRUCK AT US.

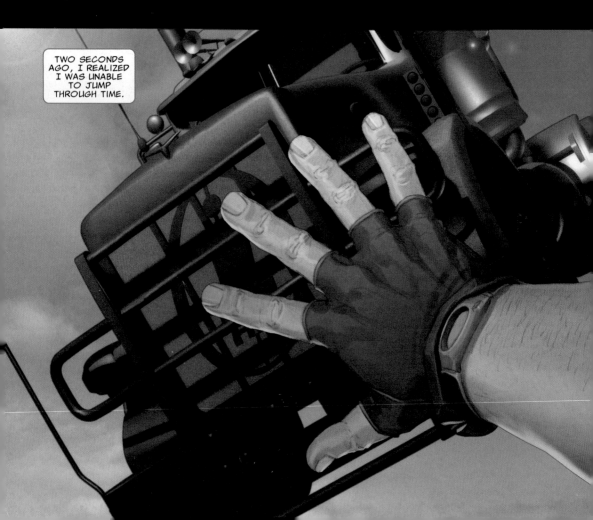

TWO SECONDS AGO, I REALIZED I WAS UNABLE TO JUMP THROUGH TIME.

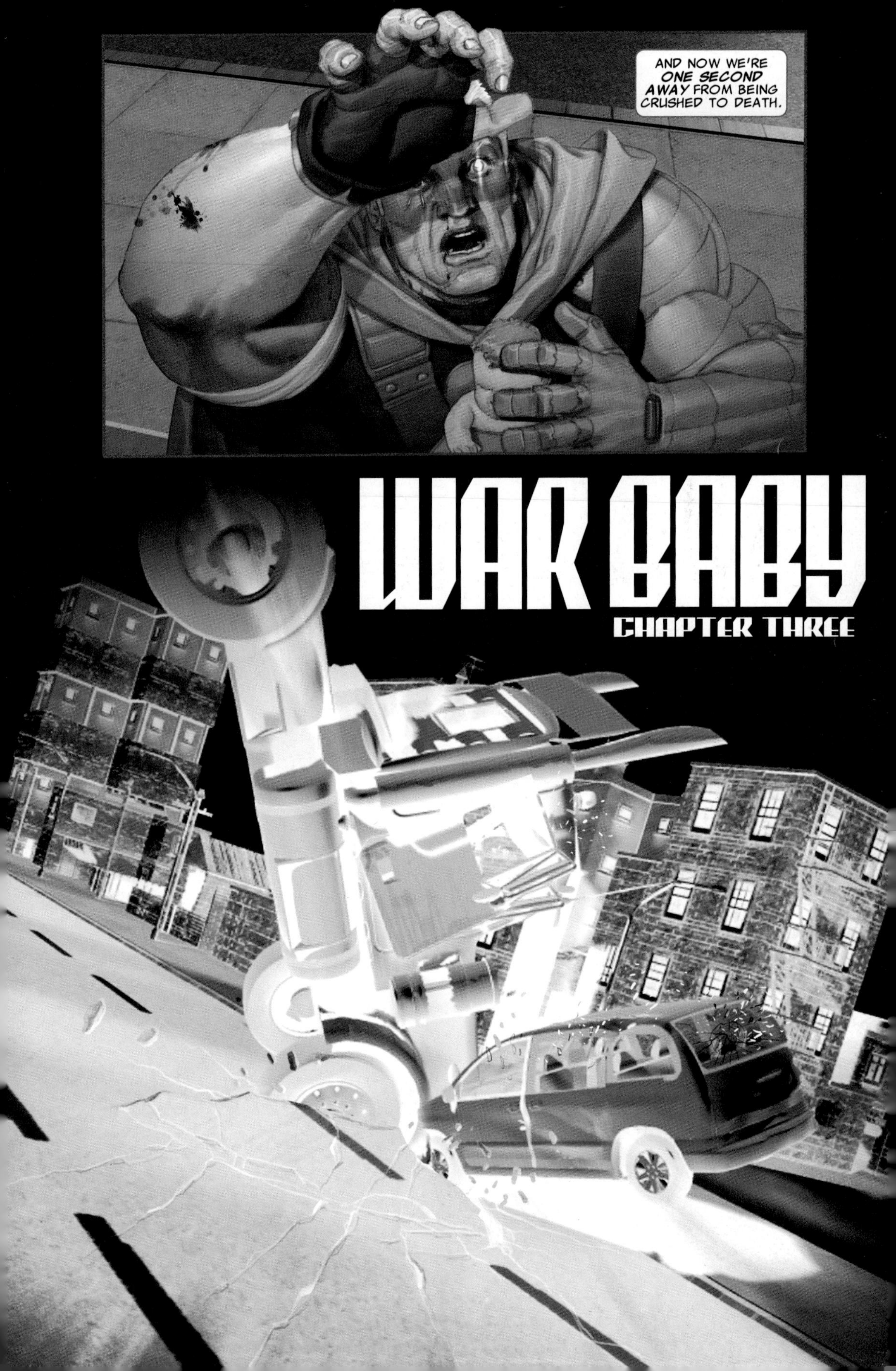
AND NOW WE'RE ONE SECOND AWAY FROM BEING CRUSHED TO DEATH.
WAR BABY
CHAPTER THREE

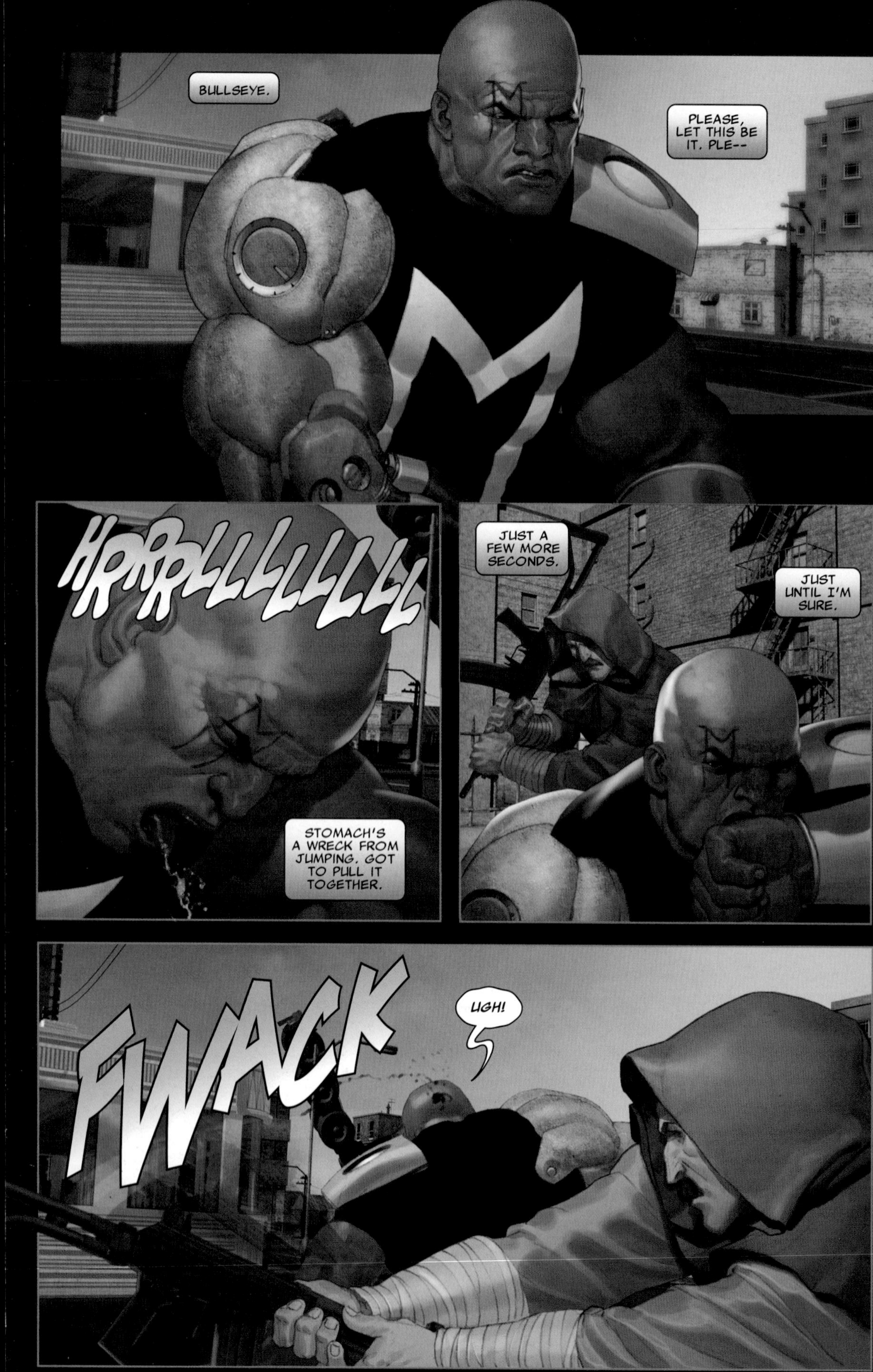
BULLSEYE.
PLEASE, LET THIS BE IT. PLE--
HRRRLLLLLLLL
STOMACH'S A WRECK FROM JUMPING. GOT TO PULL IT TOGETHER.
JUST A FEW MORE SECONDS.
JUST UNTIL I'M SURE.
FWACK
UGH!

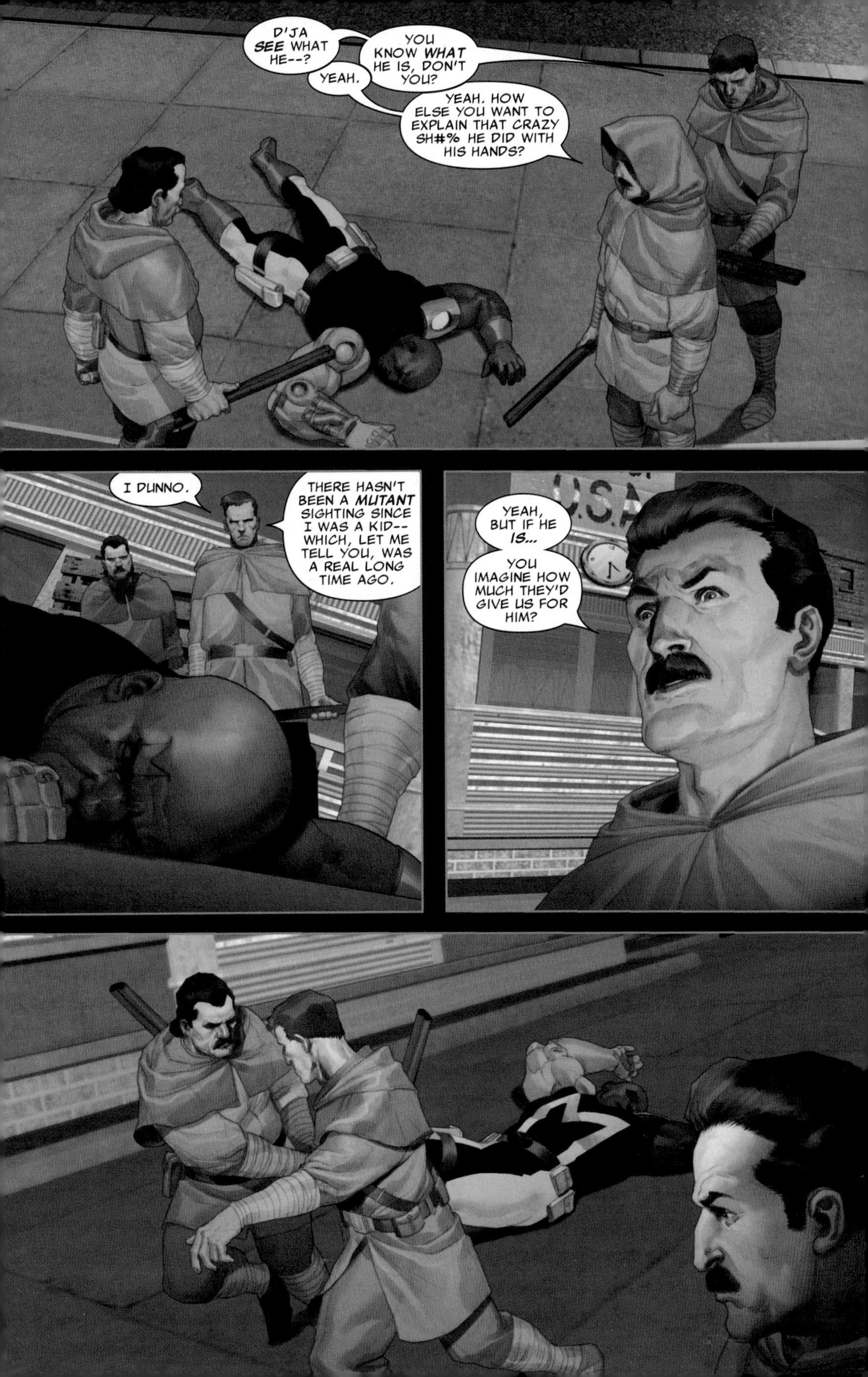
D'JA **SEE** WHAT HE--?
YEAH.
YOU KNOW **WHAT** HE IS, DON'T YOU?
YEAH. HOW ELSE YOU WANT TO EXPLAIN THAT CRAZY SH#% HE DID WITH HIS HANDS?
I DUNNO.
THERE HASN'T BEEN A ***MUTANT*** SIGHTING SINCE I WAS A KID-- WHICH, LET ME TELL YOU, WAS A REAL LONG TIME AGO.
YEAH, BUT IF HE ***IS...***
YOU IMAGINE HOW MUCH THEY'D GIVE US FOR HIM?

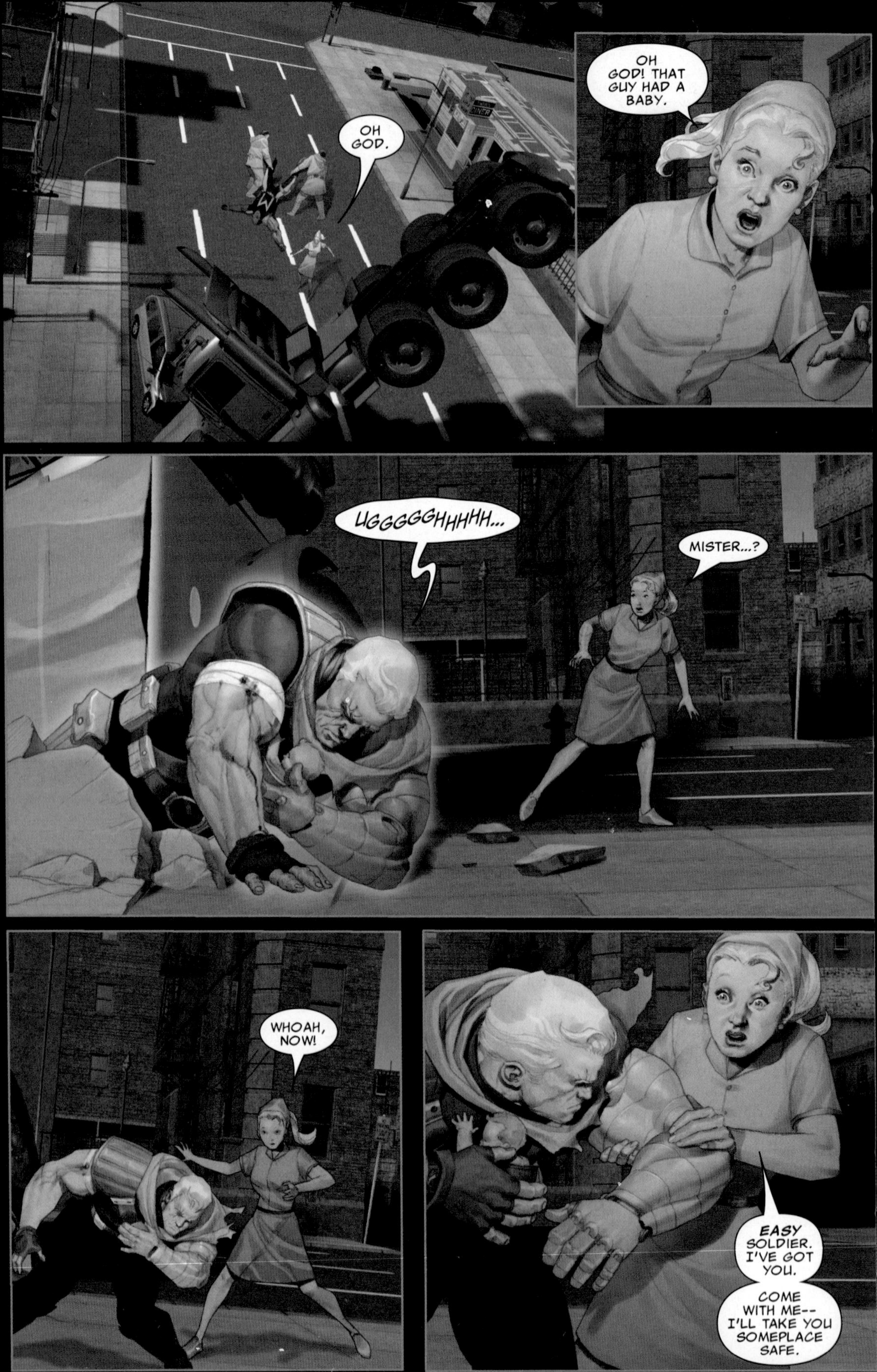
OH GOD.
OH GOD! THAT GUY HAD A BABY.
UGGGGGHHHHH...
MISTER...?
WHOAH, NOW!
EASY SOLDIER. I'VE GOT YOU.
COME WITH ME-- I'LL TAKE YOU SOMEPLACE SAFE.

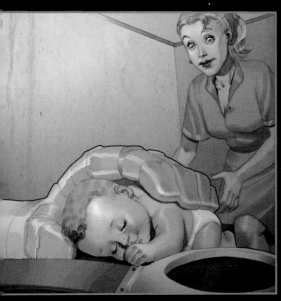

NO.

I WAS JUST--

YOU PASSED OUT AND THE BABY--

I DIDN'T MEAN ANY--

NOBODY HOLDS HER BUT ME.

I GET IT, I GET IT.

LISTEN, MISTER, YOU'RE HURT REAL BAD. WE'VE GOT TO FIND YOU A DOCTOR.

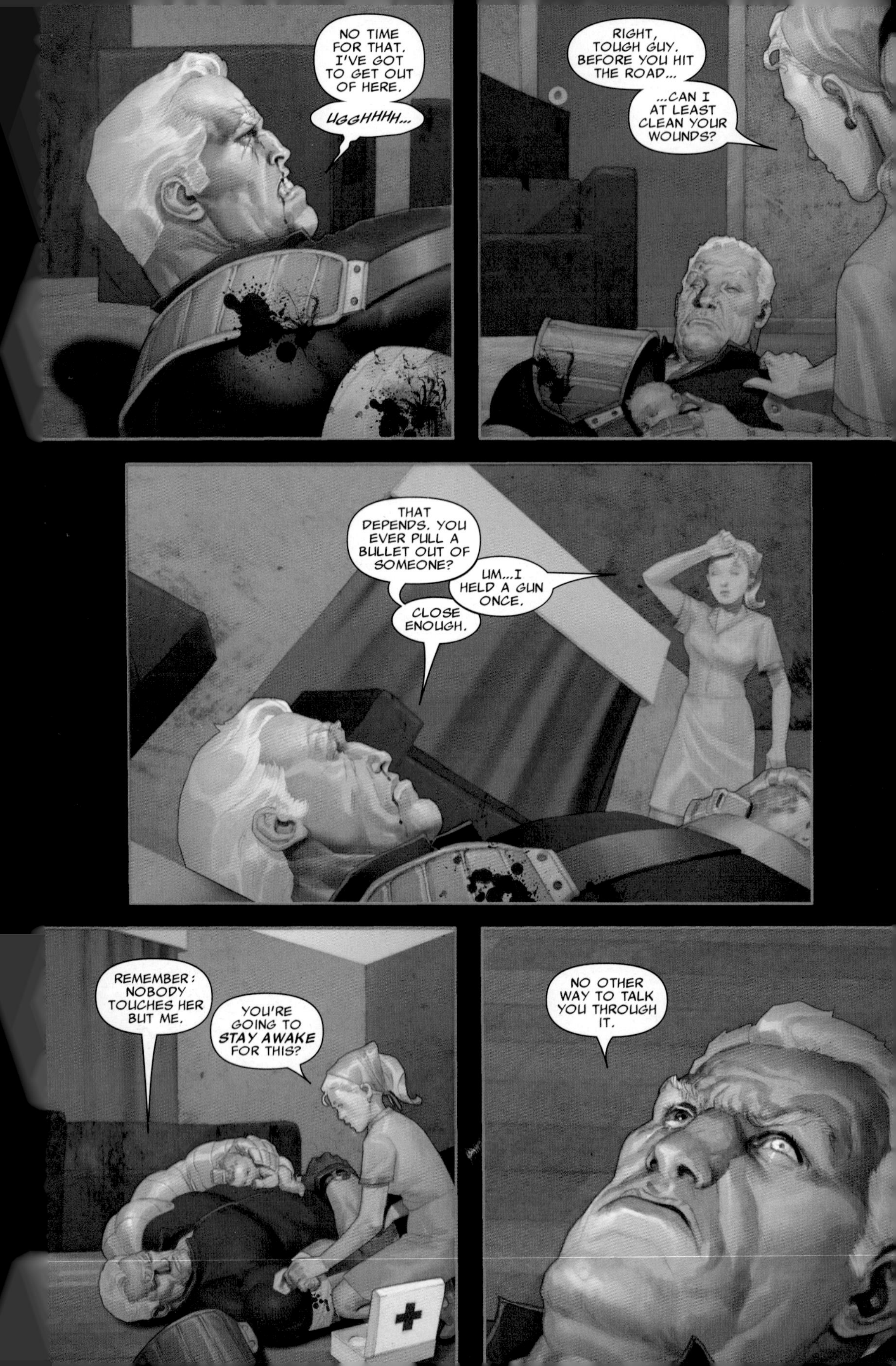
NO TIME FOR THAT. I'VE GOT TO GET OUT OF HERE.
UGGHHHH...
RIGHT, TOUGH GUY. BEFORE YOU HIT THE ROAD...
...CAN I AT LEAST CLEAN YOUR WOUNDS?
THAT DEPENDS. YOU EVER PULL A BULLET OUT OF SOMEONE?
UM...I HELD A GUN ONCE.
CLOSE ENOUGH.
REMEMBER: NOBODY TOUCHES HER BUT ME.
YOU'RE GOING TO STAY AWAKE FOR THIS?
NO OTHER WAY TO TALK YOU THROUGH IT.

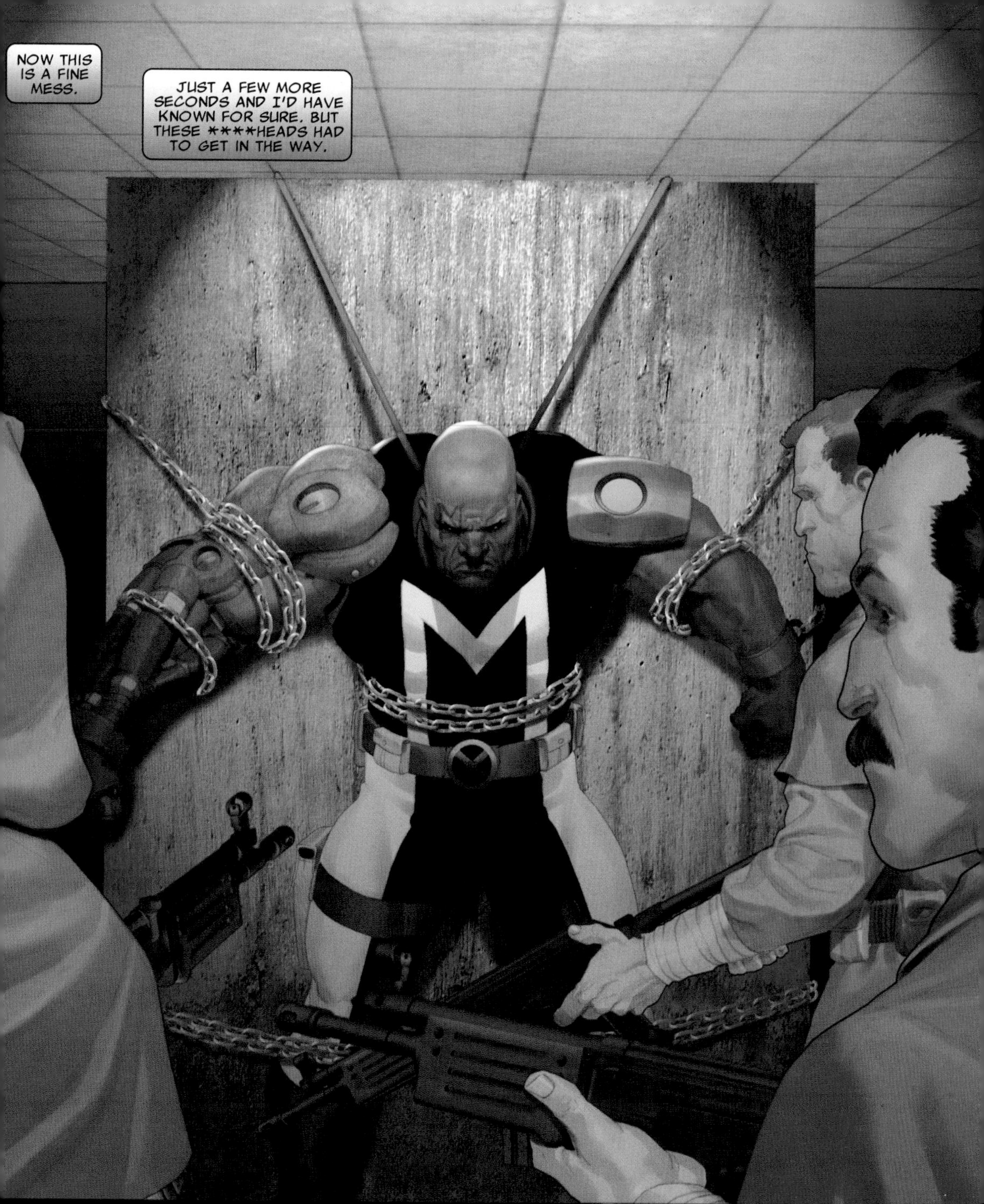
NOW THIS IS A FINE MESS.
JUST A FEW MORE SECONDS AND I'D HAVE KNOWN FOR SURE. BUT THESE ****HEADS HAD TO GET IN THE WAY.

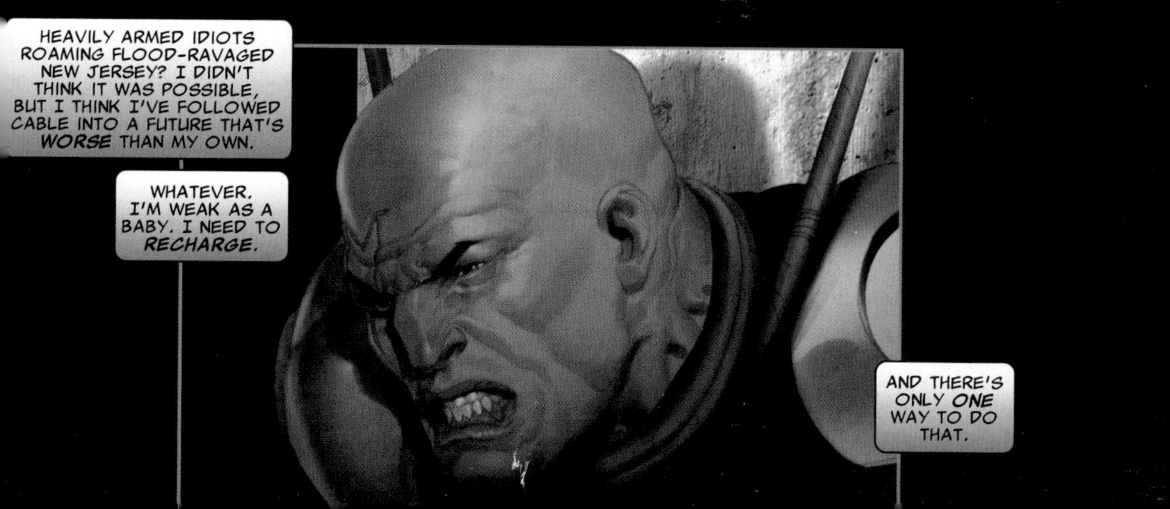
HEAVILY ARMED IDIOTS ROAMING FLOOD-RAVAGED NEW JERSEY? I DIDN'T THINK IT WAS POSSIBLE, BUT I THINK I'VE FOLLOWED CABLE INTO A FUTURE THAT'S *WORSE* THAN MY OWN.
WHATEVER. I'M WEAK AS A BABY. I NEED TO *RECHARGE*.
AND THERE'S ONLY *ONE* WAY TO DO THAT.

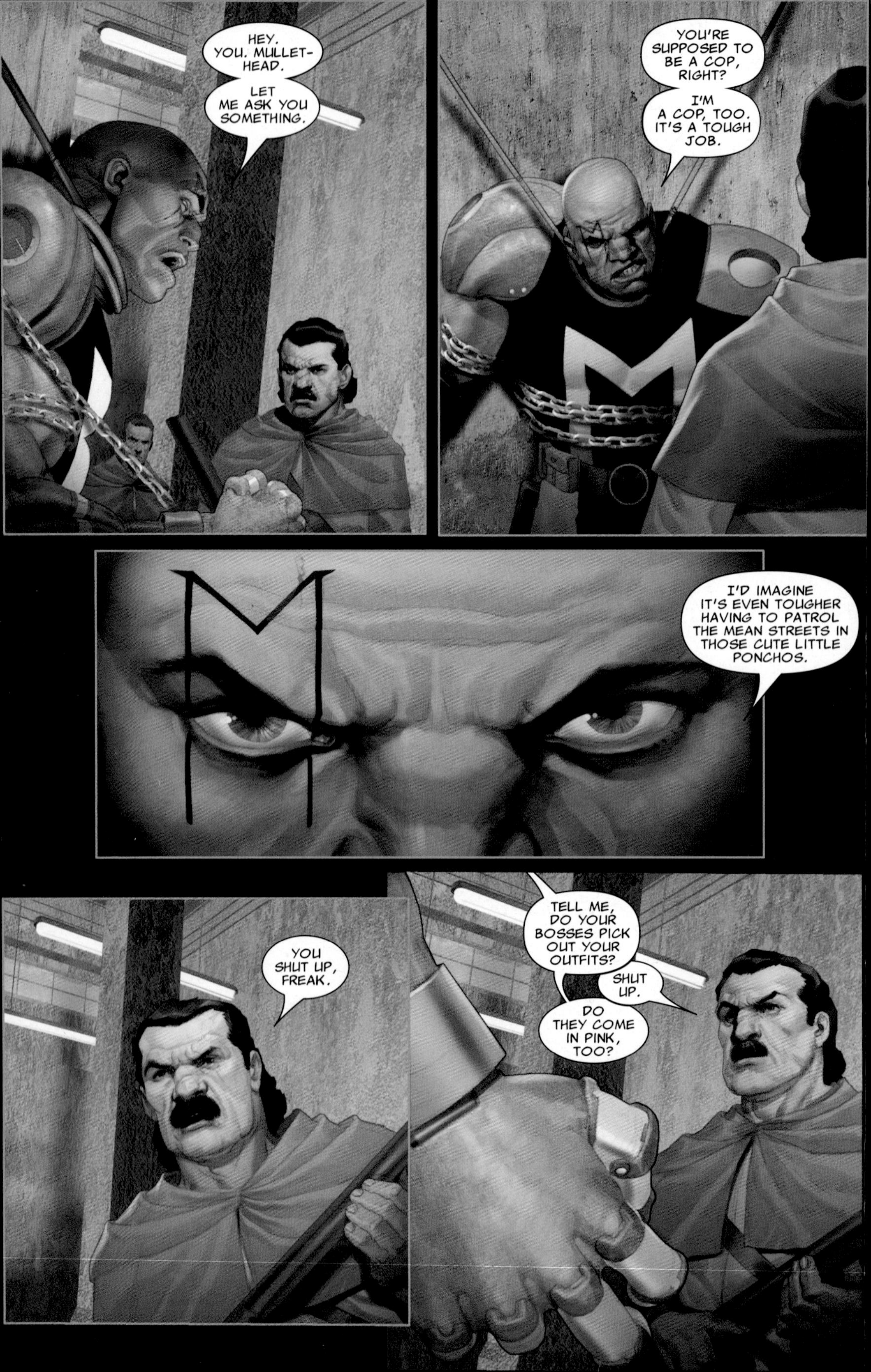
HEY. YOU. MULLET-HEAD.
LET ME ASK YOU SOMETHING.
YOU'RE SUPPOSED TO BE A COP, RIGHT?
I'M A COP, TOO. IT'S A TOUGH JOB.
I'D IMAGINE IT'S EVEN TOUGHER HAVING TO PATROL THE MEAN STREETS IN THOSE CUTE LITTLE PONCHOS.
YOU SHUT UP, FREAK.
TELL ME, DO YOUR BOSSES PICK OUT YOUR OUTFITS?
SHUT UP.
DO THEY COME IN PINK, TOO?

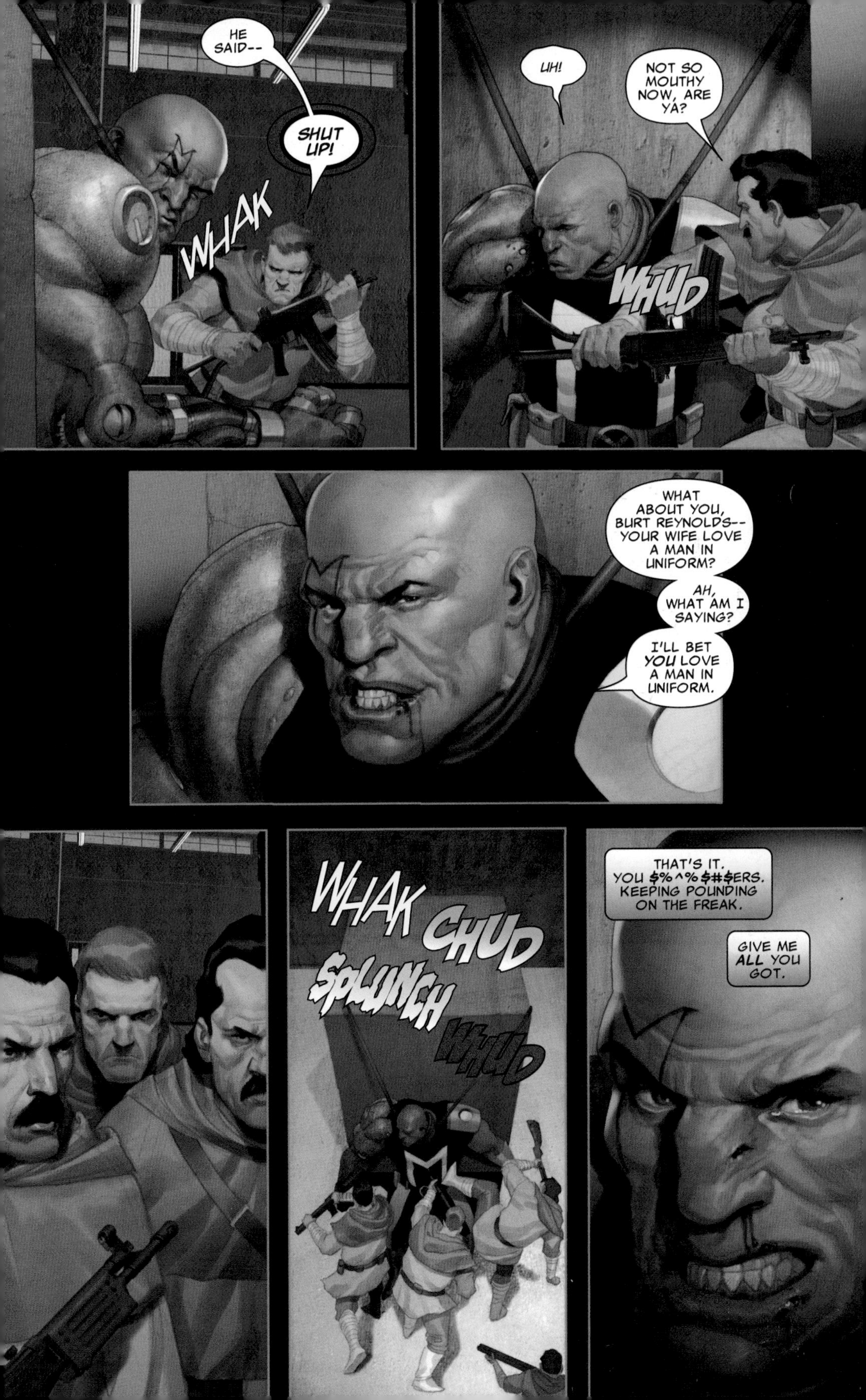
HE SAID--
SHUT UP!
WHAK
UH!
NOT SO MOUTHY NOW, ARE YA?
WHUD
WHAT ABOUT YOU, BURT REYNOLDS-- YOUR WIFE LOVE A MAN IN UNIFORM?
AH, WHAT AM I SAYING?
I'LL BET YOU LOVE A MAN IN UNIFORM.
WHAK
CHUD
SPLUNCH
WHUD
THAT'S IT. YOU $%^%$#$ERS. KEEPING POUNDING ON THE FREAK.
GIVE ME ALL YOU GOT.

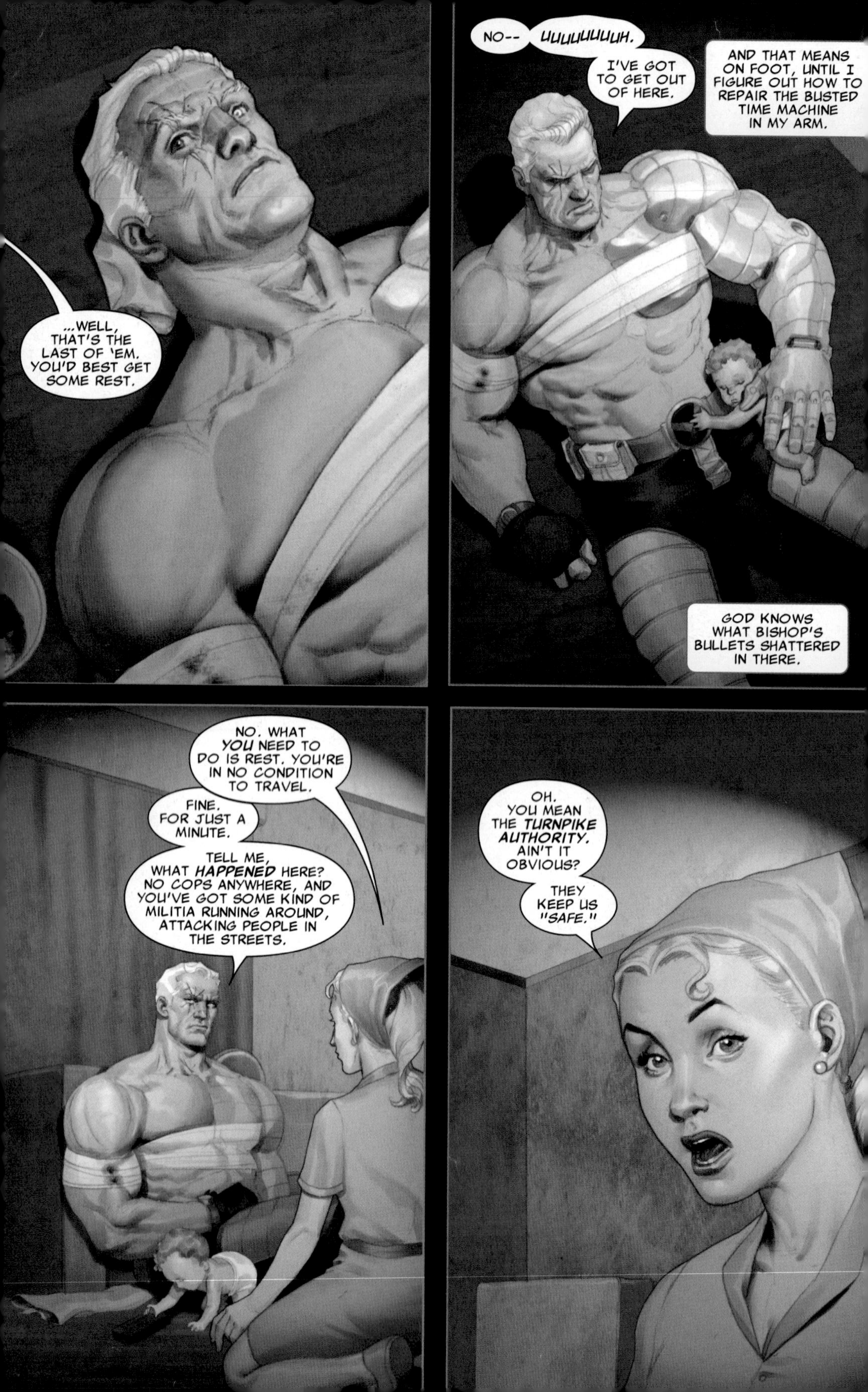
...WELL, THAT'S THE LAST OF 'EM. YOU'D BEST GET SOME REST.
NO--
UUUUUUUUH.
I'VE GOT TO GET OUT OF HERE.
AND THAT MEANS ON FOOT, UNTIL I FIGURE OUT HOW TO REPAIR THE BUSTED TIME MACHINE IN MY ARM.
GOD KNOWS WHAT BISHOP'S BULLETS SHATTERED IN THERE.
NO. WHAT YOU NEED TO DO IS REST. YOU'RE IN NO CONDITION TO TRAVEL.
FINE. FOR JUST A MINUTE.
TELL ME, WHAT HAPPENED HERE? NO COPS ANYWHERE, AND YOU'VE GOT SOME KIND OF MILITIA RUNNING AROUND, ATTACKING PEOPLE IN THE STREETS.
OH. YOU MEAN THE TURNPIKE AUTHORITY. AIN'T IT OBVIOUS?
THEY KEEP US "SAFE."

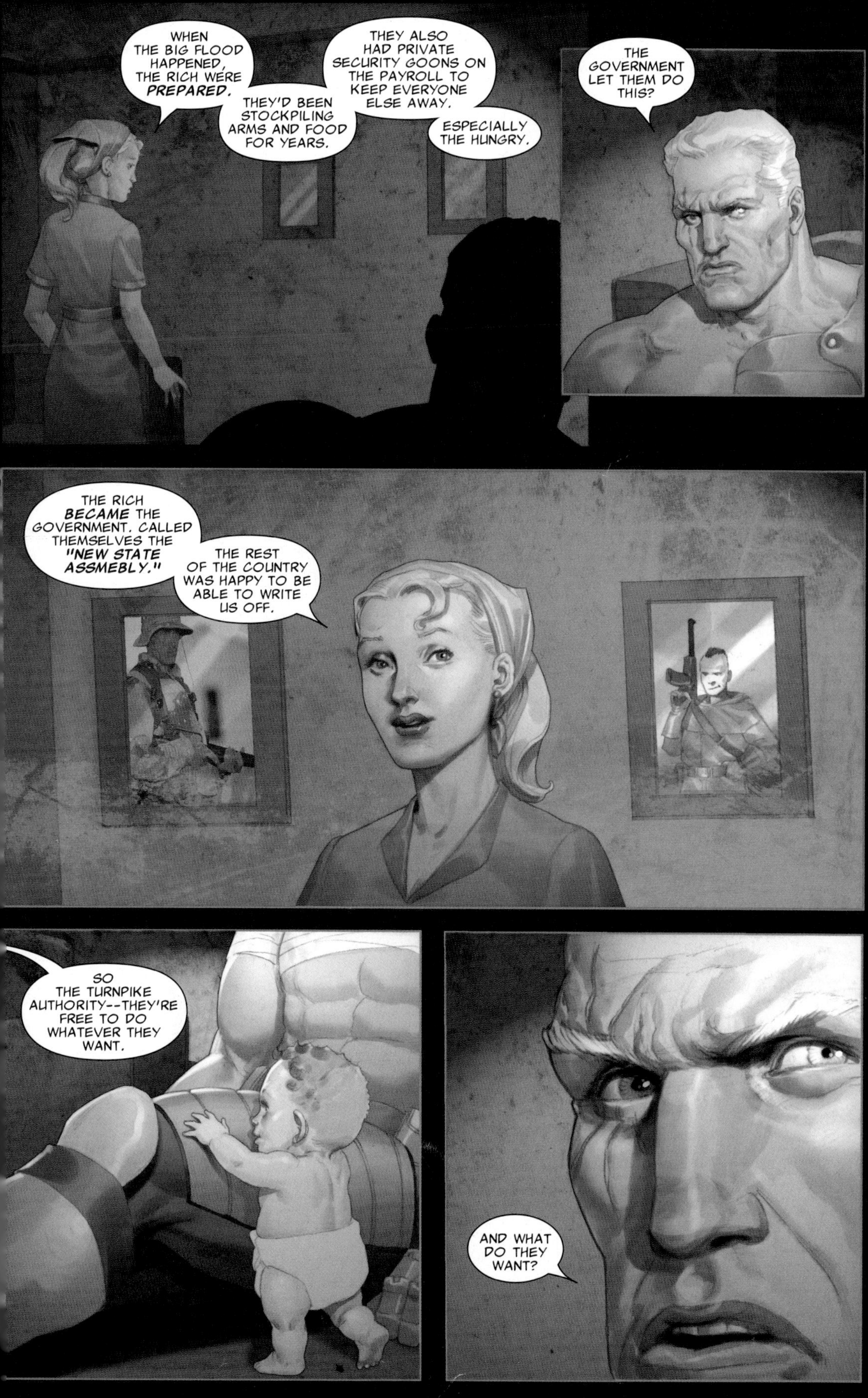

WHEN THE BIG FLOOD HAPPENED, THE RICH WERE PREPARED.
THEY'D BEEN STOCKPILING ARMS AND FOOD FOR YEARS.
THEY ALSO HAD PRIVATE SECURITY GOONS ON THE PAYROLL TO KEEP EVERYONE ELSE AWAY.
ESPECIALLY THE HUNGRY.
THE GOVERNMENT LET THEM DO THIS?
THE RICH BECAME THE GOVERNMENT. CALLED THEMSELVES THE "NEW STATE ASSMEBLY."
THE REST OF THE COUNTRY WAS HAPPY TO BE ABLE TO WRITE US OFF.
SO THE TURNPIKE AUTHORITY--THEY'RE FREE TO DO WHATEVER THEY WANT.
AND WHAT DO THEY WANT?

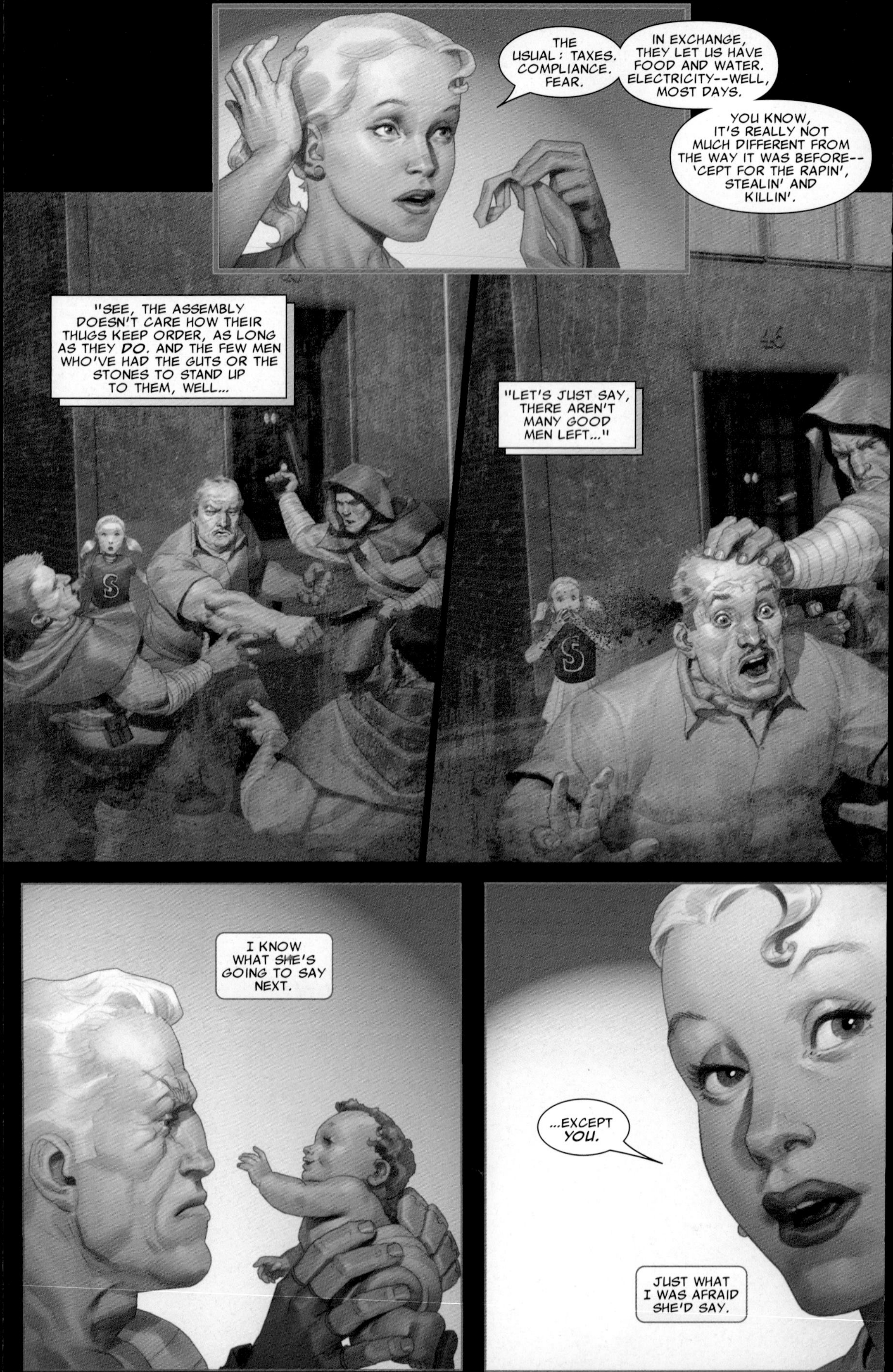

THE USUAL: TAXES. COMPLIANCE. FEAR.
IN EXCHANGE, THEY LET US HAVE FOOD AND WATER. ELECTRICITY--WELL, MOST DAYS.
YOU KNOW, IT'S REALLY NOT MUCH DIFFERENT FROM THE WAY IT WAS BEFORE--'CEPT FOR THE RAPIN', STEALIN' AND KILLIN'.
"SEE, THE ASSEMBLY DOESN'T CARE HOW THEIR THUGS KEEP ORDER, AS LONG AS THEY DO. AND THE FEW MEN WHO'VE HAD THE GUTS OR THE STONES TO STAND UP TO THEM, WELL...
"LET'S JUST SAY, THERE AREN'T MANY GOOD MEN LEFT..."
I KNOW WHAT SHE'S GOING TO SAY NEXT.
...EXCEPT YOU.
JUST WHAT I WAS AFRAID SHE'D SAY.

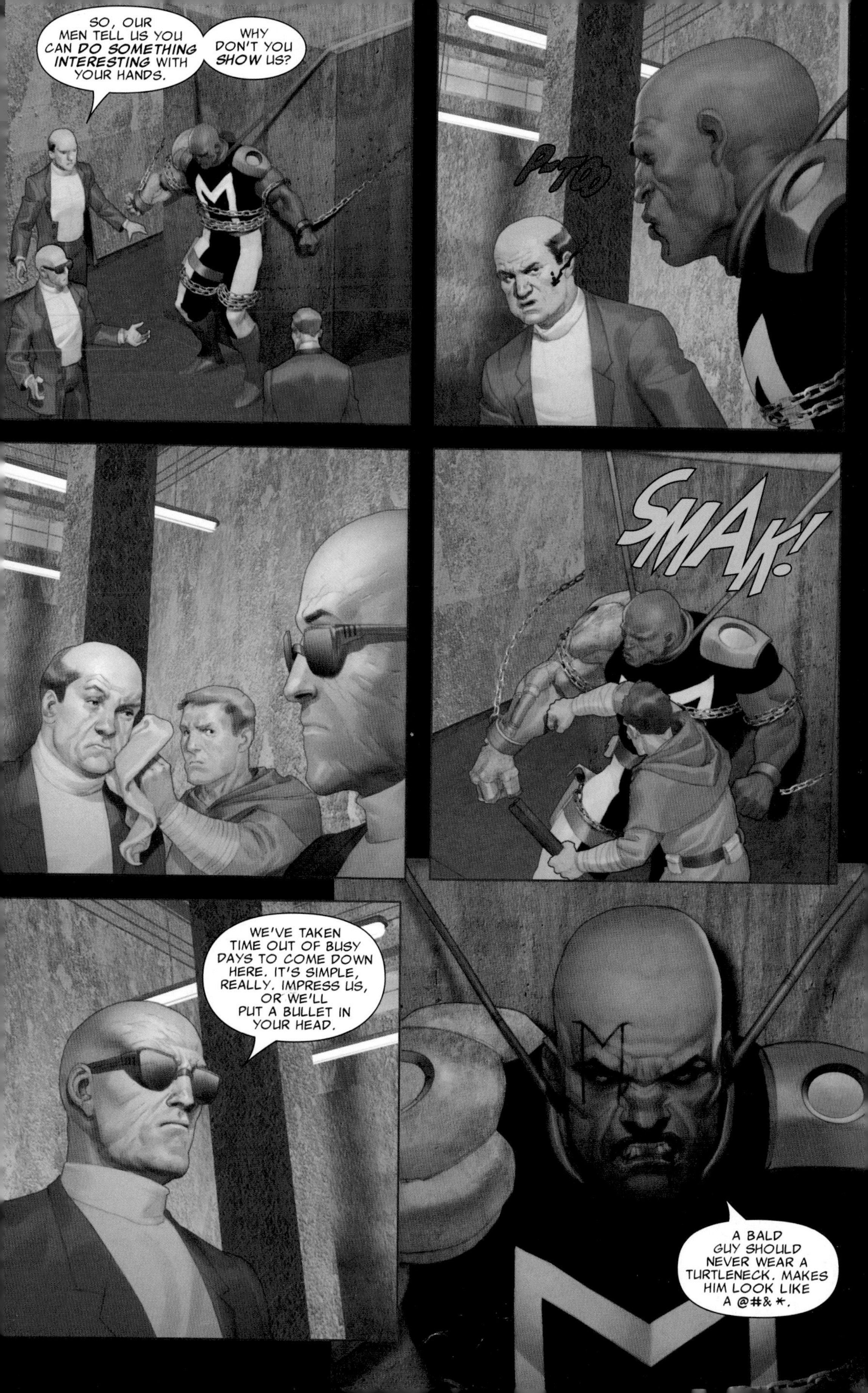
SO, OUR MEN TELL US YOU CAN DO SOMETHING INTERESTING WITH YOUR HANDS.
WHY DON'T YOU SHOW US?
SMAK!
WE'VE TAKEN TIME OUT OF BUSY DAYS TO COME DOWN HERE. IT'S SIMPLE, REALLY. IMPRESS US, OR WE'LL PUT A BULLET IN YOUR HEAD.
A BALD GUY SHOULD NEVER WEAR A TURTLENECK. MAKES HIM LOOK LIKE A @#&*.

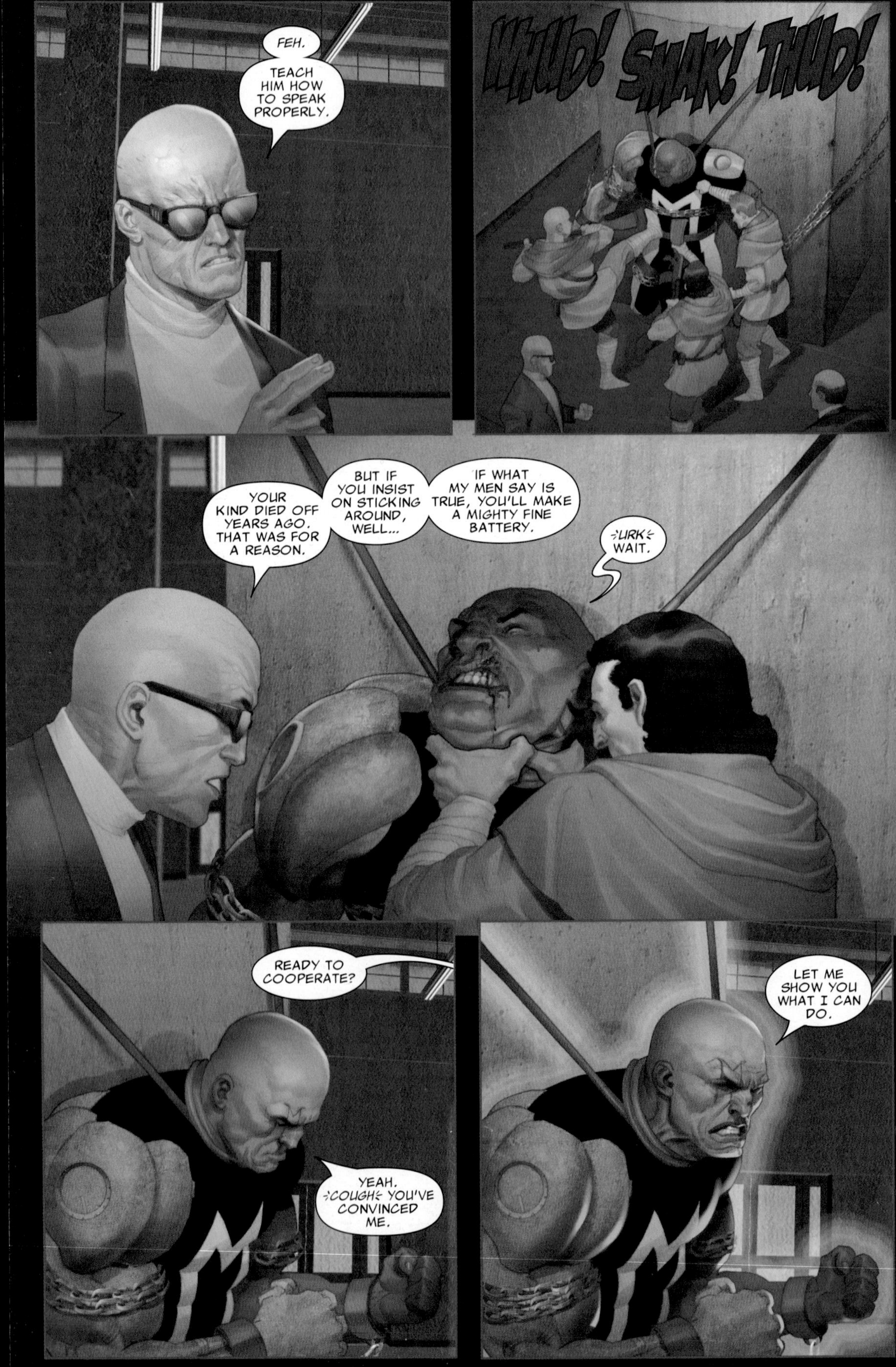

FEH.
TEACH HIM HOW TO SPEAK PROPERLY.
WHUD! SHAK! THUD!
YOUR KIND DIED OFF YEARS AGO. THAT WAS FOR A REASON.
BUT IF YOU INSIST ON STICKING AROUND, WELL...
IF WHAT MY MEN SAY IS TRUE, YOU'LL MAKE A MIGHTY FINE BATTERY.
URK WAIT.
READY TO COOPERATE?
YEAH. COUGH YOU'VE CONVINCED ME.
LET ME SHOW YOU WHAT I CAN DO.

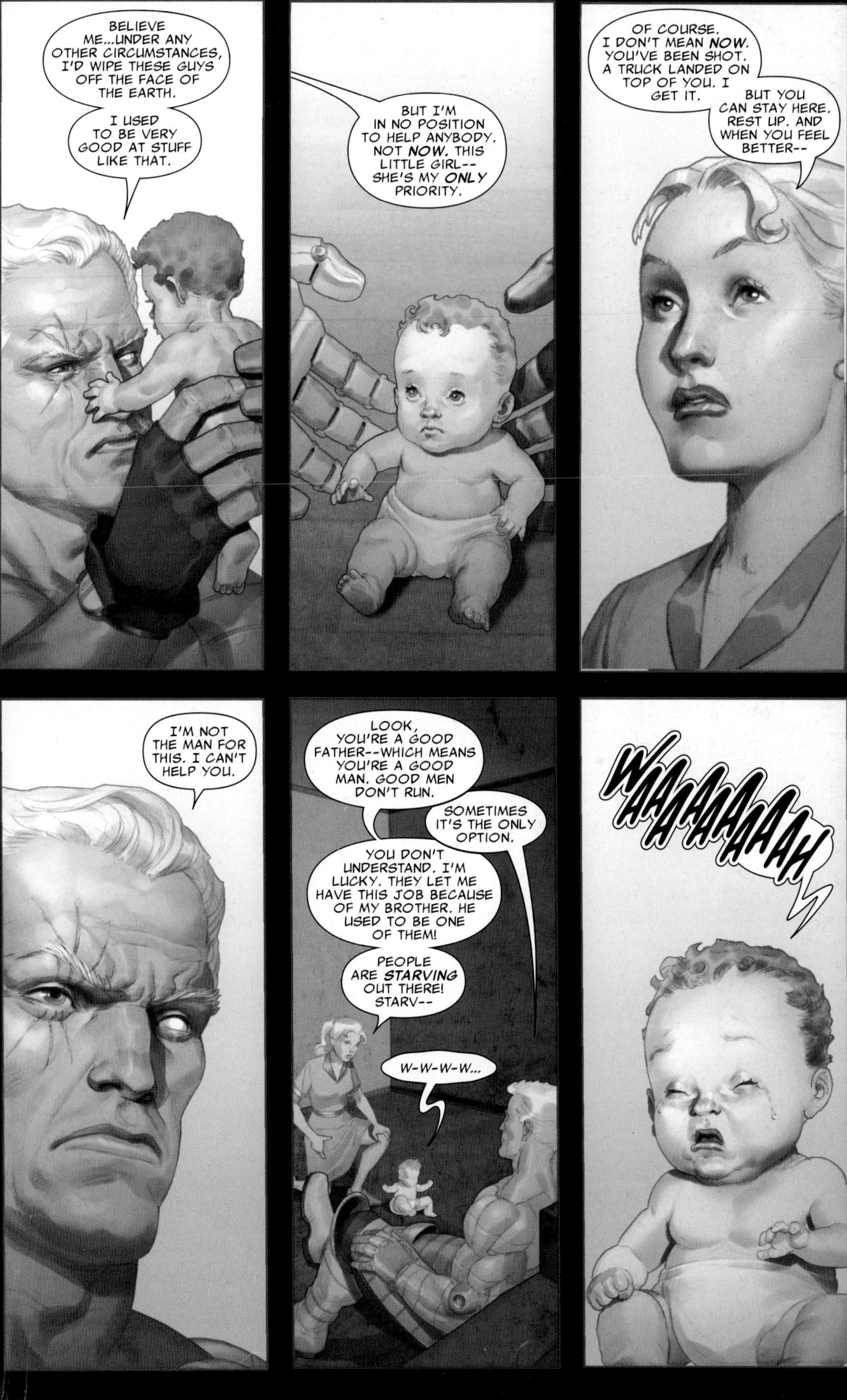

BELIEVE ME...UNDER ANY OTHER CIRCUMSTANCES, I'D WIPE THESE GUYS OFF THE FACE OF THE EARTH.
I USED TO BE VERY GOOD AT STUFF LIKE THAT.
BUT I'M IN NO POSITION TO HELP ANYBODY. NOT NOW. THIS LITTLE GIRL-- SHE'S MY ONLY PRIORITY.
OF COURSE. I DON'T MEAN NOW. YOU'VE BEEN SHOT. A TRUCK LANDED ON TOP OF YOU. I GET IT.
BUT YOU CAN STAY HERE. REST UP. AND WHEN YOU FEEL BETTER--
I'M NOT THE MAN FOR THIS. I CAN'T HELP YOU.
LOOK, YOU'RE A GOOD FATHER--WHICH MEANS YOU'RE A GOOD MAN. GOOD MEN DON'T RUN.
SOMETIMES IT'S THE ONLY OPTION.
YOU DON'T UNDERSTAND. I'M LUCKY. THEY LET ME HAVE THIS JOB BECAUSE OF MY BROTHER. HE USED TO BE ONE OF THEM!
PEOPLE ARE STARVING OUT THERE! STARV--
W-W-W-W...
WAAAAAAAAAH

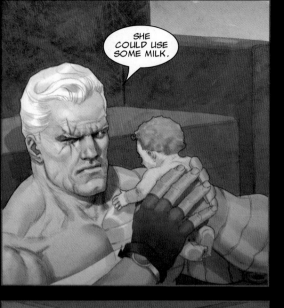

SHE COULD USE SOME MILK.

YOU DON'T FEED A BABY COW'S MILK. WHAT'S WRONG WITH YOU?

LUCKY FOR YOU I HAVE SOME VITAMIN-FORTIFIED PROTEIN WATER.

ONE OF THE BENEFITS OF WORKING AT THE DINER.

I GET TO SNEAK HOME REAL FOOD EVERY SO OFTEN.

YOUR NAME TAG SAYS "SOPHIE." I'M NATHAN.

NICE TO MEET YOU, NATHAN.

SOPHIE, NONE OF THIS WAS SUPPOSED TO HAPPEN.

WHAT DO YOU MEAN?

I...

I DON'T EXPECT YOU TO UNDERSTAND, BUT I'M TRYING TO PREVENT ALL OF THIS. THAT'S WHY I'M HERE.

RIGHT. WELL, DON'T TAKE THIS THE WRONG WAY, NATHAN...

...BUT YOU'RE A LITTLE LATE.

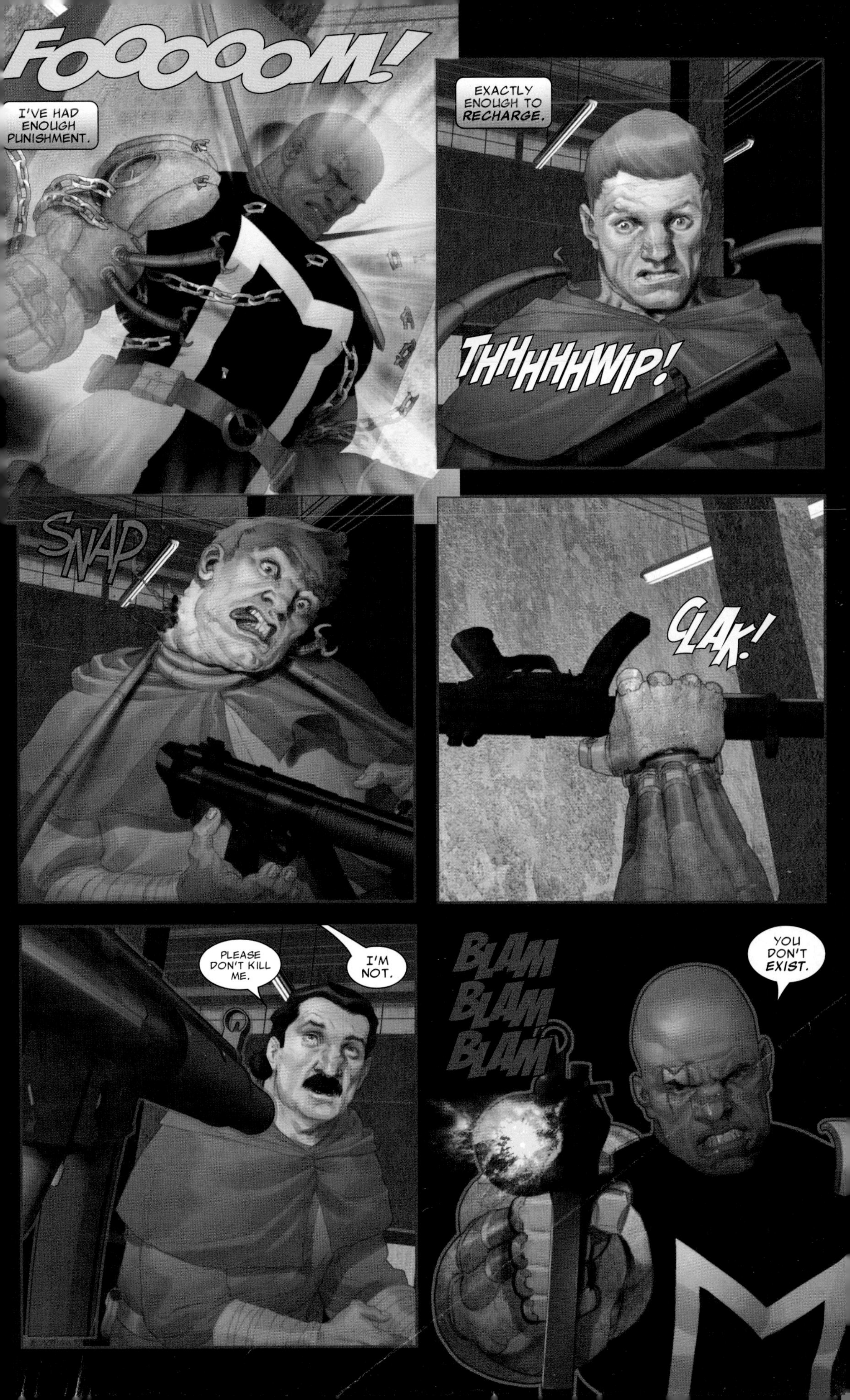
FOOOOOM!
I'VE HAD ENOUGH PUNISHMENT.
EXACTLY ENOUGH TO RECHARGE.
THHHHHWIP!
SNAP
CLAK!
PLEASE DON'T KILL ME.
I'M NOT.
BLAM BLAM BLAM
YOU DON'T EXIST.

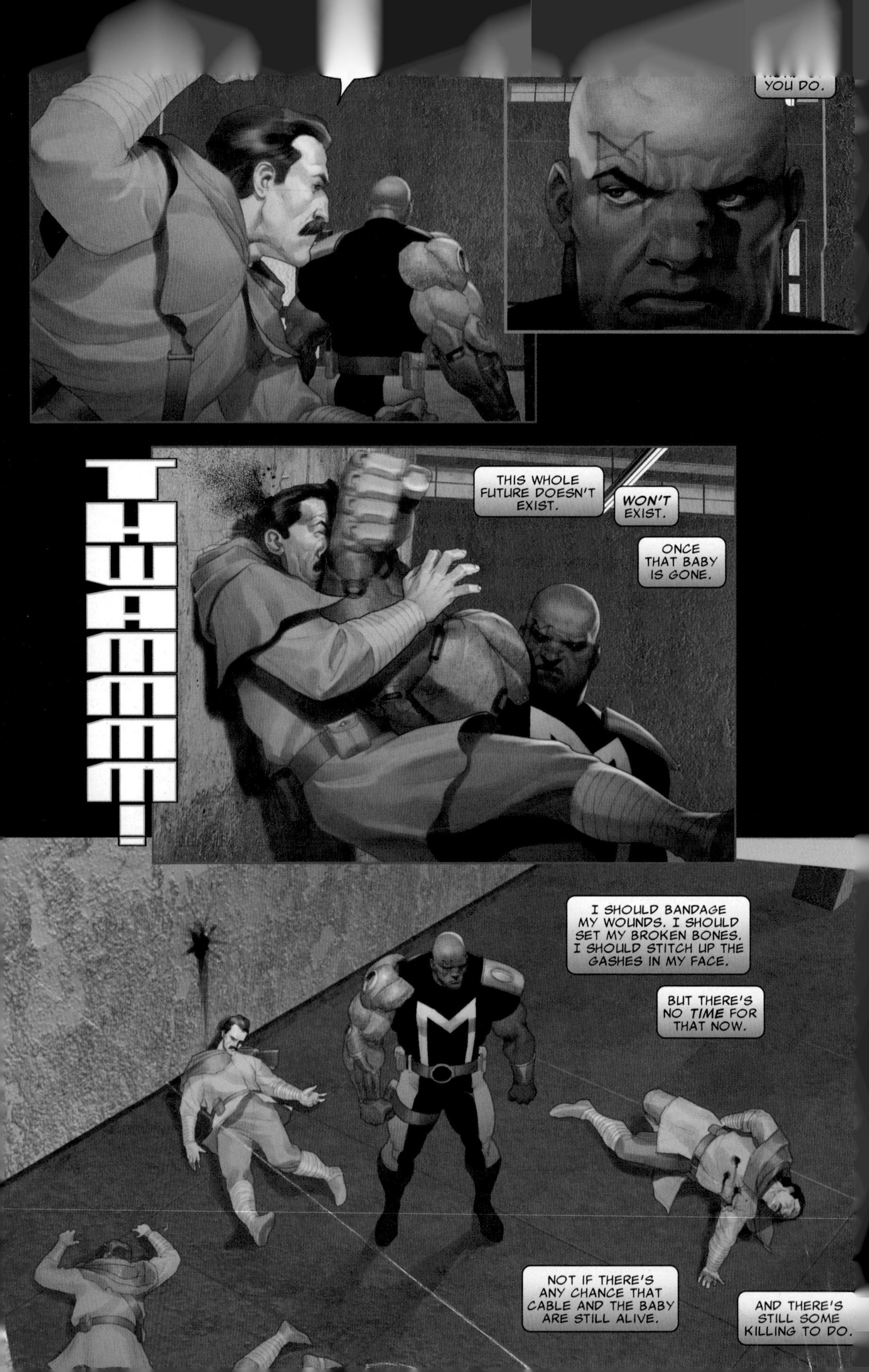

YOU DO.
THWAMMMM!
THIS WHOLE FUTURE DOESN'T EXIST.
WON'T EXIST.
ONCE THAT BABY IS GONE.
I SHOULD BANDAGE MY WOUNDS. I SHOULD SET MY BROKEN BONES. I SHOULD STITCH UP THE GASHES IN MY FACE.
BUT THERE'S NO TIME FOR THAT NOW.
NOT IF THERE'S ANY CHANCE THAT CABLE AND THE BABY ARE STILL ALIVE.
AND THERE'S STILL SOME KILLING TO DO.

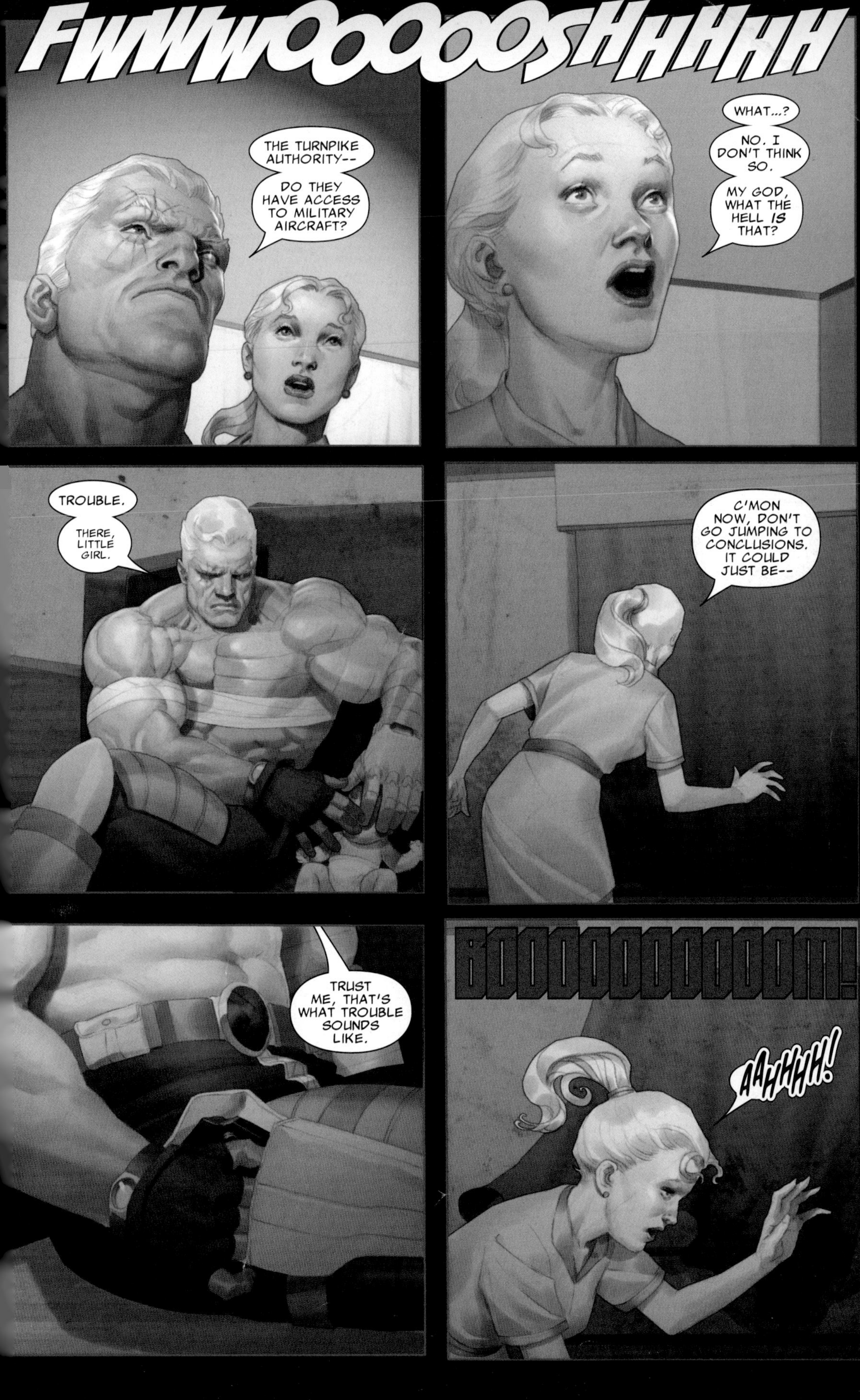
FWWWOOOOOOSHHHHH
THE TURNPIKE AUTHORITY--
DO THEY HAVE ACCESS TO MILITARY AIRCRAFT?
WHAT...?
NO. I DON'T THINK SO.
MY GOD, WHAT THE HELL IS THAT?
TROUBLE.
THERE, LITTLE GIRL.
C'MON NOW, DON'T GO JUMPING TO CONCLUSIONS. IT COULD JUST BE--
TRUST ME, THAT'S WHAT TROUBLE SOUNDS LIKE.
BOOOOOOOOOOM!
AAHHHH!

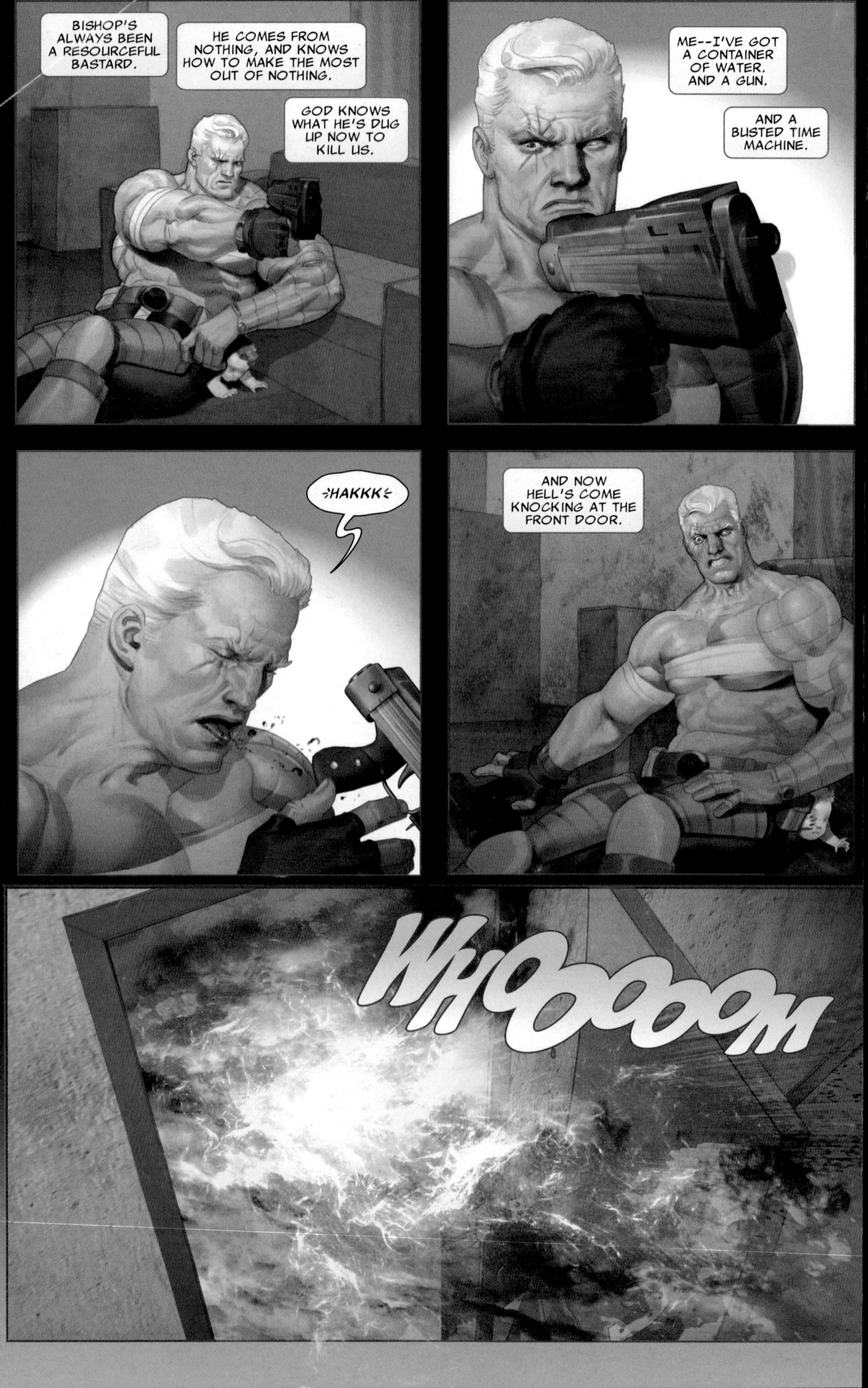
BISHOP'S ALWAYS BEEN A RESOURCEFUL BASTARD.
HE COMES FROM NOTHING, AND KNOWS HOW TO MAKE THE MOST OUT OF NOTHING.
GOD KNOWS WHAT HE'S DUG UP NOW TO KILL US.
ME--I'VE GOT A CONTAINER OF WATER. AND A GUN.
AND A BUSTED TIME MACHINE.
HAKKK
AND NOW HELL'S COME KNOCKING AT THE FRONT DOOR.
WHOOOOOM

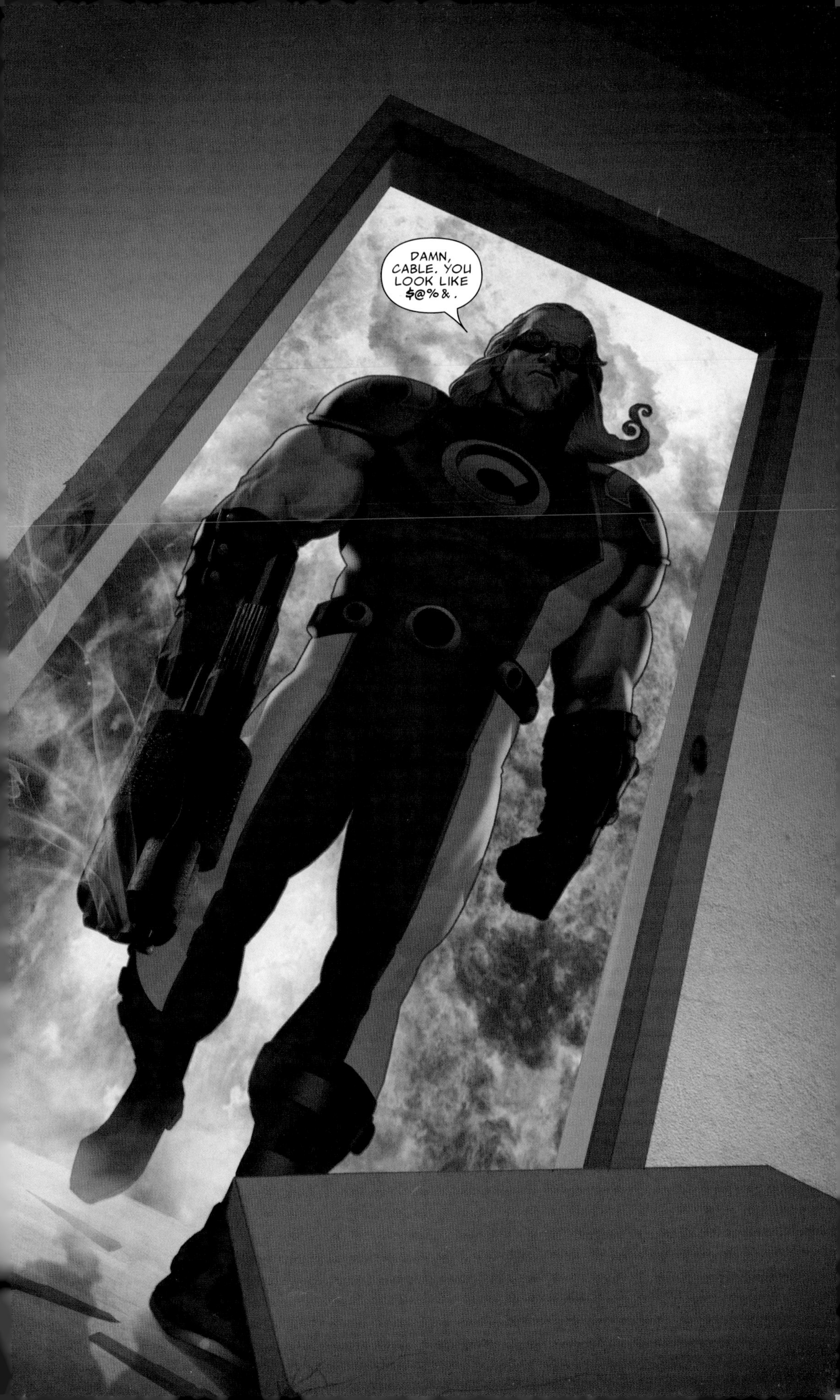
DAMN, CABLE. YOU LOOK LIKE $@%&.

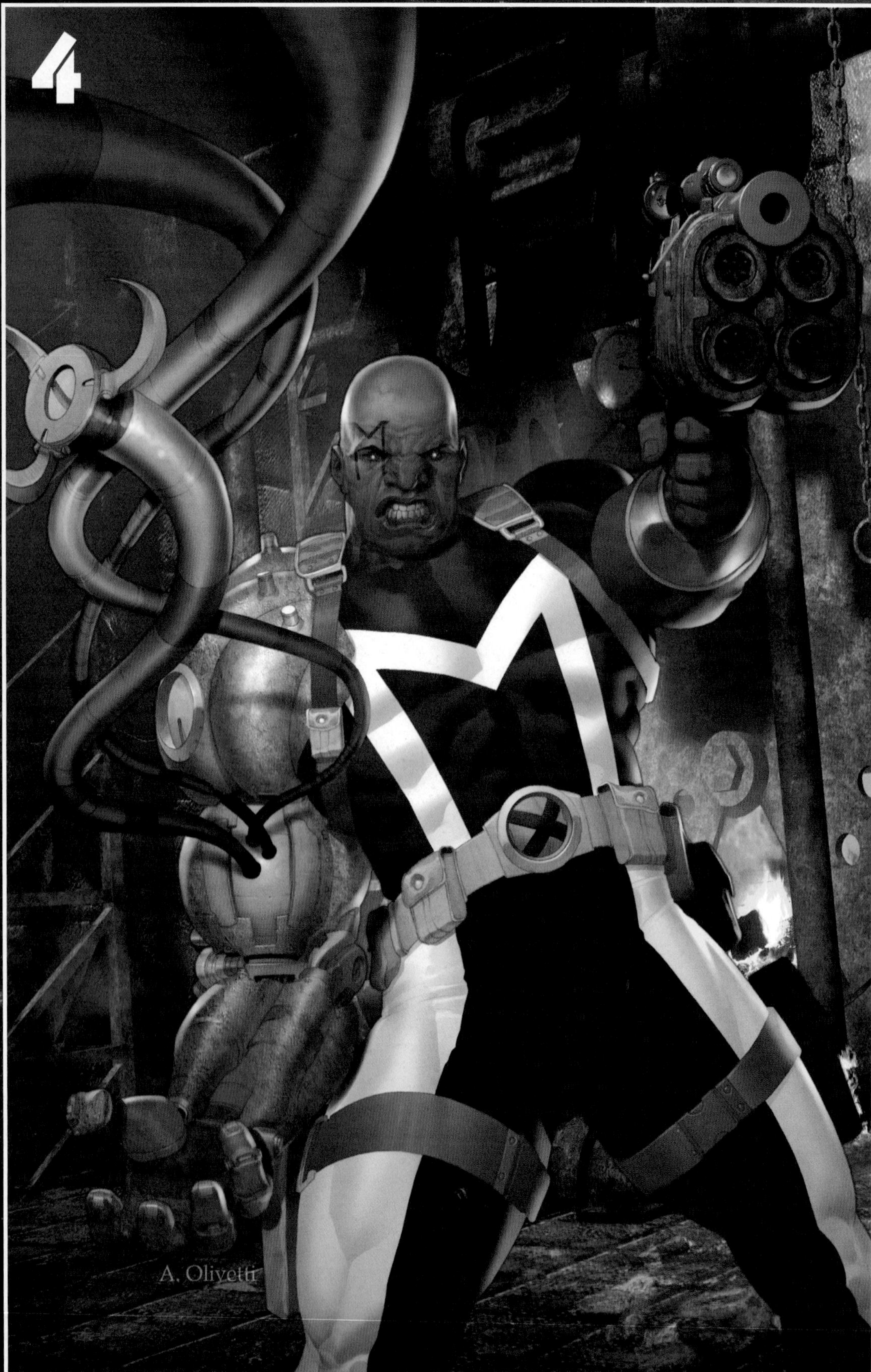
4
A. Olivetti

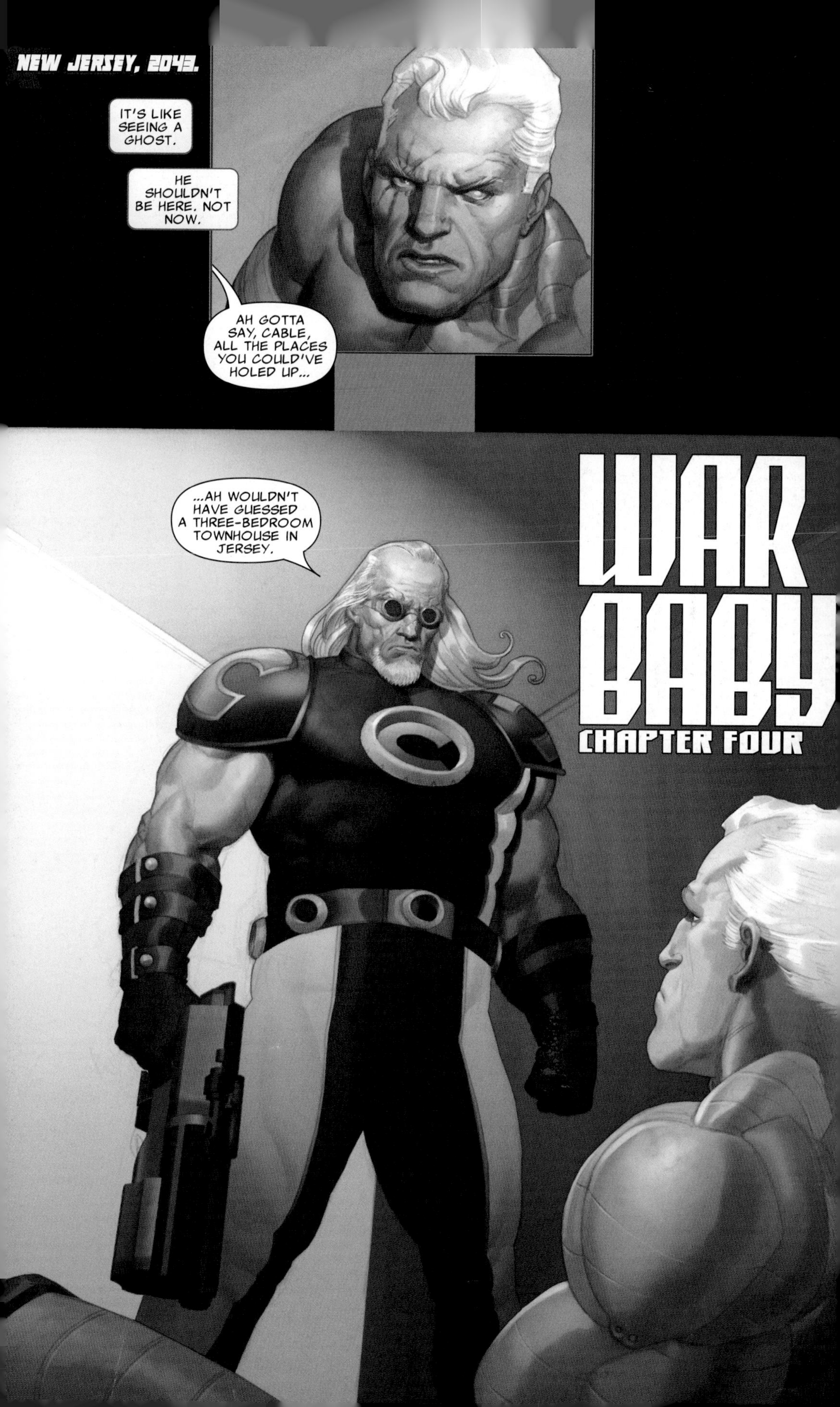
NEW JERSEY, 2043.
IT'S LIKE SEEING A GHOST.
HE SHOULDN'T BE HERE. NOT NOW.
AH GOTTA SAY, CABLE, ALL THE PLACES YOU COULD'VE HOLED UP...
...AH WOULDN'T HAVE GUESSED A THREE-BEDROOM TOWNHOUSE IN JERSEY.
WAR BABY
CHAPTER FOUR

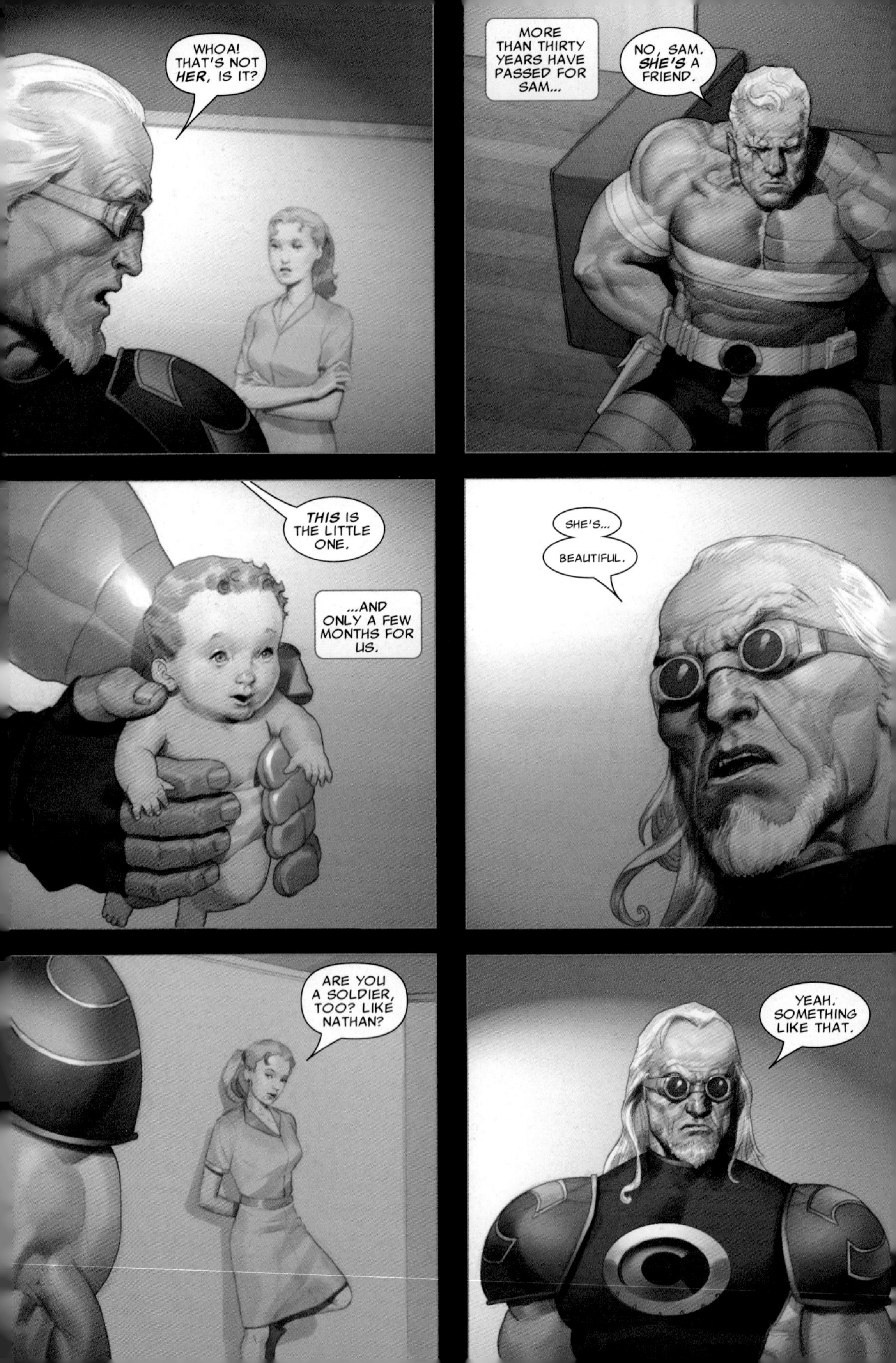
WHOA! THAT'S NOT HER, IS IT?
MORE THAN THIRTY YEARS HAVE PASSED FOR SAM...
NO, SAM. SHE'S A FRIEND.
THIS IS THE LITTLE ONE.
...AND ONLY A FEW MONTHS FOR US.
SHE'S...
BEAUTIFUL.
ARE YOU A SOLDIER, TOO? LIKE NATHAN?
YEAH. SOMETHING LIKE THAT.

KRAKKABOOM

NOTHING. NO BODIES.

THEY COULD BE ANYWHERE BY NOW. ANY TIME.

BUT I HAVE TO BE SURE.

KRUNCH

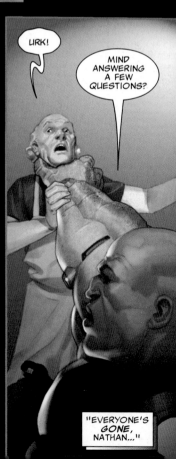

URK!

MIND ANSWERING A FEW QUESTIONS?

"EVERYONE'S GONE, NATHAN..."

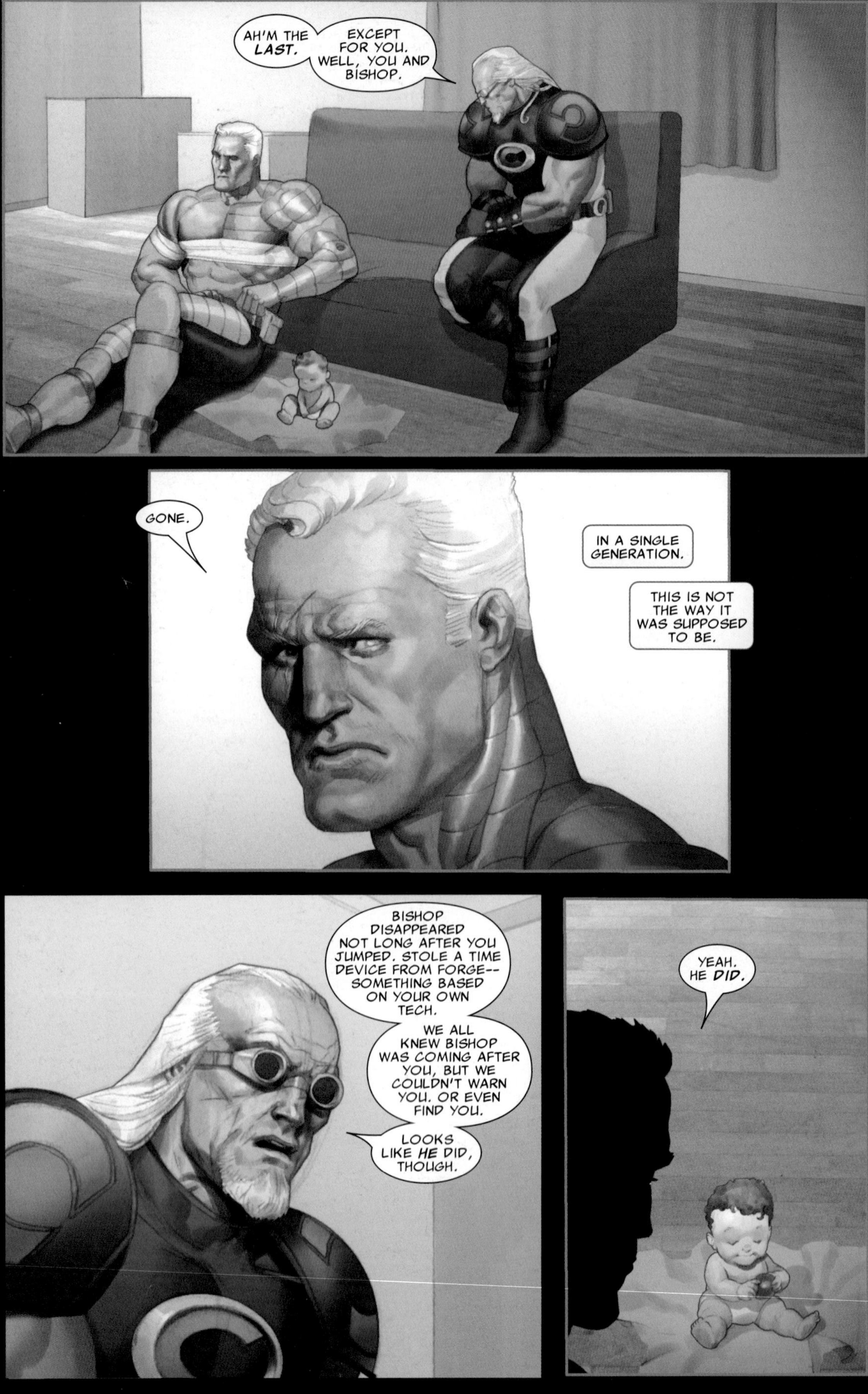
AH'M THE LAST.
EXCEPT FOR YOU. WELL, YOU AND BISHOP.
GONE.
IN A SINGLE GENERATION.
THIS IS NOT THE WAY IT WAS SUPPOSED TO BE.
BISHOP DISAPPEARED NOT LONG AFTER YOU JUMPED. STOLE A TIME DEVICE FROM FORGE-- SOMETHING BASED ON YOUR OWN TECH.
WE ALL KNEW BISHOP WAS COMING AFTER YOU, BUT WE COULDN'T WARN YOU. OR EVEN FIND YOU.
LOOKS LIKE HE DID, THOUGH.
YEAH. HE DID.

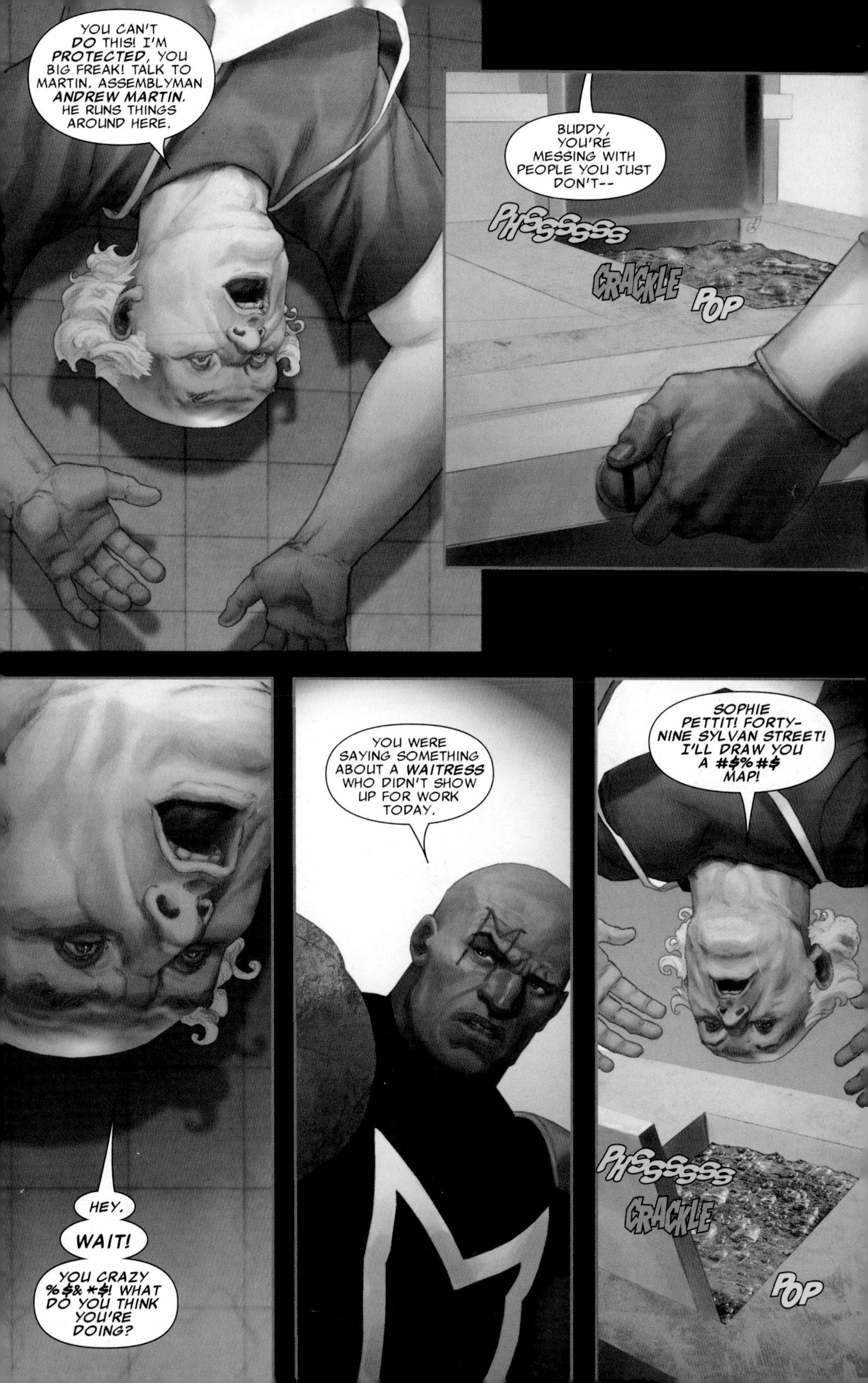
YOU CAN'T DO THIS! I'M PROTECTED, YOU BIG FREAK! TALK TO MARTIN. ASSEMBLYMAN ANDREW MARTIN. HE RUNS THINGS AROUND HERE.
BUDDY, YOU'RE MESSING WITH PEOPLE YOU JUST DON'T--
PHSSSSSS
CRACKLE
POP
HEY.
WAIT!
YOU CRAZY %$& *$! WHAT DO YOU THINK YOU'RE DOING?
YOU WERE SAYING SOMETHING ABOUT A WAITRESS WHO DIDN'T SHOW UP FOR WORK TODAY.
SOPHIE PETTIT! FORTY-NINE SYLVAN STREET! I'LL DRAW YOU A #$%#$ MAP!
PHSSSSSS
CRACKLE
POP

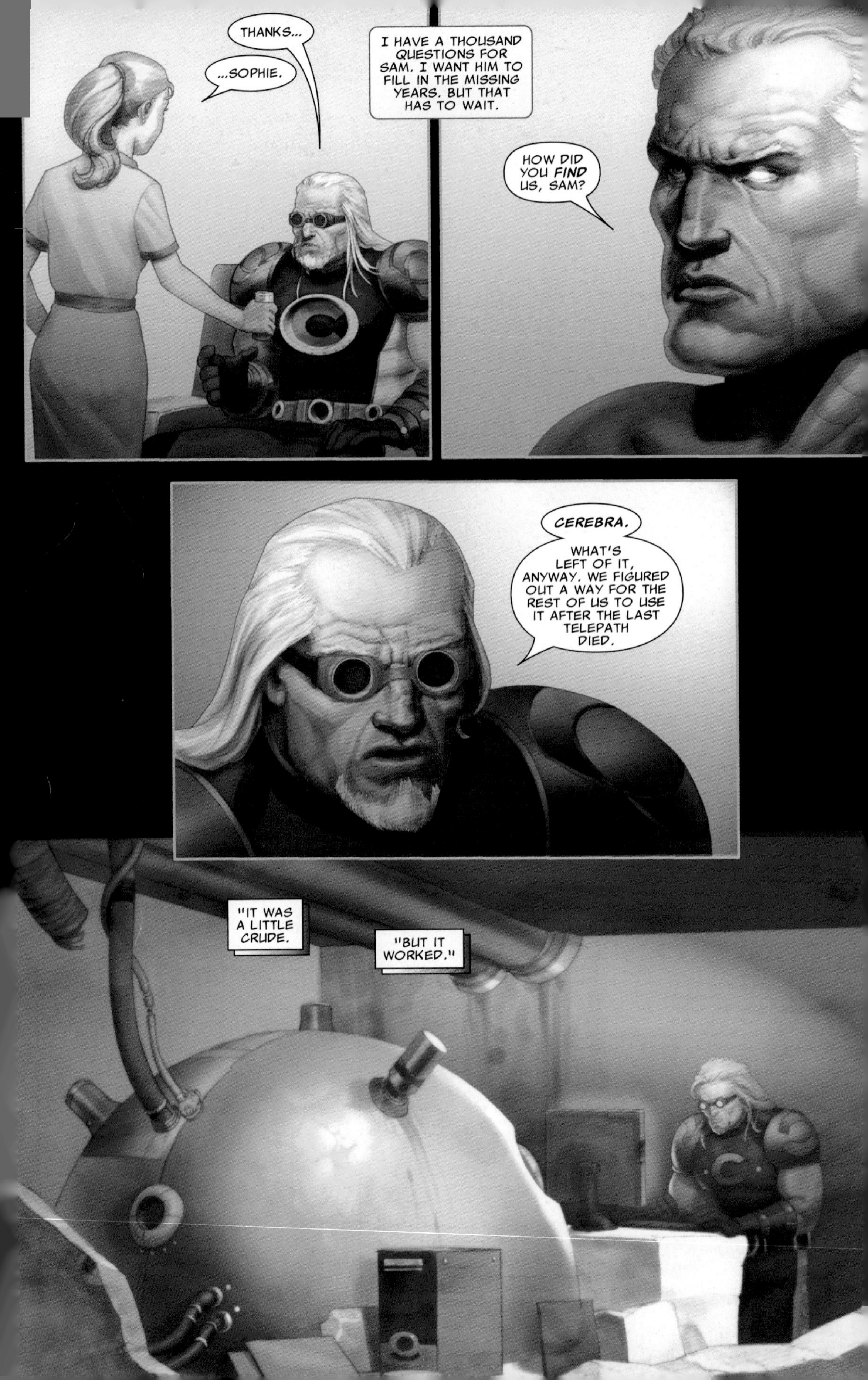
THANKS...
...SOPHIE.
I HAVE A THOUSAND QUESTIONS FOR SAM. I WANT HIM TO FILL IN THE MISSING YEARS. BUT THAT HAS TO WAIT.
HOW DID YOU FIND US, SAM?
CEREBRA.
WHAT'S LEFT OF IT, ANYWAY. WE FIGURED OUT A WAY FOR THE REST OF US TO USE IT AFTER THE LAST TELEPATH DIED.
"IT WAS A LITTLE CRUDE.
"BUT IT WORKED."

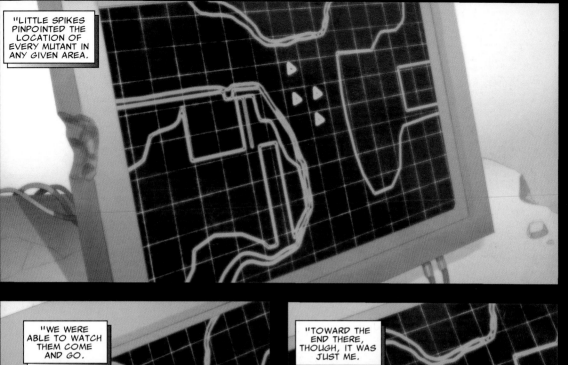

"LITTLE SPIKES PINPOINTED THE LOCATION OF EVERY MUTANT IN ANY GIVEN AREA.

"WE WERE ABLE TO WATCH THEM COME AND GO.

"TOWARD THE END THERE, THOUGH, IT WAS JUST ME.

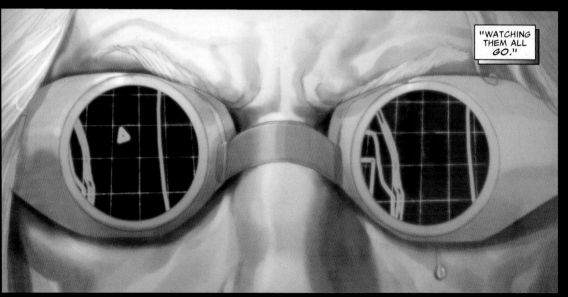

"WATCHING THEM ALL GO."

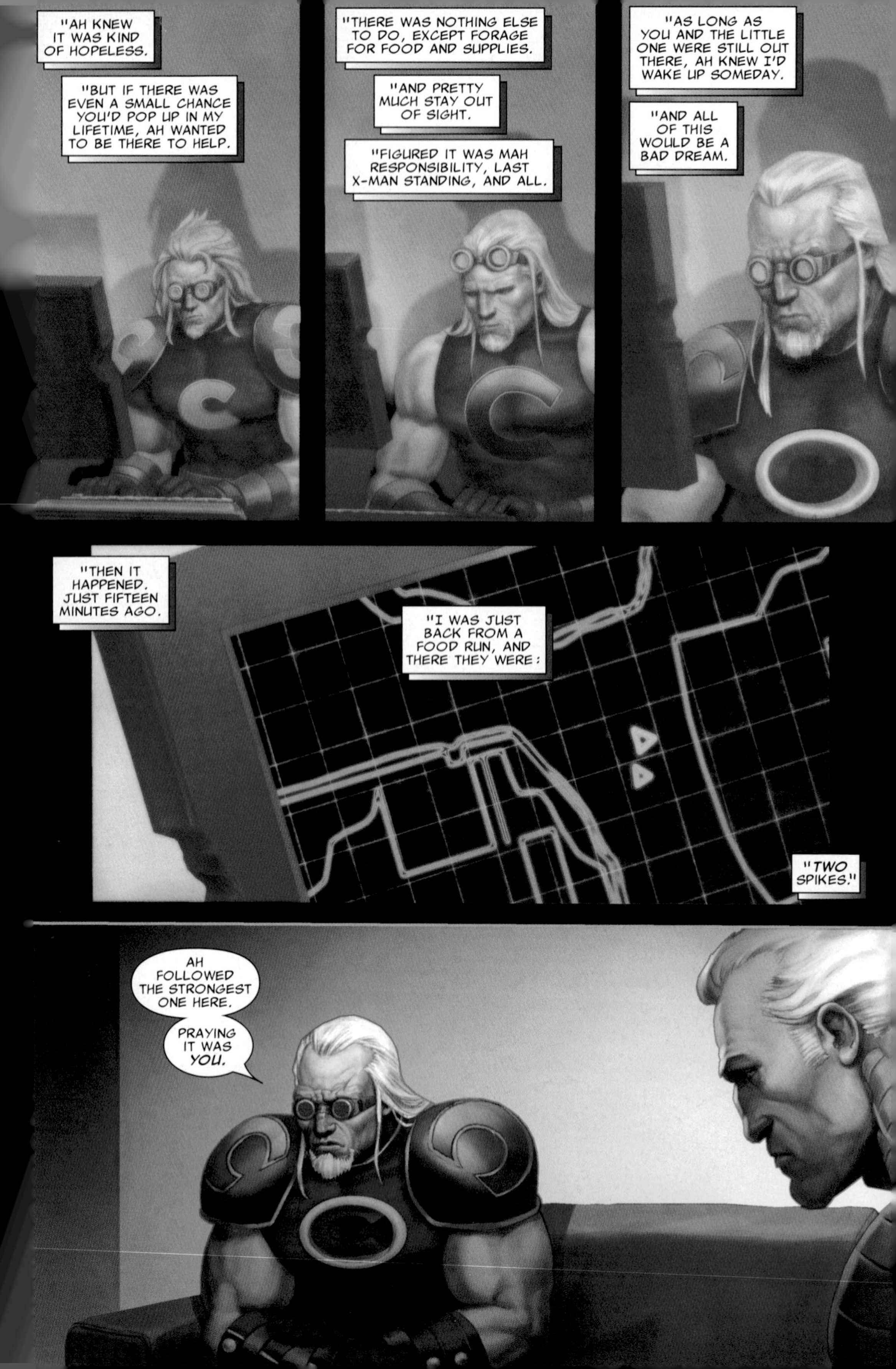
"AH KNEW IT WAS KIND OF HOPELESS.
"BUT IF THERE WAS EVEN A SMALL CHANCE YOU'D POP UP IN MY LIFETIME, AH WANTED TO BE THERE TO HELP.
"THERE WAS NOTHING ELSE TO DO, EXCEPT FORAGE FOR FOOD AND SUPPLIES.
"AND PRETTY MUCH STAY OUT OF SIGHT.
"FIGURED IT WAS MAH RESPONSIBILITY, LAST X-MAN STANDING, AND ALL.
"AS LONG AS YOU AND THE LITTLE ONE WERE STILL OUT THERE, AH KNEW I'D WAKE UP SOMEDAY.
"AND ALL OF THIS WOULD BE A BAD DREAM.
"THEN IT HAPPENED. JUST FIFTEEN MINUTES AGO.
"I WAS JUST BACK FROM A FOOD RUN, AND THERE THEY WERE:
"TWO SPIKES."
AH FOLLOWED THE STRONGEST ONE HERE.
PRAYING IT WAS YOU.

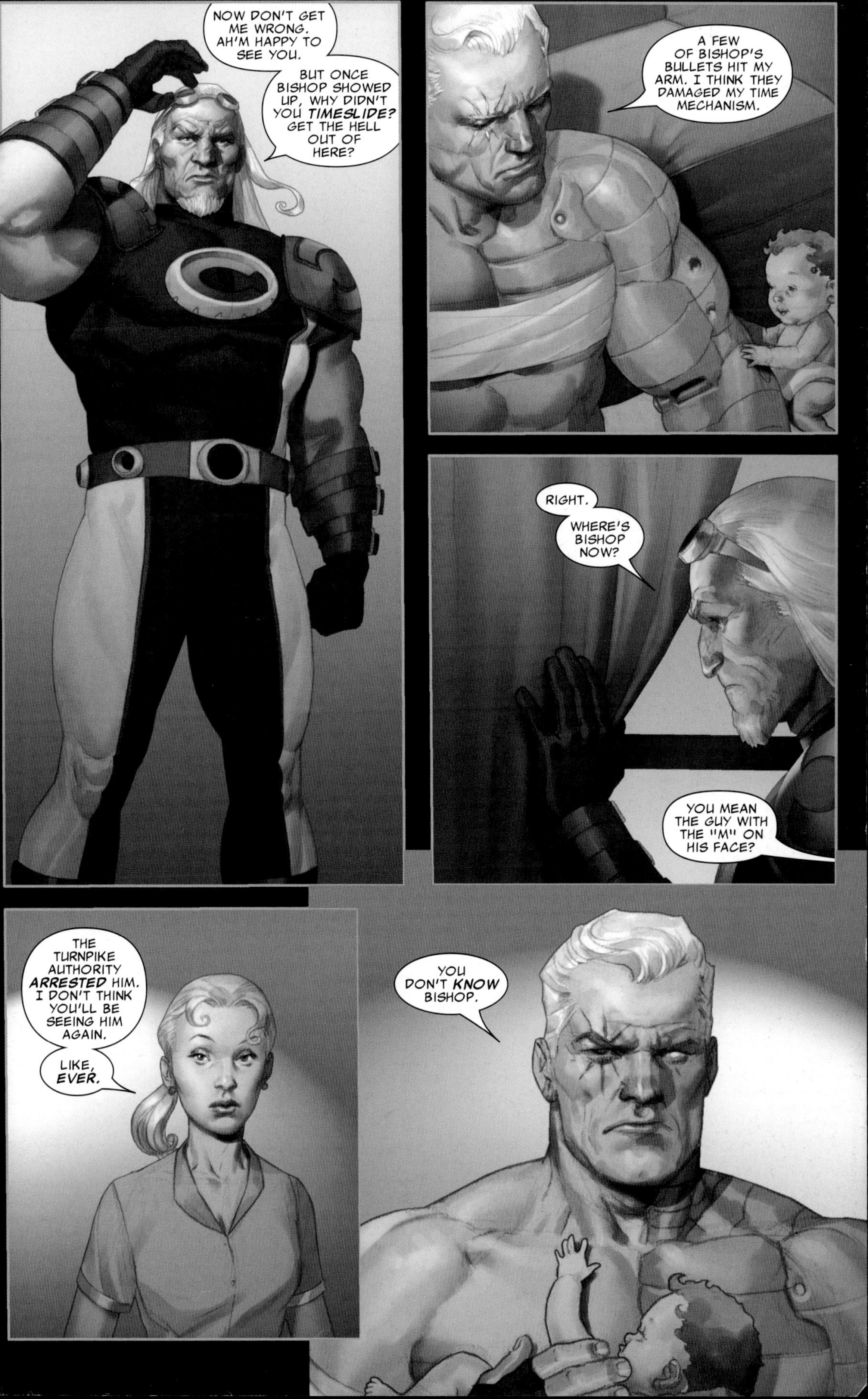
NOW DON'T GET ME WRONG. AH'M HAPPY TO SEE YOU.
BUT ONCE BISHOP SHOWED UP, WHY DIDN'T YOU *TIMESLIDE?* GET THE HELL OUT OF HERE?
A FEW OF BISHOP'S BULLETS HIT MY ARM. I THINK THEY DAMAGED MY TIME MECHANISM.
RIGHT.
WHERE'S BISHOP NOW?
YOU MEAN THE GUY WITH THE "M" ON HIS FACE?
THE TURNPIKE AUTHORITY *ARRESTED* HIM. I DON'T THINK YOU'LL BE SEEING HIM AGAIN.
LIKE, *EVER.*
YOU DON'T *KNOW* BISHOP.

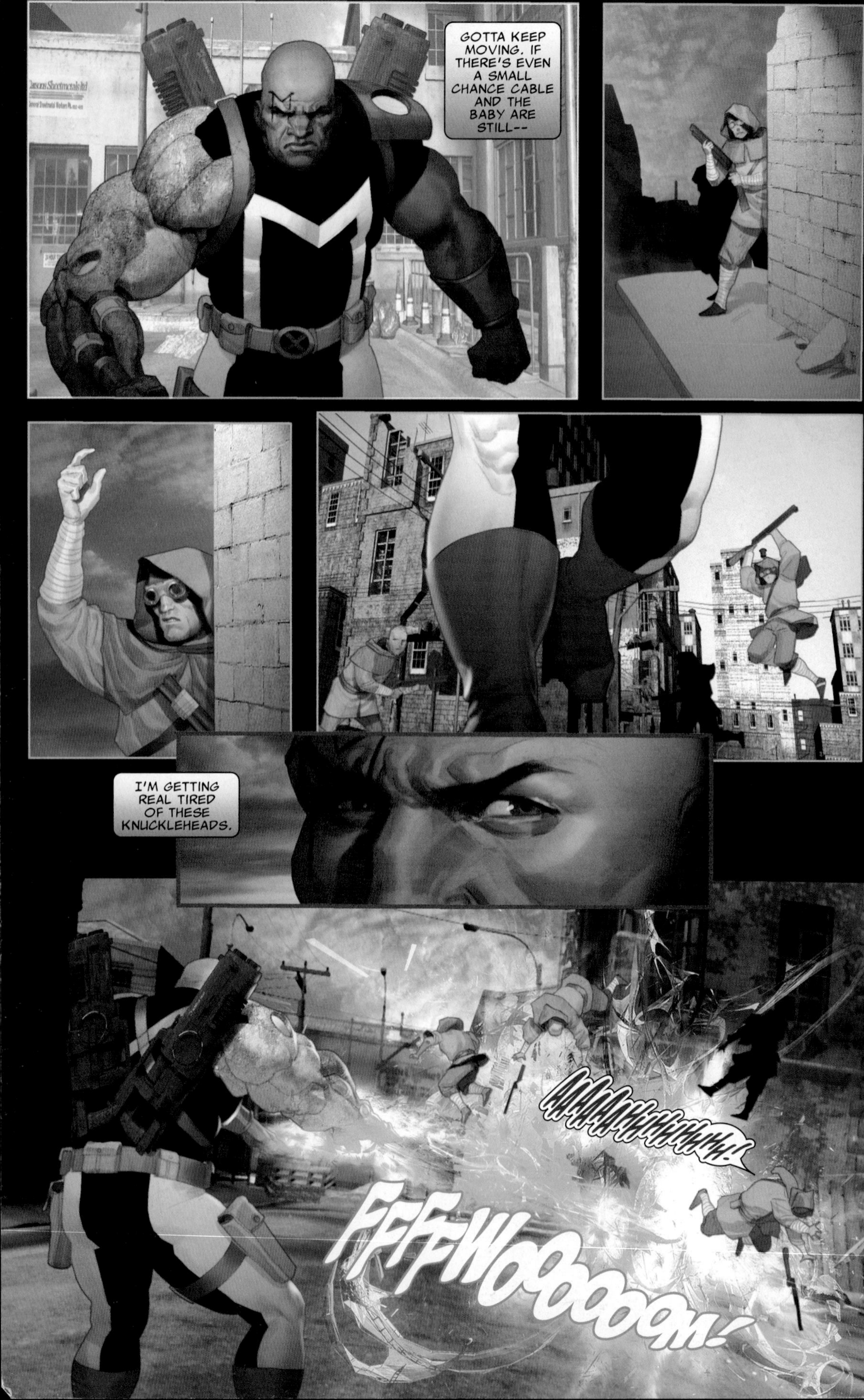
GOTTA KEEP MOVING. IF THERE'S EVEN A SMALL CHANCE CABLE AND THE BABY ARE STILL--
I'M GETTING REAL TIRED OF THESE KNUCKLEHEADS.
AAAAAAHHHHHHH!
FFFWOOOOOOM!

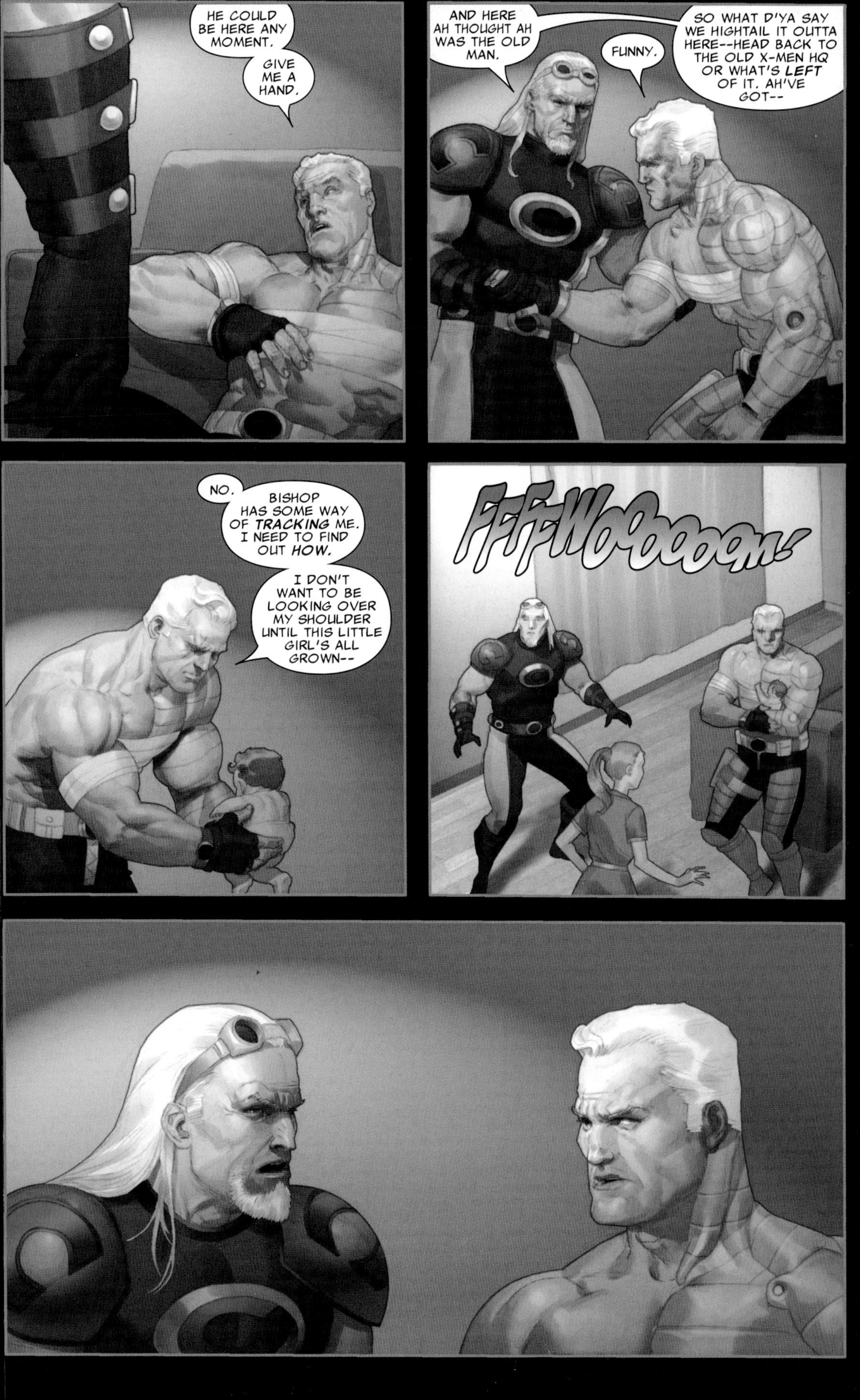
HE COULD BE HERE ANY MOMENT.
GIVE ME A HAND.
AND HERE AH THOUGHT AH WAS THE OLD MAN.
FUNNY.
SO WHAT D'YA SAY WE HIGHTAIL IT OUTTA HERE--HEAD BACK TO THE OLD X-MEN HQ OR WHAT'S **LEFT** OF IT. AH'VE GOT--
NO.
BISHOP HAS SOME WAY OF **TRACKING** ME. I NEED TO FIND OUT **HOW.**
I DON'T WANT TO BE LOOKING OVER MY SHOULDER UNTIL THIS LITTLE GIRL'S ALL GROWN--
FFFWOOOOOOM!

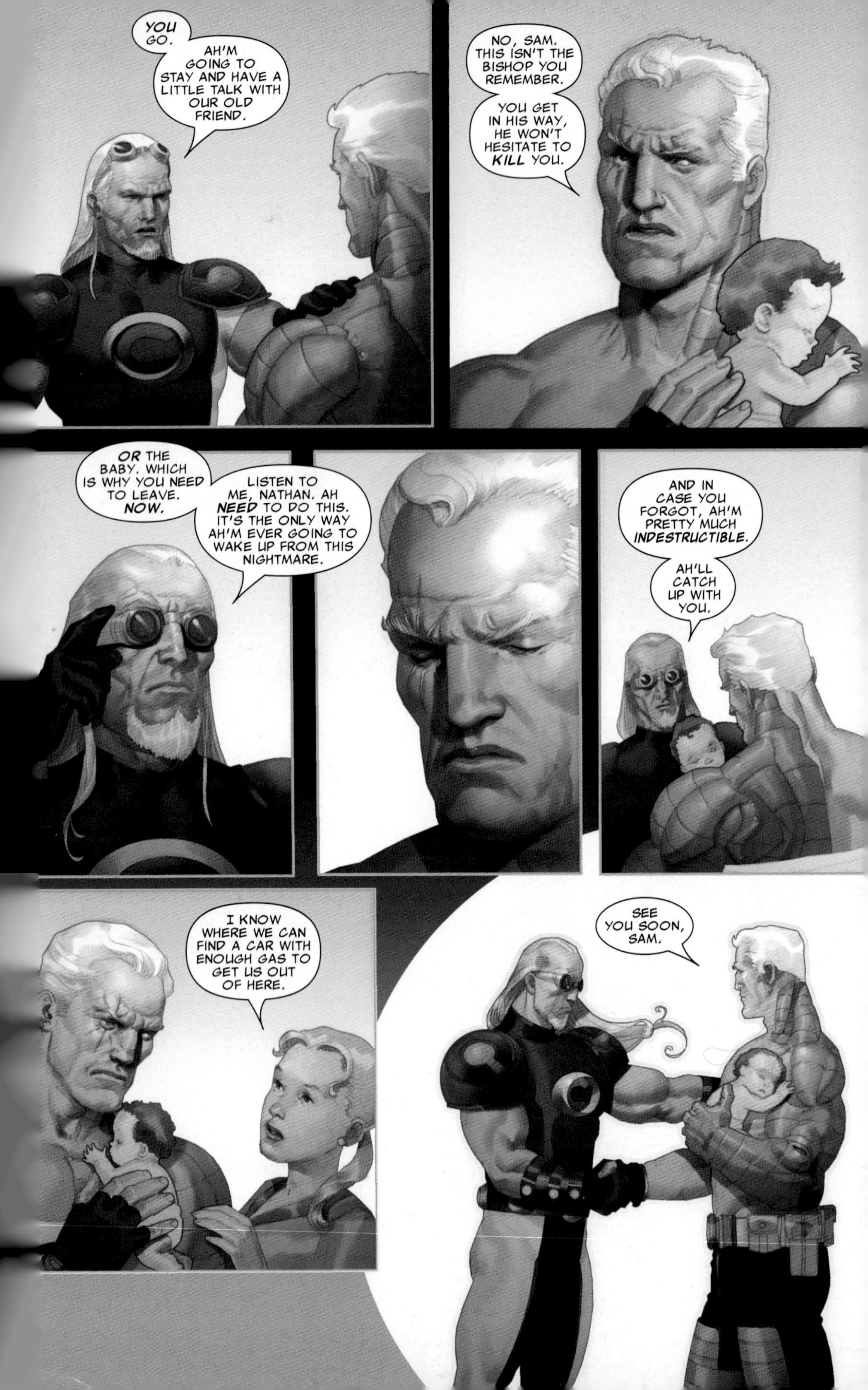
YOU GO.
AH'M GOING TO STAY AND HAVE A LITTLE TALK WITH OUR OLD FRIEND.
NO, SAM. THIS ISN'T THE BISHOP YOU REMEMBER.
YOU GET IN HIS WAY, HE WON'T HESITATE TO KILL YOU.
OR THE BABY. WHICH IS WHY YOU NEED TO LEAVE. NOW.
LISTEN TO ME, NATHAN. AH NEED TO DO THIS. IT'S THE ONLY WAY AH'M EVER GOING TO WAKE UP FROM THIS NIGHTMARE.
AND IN CASE YOU FORGOT, AH'M PRETTY MUCH INDESTRUCTIBLE.
AH'LL CATCH UP WITH YOU.
I KNOW WHERE WE CAN FIND A CAR WITH ENOUGH GAS TO GET US OUT OF HERE.
SEE YOU SOON, SAM.

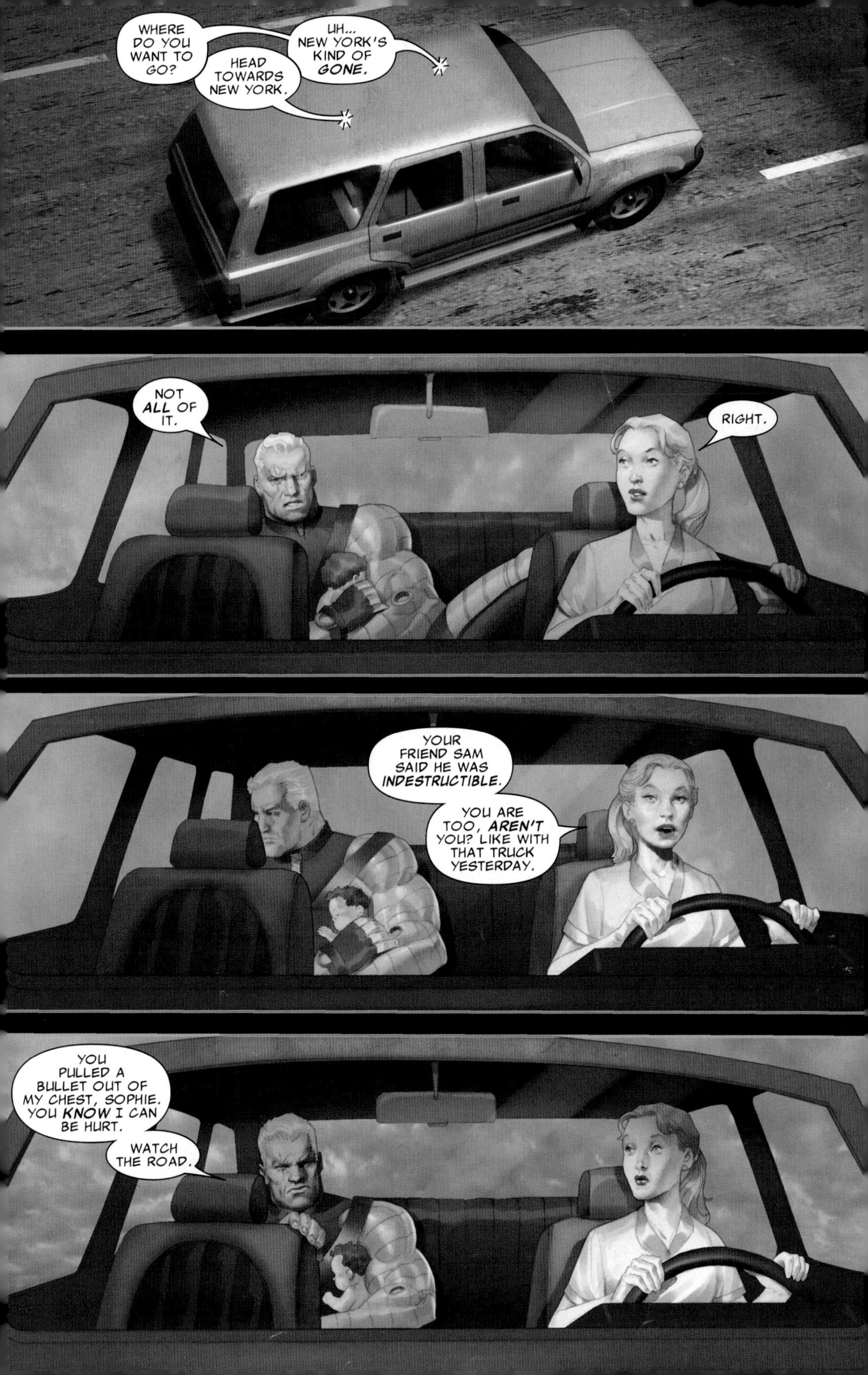
WHERE DO YOU WANT TO GO?
HEAD TOWARDS NEW YORK.
UH... NEW YORK'S KIND OF GONE.
NOT ALL OF IT.
RIGHT.
YOUR FRIEND SAM SAID HE WAS INDESTRUCTIBLE.
YOU ARE TOO, AREN'T YOU? LIKE WITH THAT TRUCK YESTERDAY.
YOU PULLED A BULLET OUT OF MY CHEST, SOPHIE. YOU KNOW I CAN BE HURT.
WATCH THE ROAD.

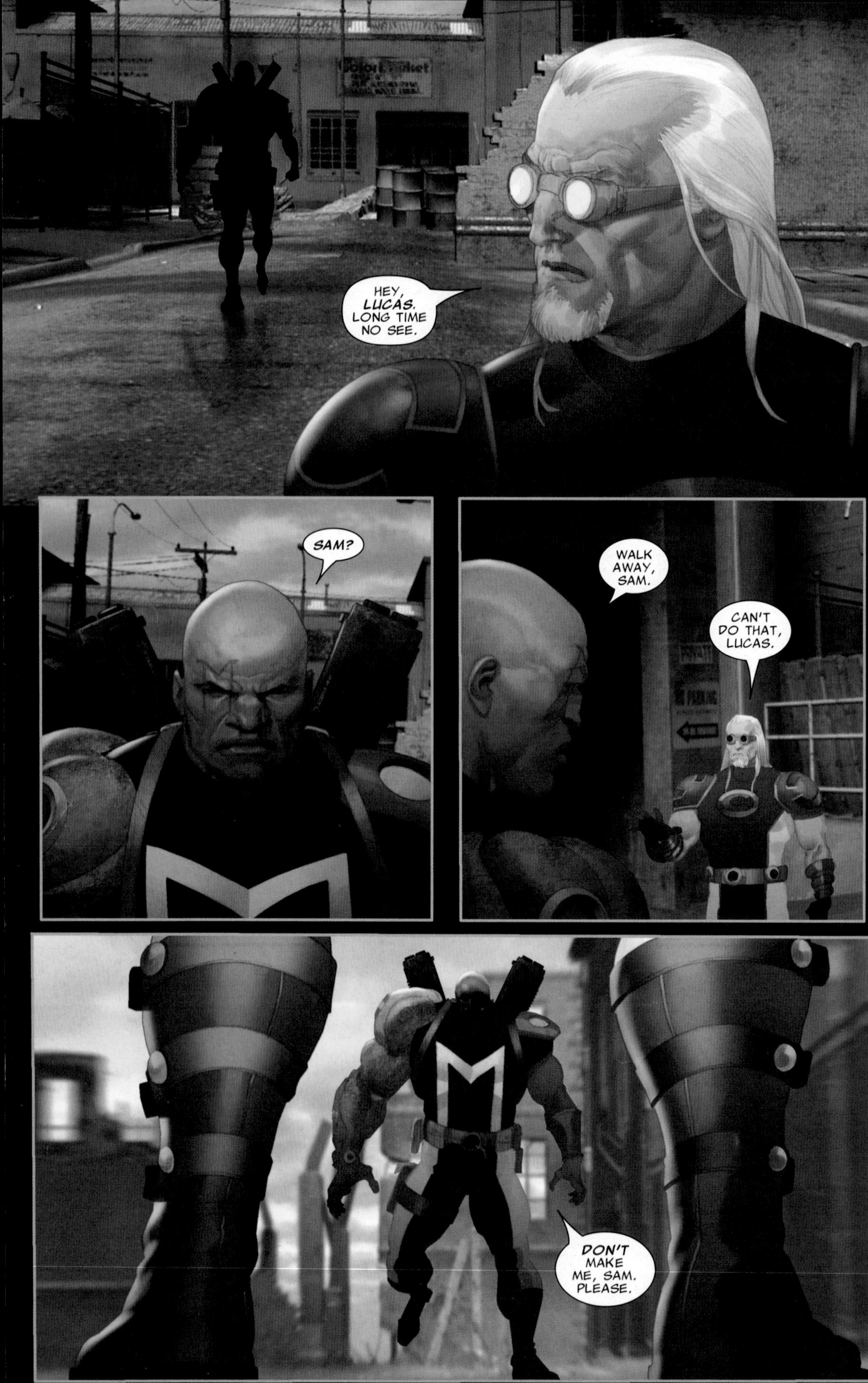
HEY, LUCAS. LONG TIME NO SEE.
SAM?
WALK AWAY, SAM.
CAN'T DO THAT, LUCAS.
DON'T MAKE ME, SAM. PLEASE.

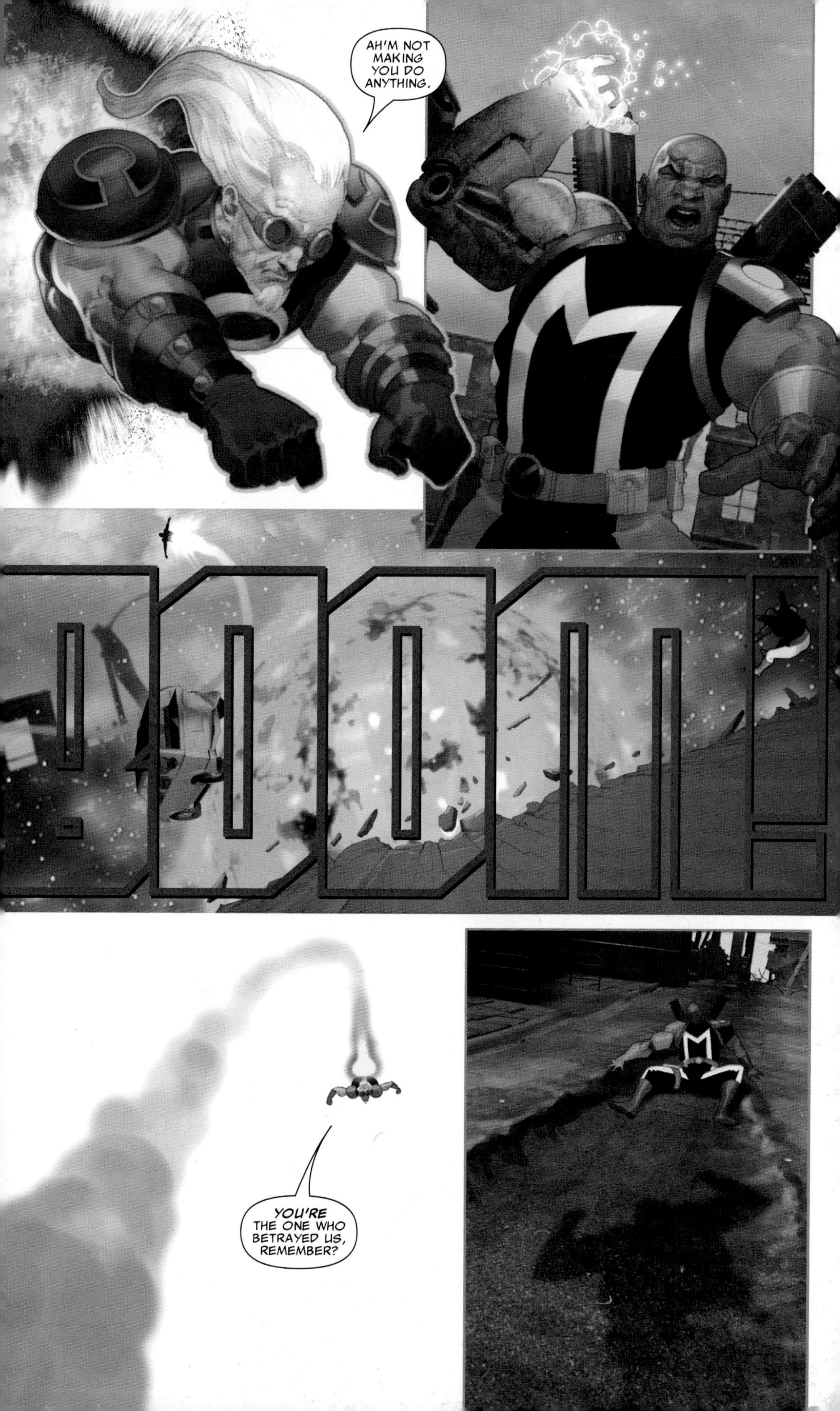
AH'M NOT MAKING YOU DO ANYTHING.
BOOM!
YOU'RE THE ONE WHO BETRAYED US, REMEMBER?

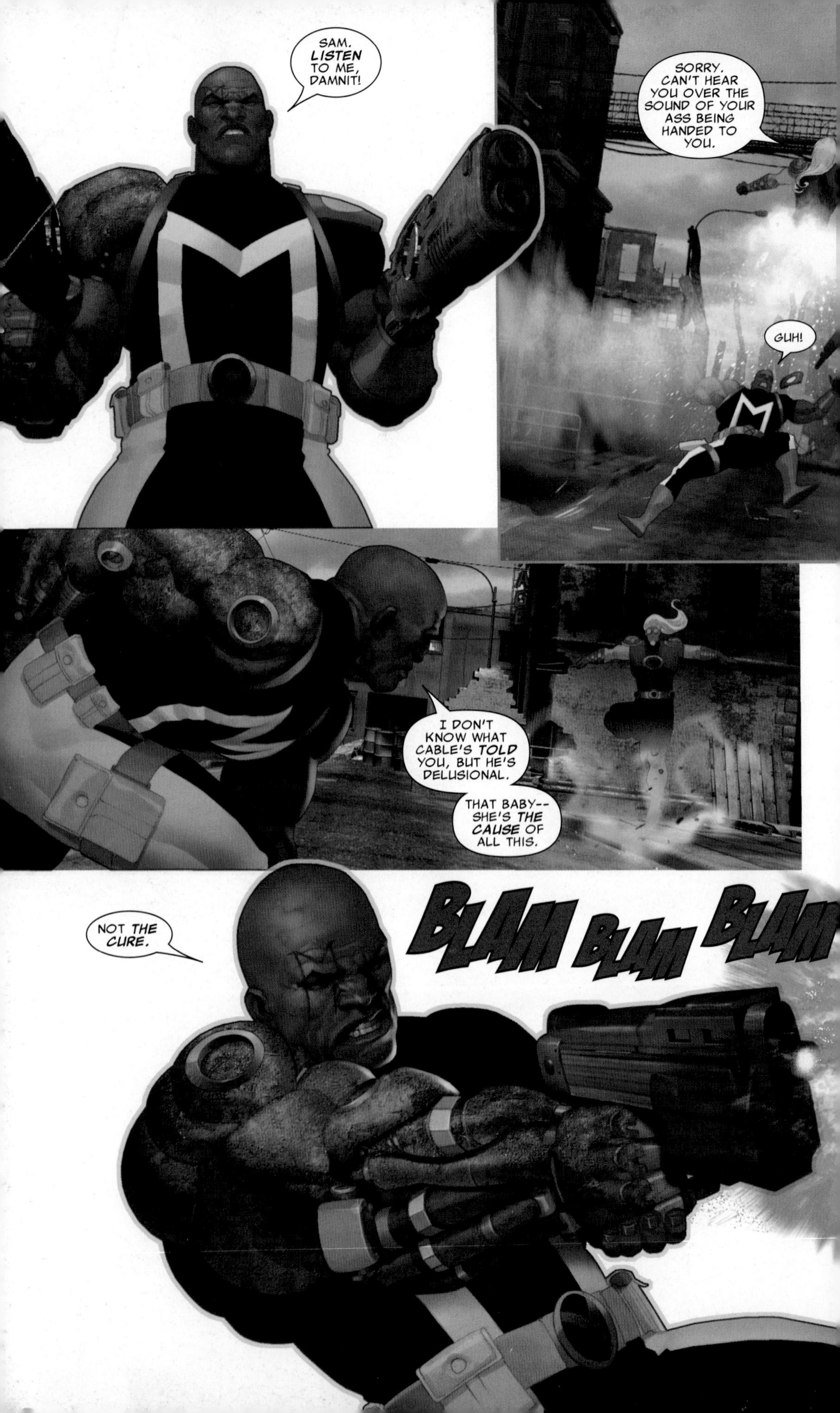
SAM. LISTEN TO ME, DAMNIT!
SORRY. CAN'T HEAR YOU OVER THE SOUND OF YOUR ASS BEING HANDED TO YOU.
GUH!
I DON'T KNOW WHAT CABLE'S TOLD YOU, BUT HE'S DELUSIONAL.
THAT BABY-- SHE'S THE CAUSE OF ALL THIS.
NOT THE CURE.
BLAM BLAM BLAM

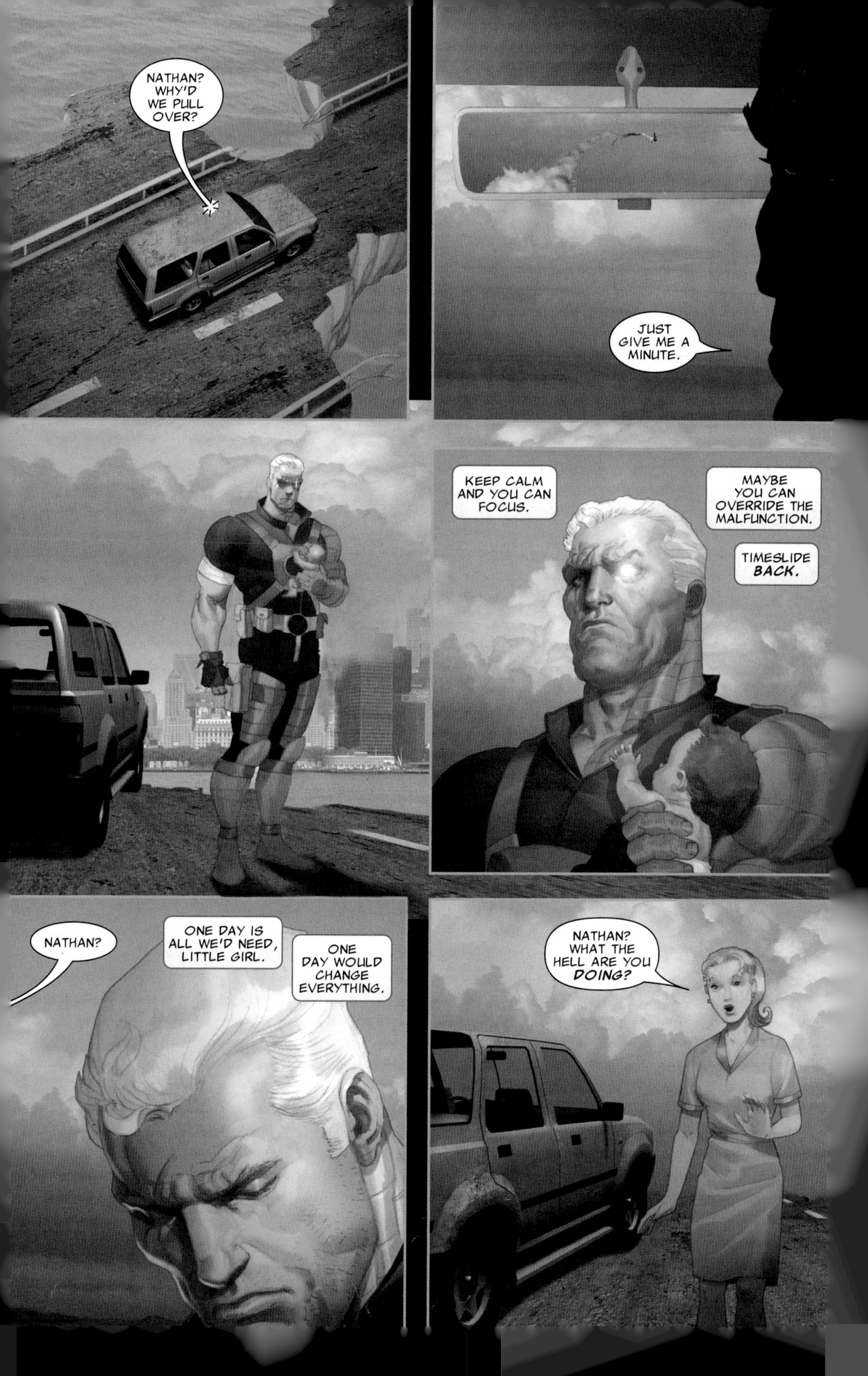
NATHAN? WHY'D WE PULL OVER?
JUST GIVE ME A MINUTE.
KEEP CALM AND YOU CAN FOCUS.
MAYBE YOU CAN OVERRIDE THE MALFUNCTION.
TIMESLIDE BACK.
NATHAN?
ONE DAY IS ALL WE'D NEED, LITTLE GIRL.
ONE DAY WOULD CHANGE EVERYTHING.
NATHAN? WHAT THE HELL ARE YOU DOING?

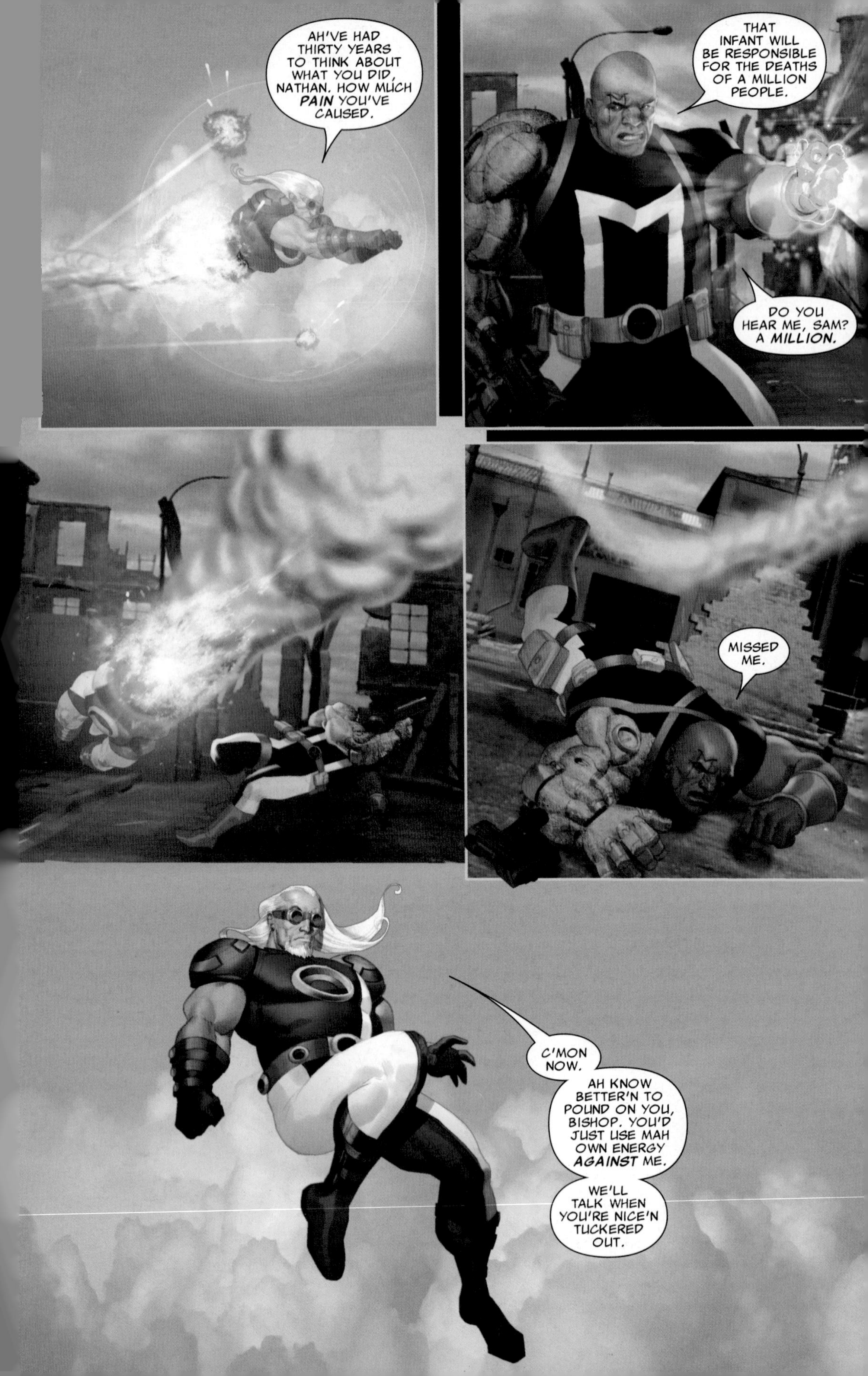
AH'VE HAD THIRTY YEARS TO THINK ABOUT WHAT YOU DID, NATHAN. HOW MUCH PAIN YOU'VE CAUSED.
THAT INFANT WILL BE RESPONSIBLE FOR THE DEATHS OF A MILLION PEOPLE.
DO YOU HEAR ME, SAM? A MILLION.
MISSED ME.
C'MON NOW.
AH KNOW BETTER'N TO POUND ON YOU, BISHOP. YOU'D JUST USE MAH OWN ENERGY AGAINST ME.
WE'LL TALK WHEN YOU'RE NICE'N TUCKERED OUT.

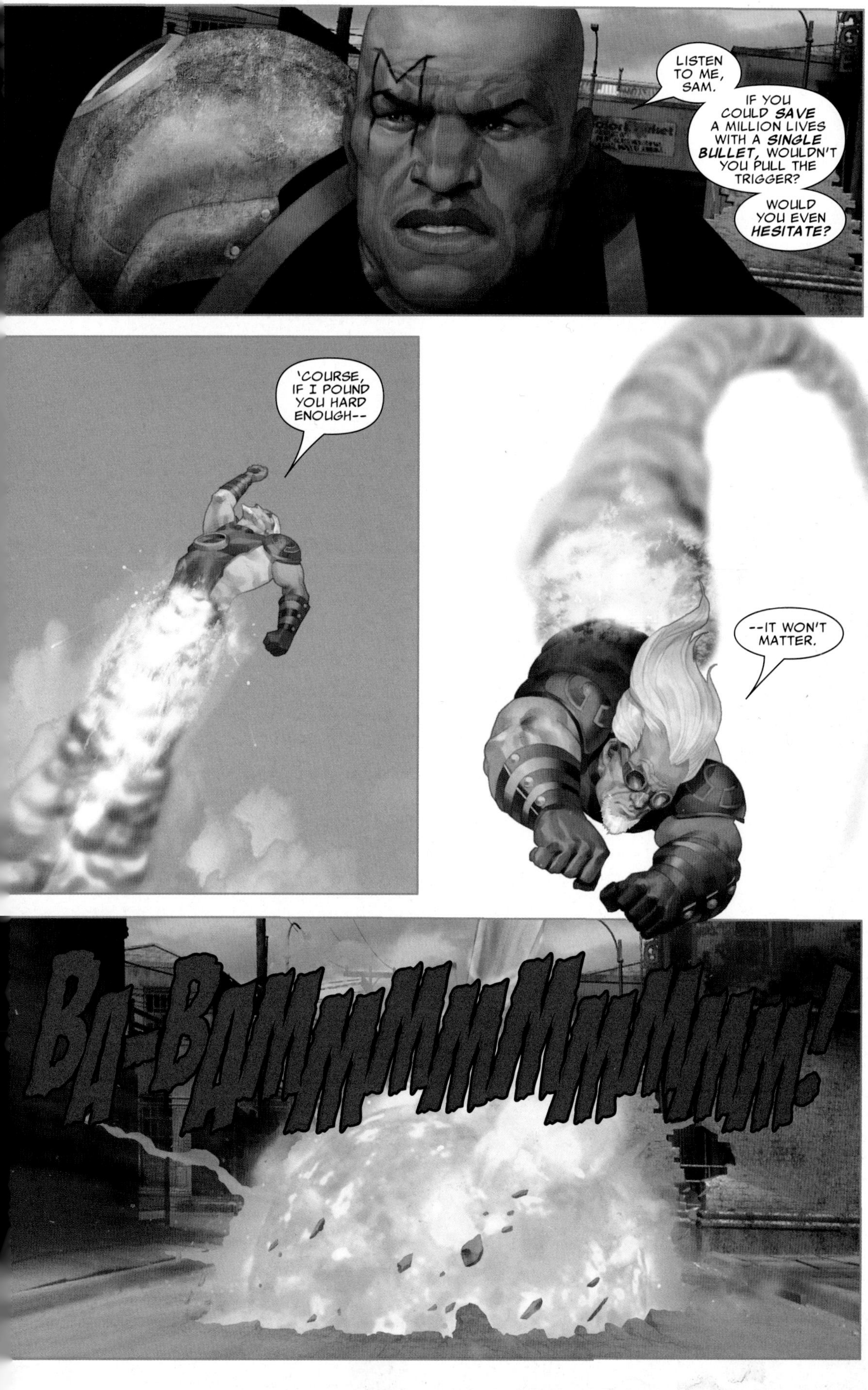
LISTEN TO ME, SAM.
IF YOU COULD SAVE A MILLION LIVES WITH A SINGLE BULLET, WOULDN'T YOU PULL THE TRIGGER?
WOULD YOU EVEN HESITATE?
'COURSE, IF I POUND YOU HARD ENOUGH--
--IT WON'T MATTER.
BA-BAMMMMMMMMMMMMM!

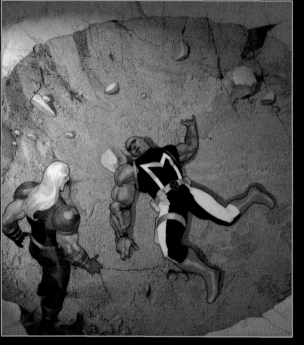

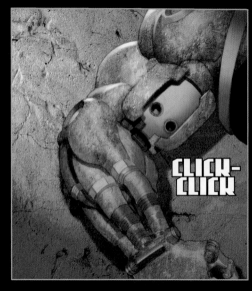

CLICK-
CLICK

WHAT THE--

ULK!

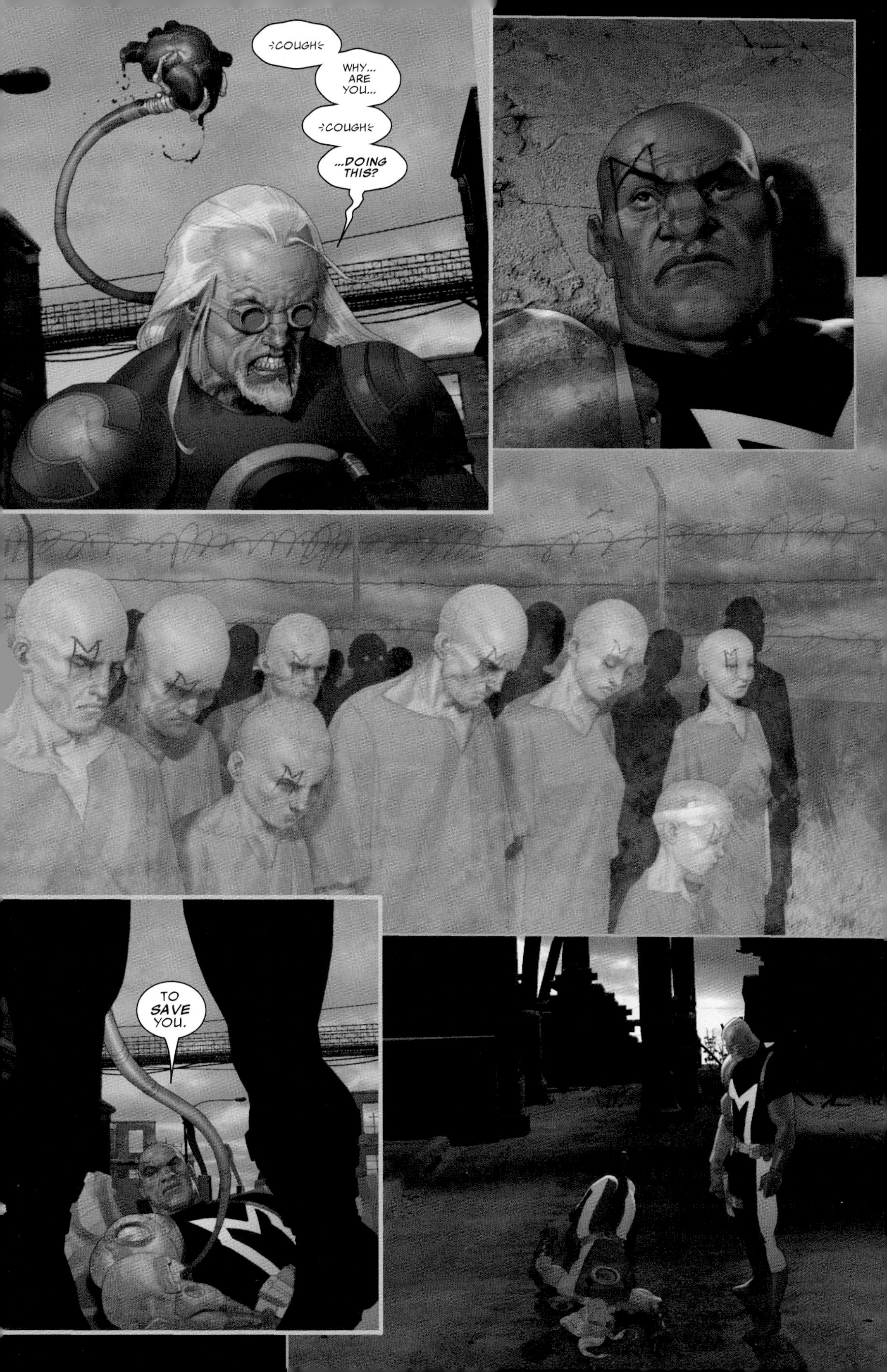

-COUGH-
WHY... ARE YOU...
-COUGH-
...DOING THIS?
TO SAVE YOU.

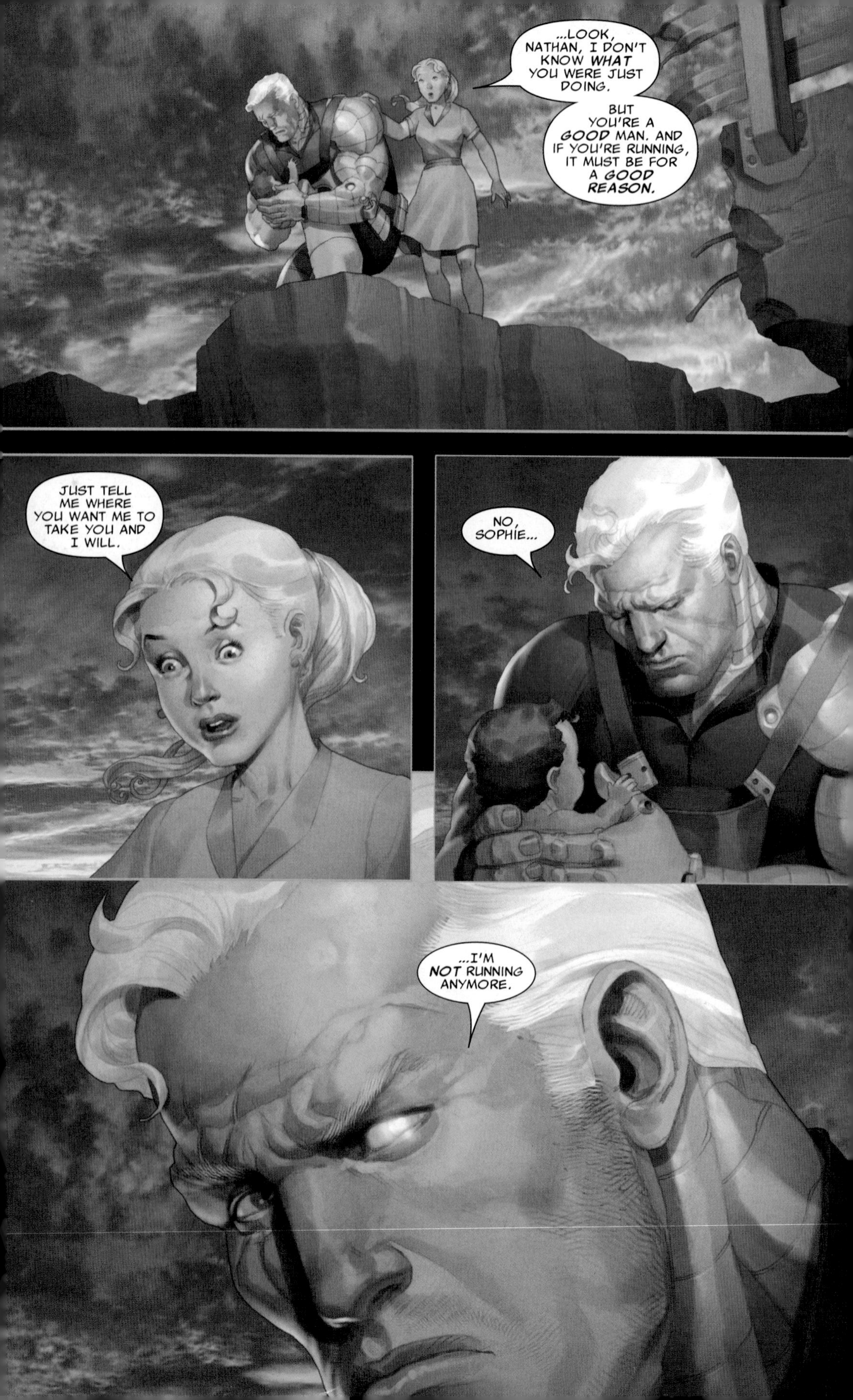
...LOOK, NATHAN, I DON'T KNOW WHAT YOU WERE JUST DOING.
BUT YOU'RE A GOOD MAN. AND IF YOU'RE RUNNING, IT MUST BE FOR A GOOD REASON.
JUST TELL ME WHERE YOU WANT ME TO TAKE YOU AND I WILL.
NO, SOPHIE...
...I'M NOT RUNNING ANYMORE.

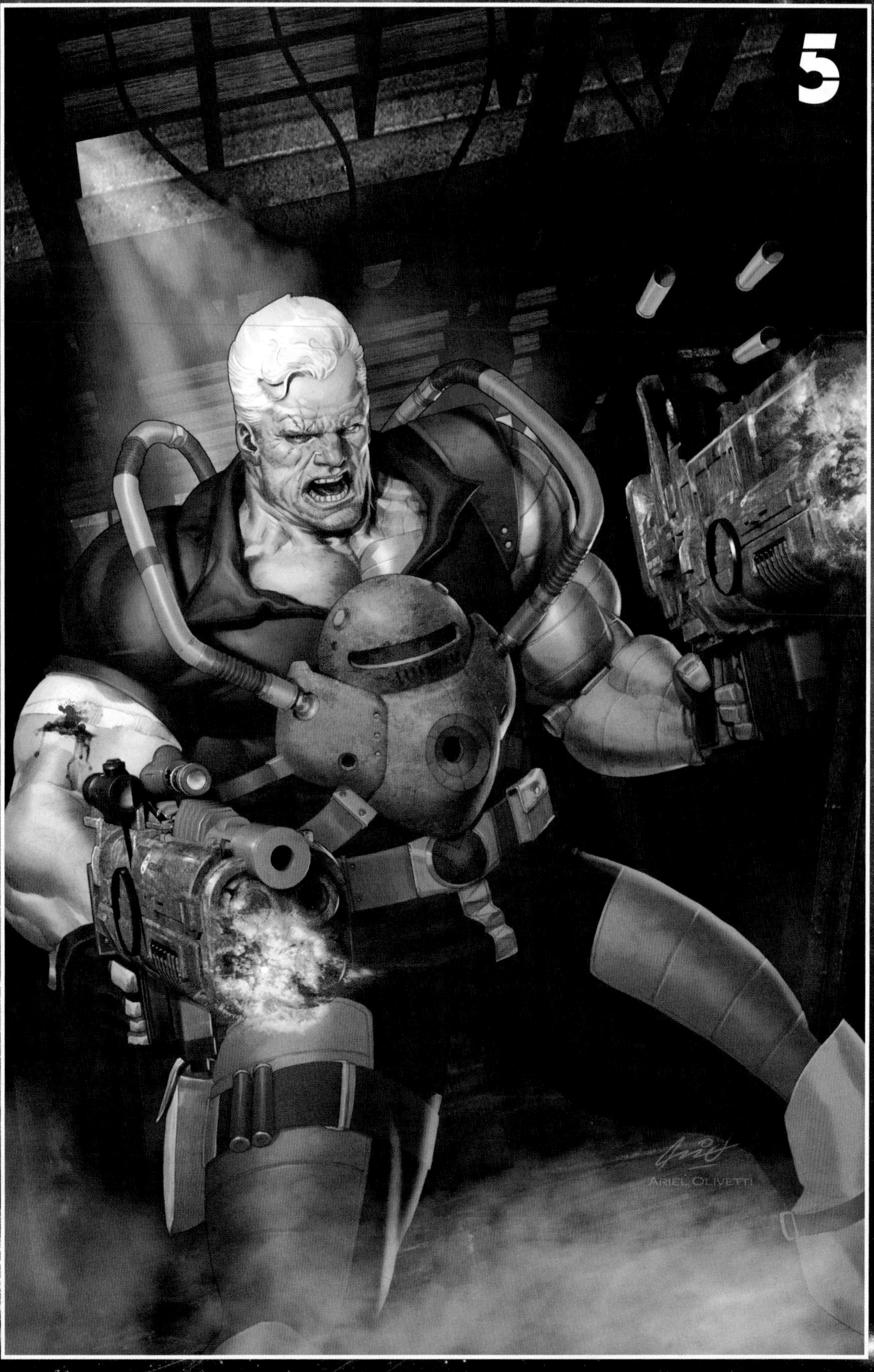
5
ARIEL OLIVETTI

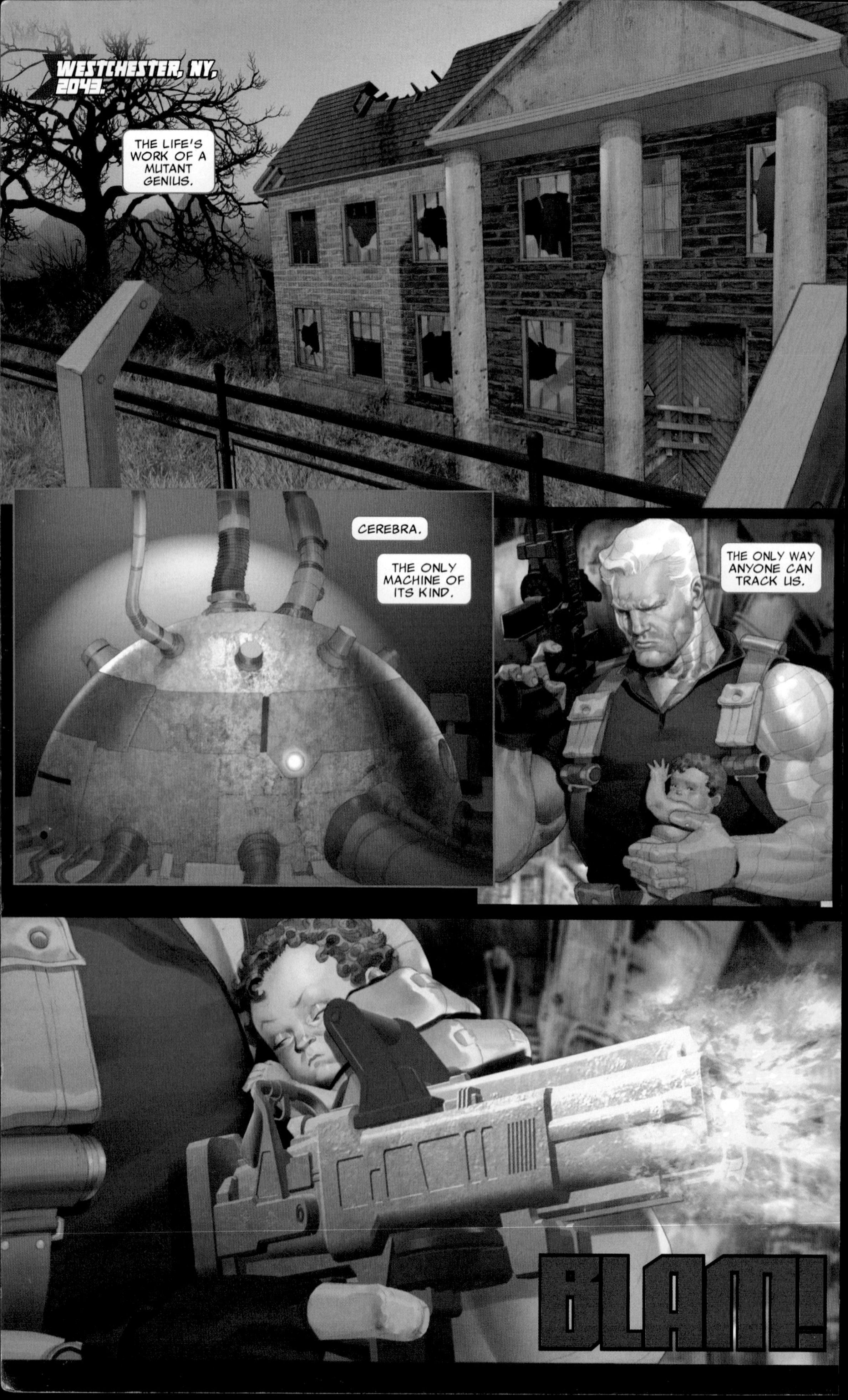
WESTCHESTER, NY, 2043.
THE LIFE'S WORK OF A MUTANT GENIUS.
CEREBRA.
THE ONLY MACHINE OF ITS KIND.
THE ONLY WAY ANYONE CAN TRACK US.
BLAM!

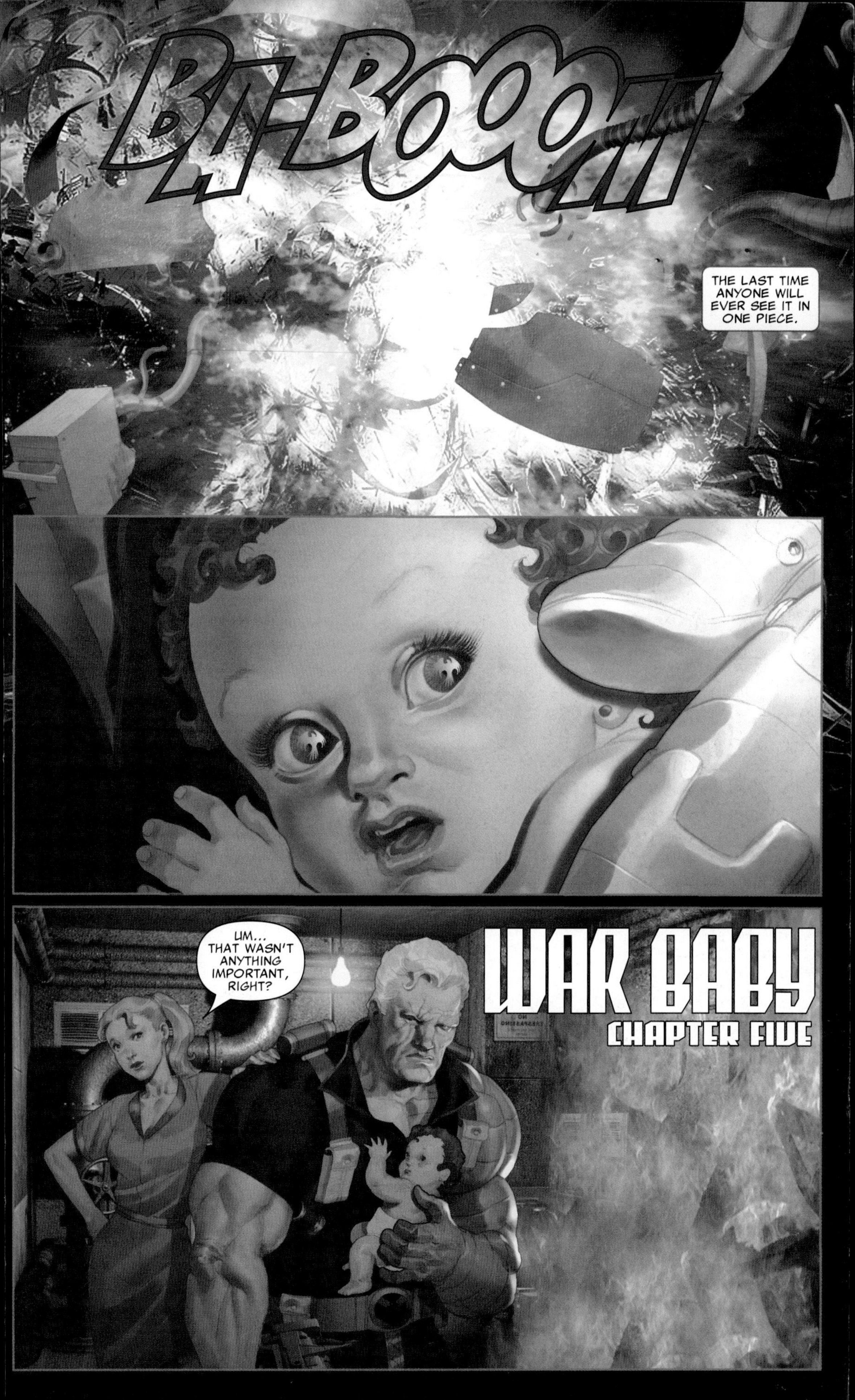
BA-BOOOM
THE LAST TIME ANYONE WILL EVER SEE IT IN ONE PIECE.
UM... THAT WASN'T ANYTHING IMPORTANT, RIGHT?
WAR BABY
CHAPTER FIVE

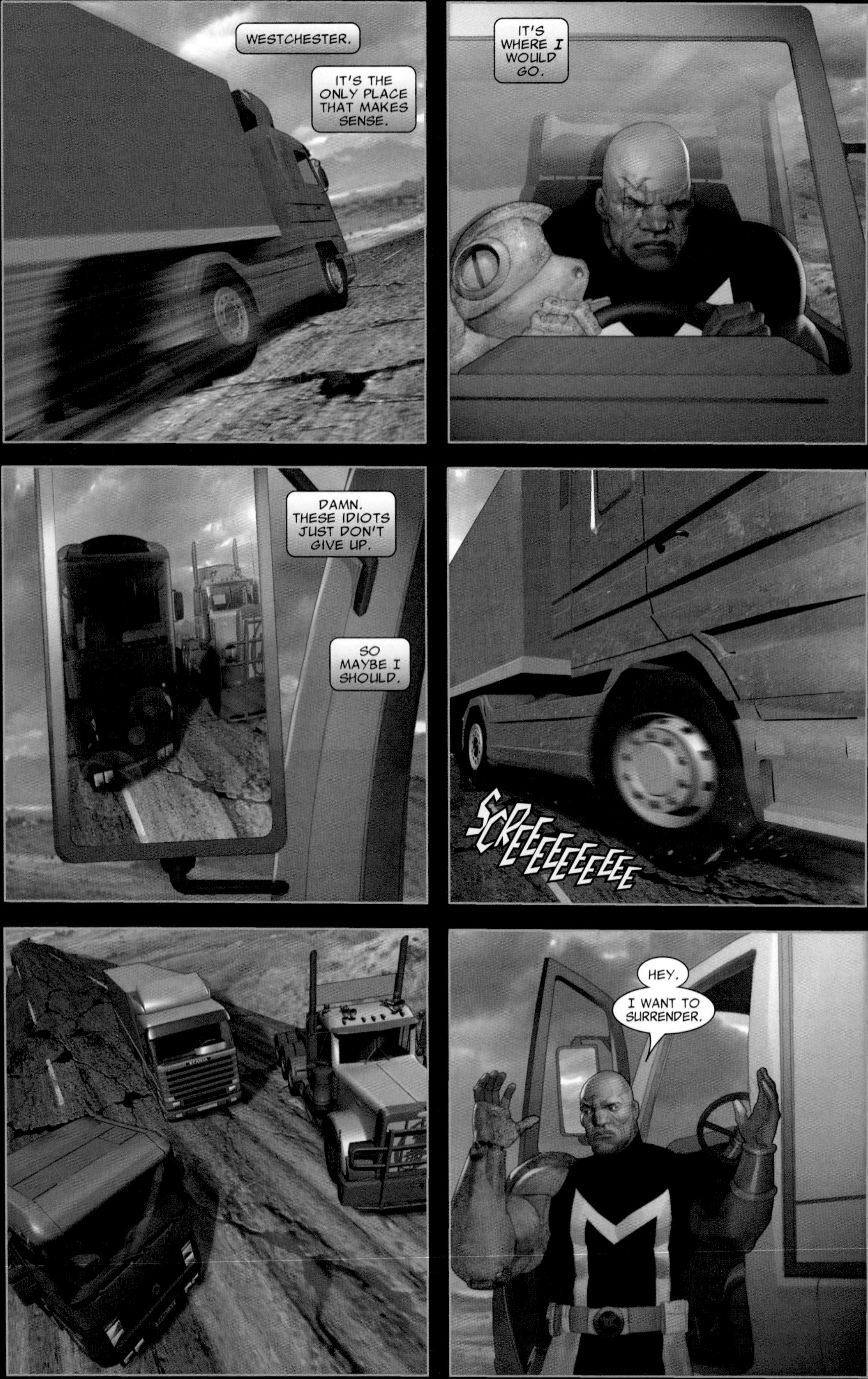
WESTCHESTER.
IT'S THE ONLY PLACE THAT MAKES SENSE.
IT'S WHERE I WOULD GO.
DAMN. THESE IDIOTS JUST DON'T GIVE UP.
SO MAYBE I SHOULD.
SCREEEEEEEEEEE
HEY.
I WANT TO SURRENDER.

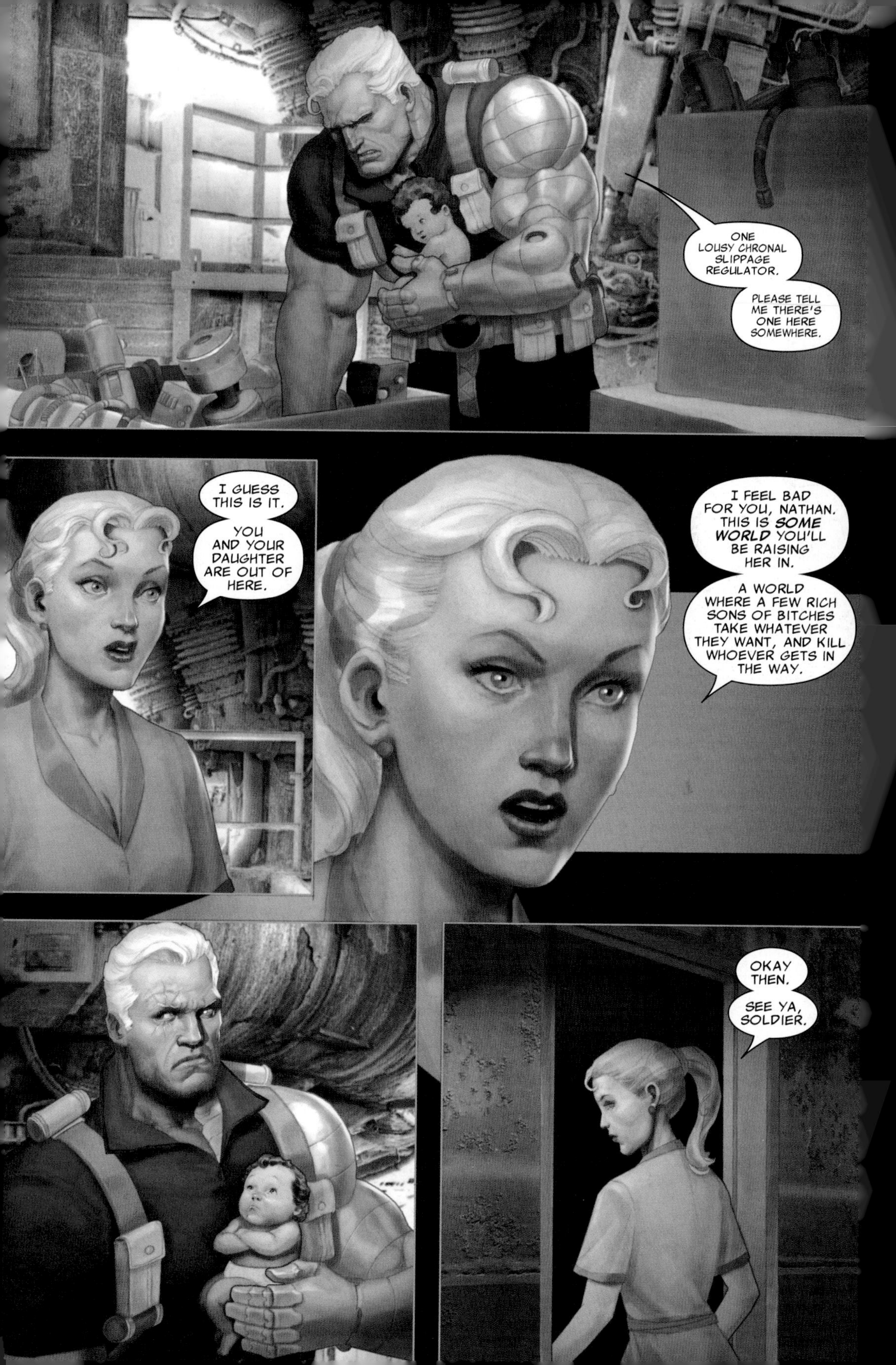
ONE LOUSY CHRONAL SLIPPAGE REGULATOR.
PLEASE TELL ME THERE'S ONE HERE SOMEWHERE.
I GUESS THIS IS IT.
YOU AND YOUR DAUGHTER ARE OUT OF HERE.
I FEEL BAD FOR YOU, NATHAN. THIS IS ***SOME WORLD*** YOU'LL BE RAISING HER IN.
A WORLD WHERE A FEW RICH SONS OF BITCHES TAKE WHATEVER THEY WANT, AND KILL WHOEVER GETS IN THE WAY.
OKAY THEN.
SEE YA, SOLDIER.

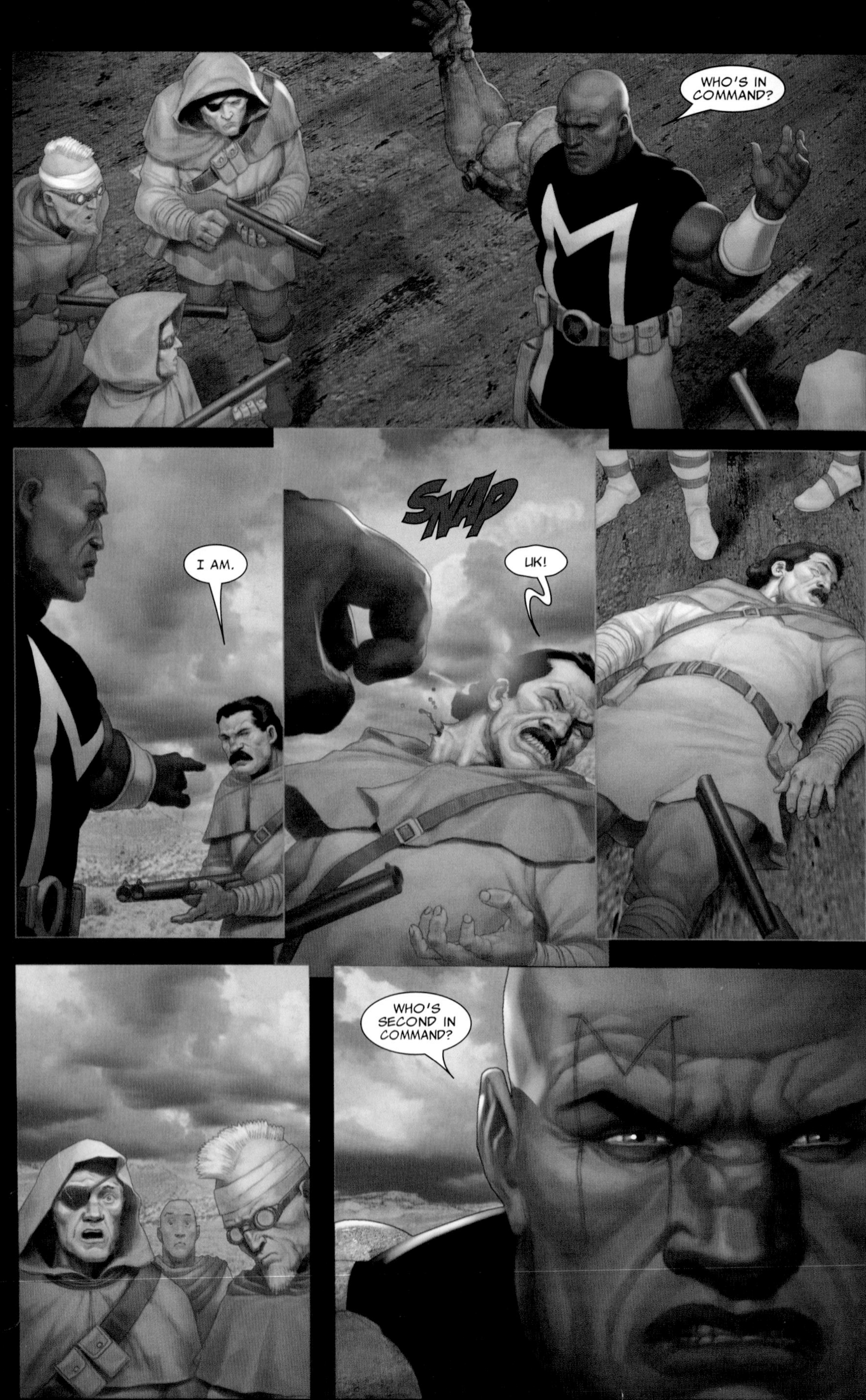
WHO'S IN COMMAND?
I AM.
SNAP
UK!
WHO'S SECOND IN COMMAND?

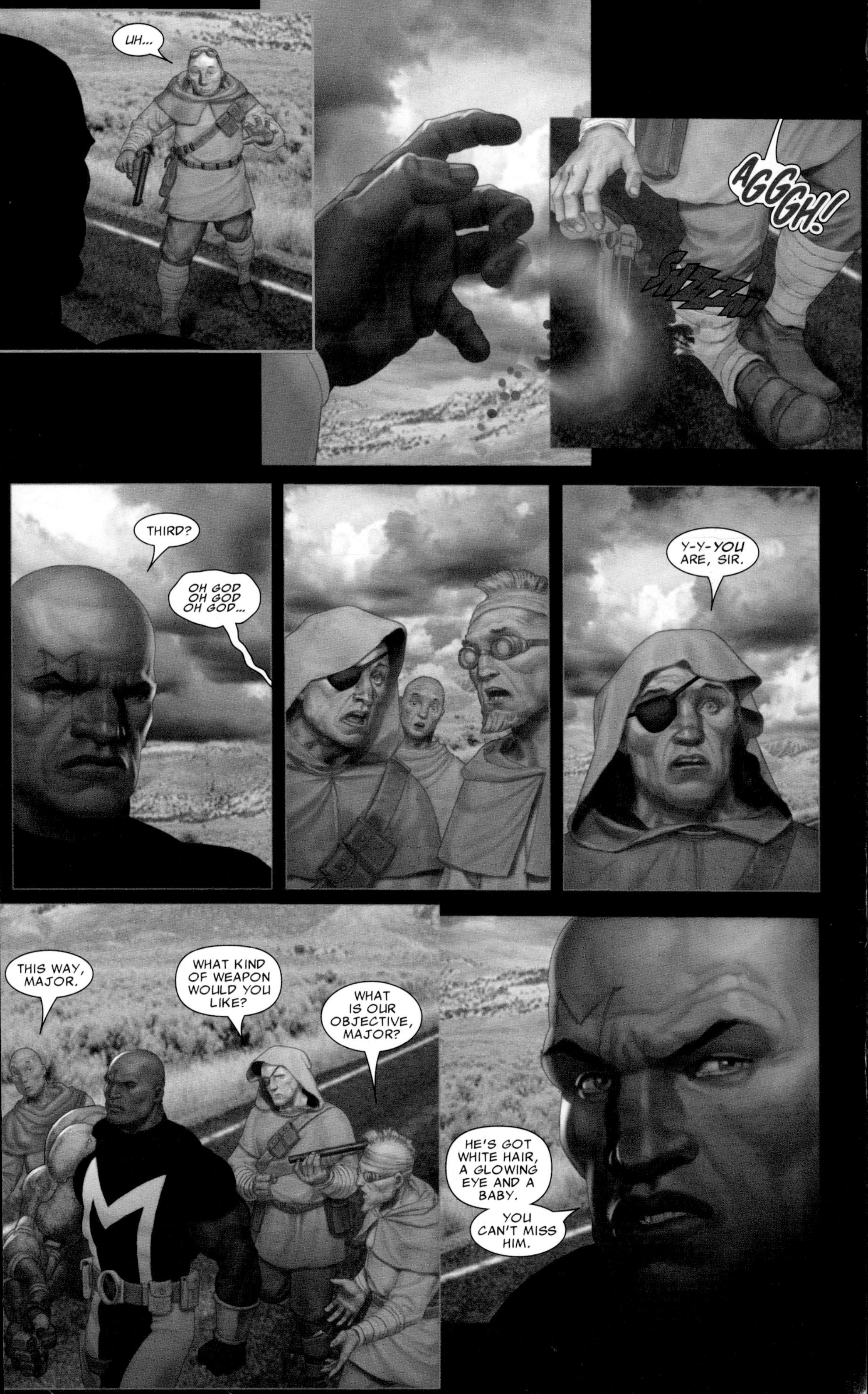
UH...
AGGGH!
SHZZZZD
THIRD?
OH GOD OH GOD OH GOD...
Y-Y-YOU ARE, SIR.
THIS WAY, MAJOR.
WHAT KIND OF WEAPON WOULD YOU LIKE?
WHAT IS OUR OBJECTIVE, MAJOR?
HE'S GOT WHITE HAIR, A GLOWING EYE AND A BABY.
YOU CAN'T MISS HIM.

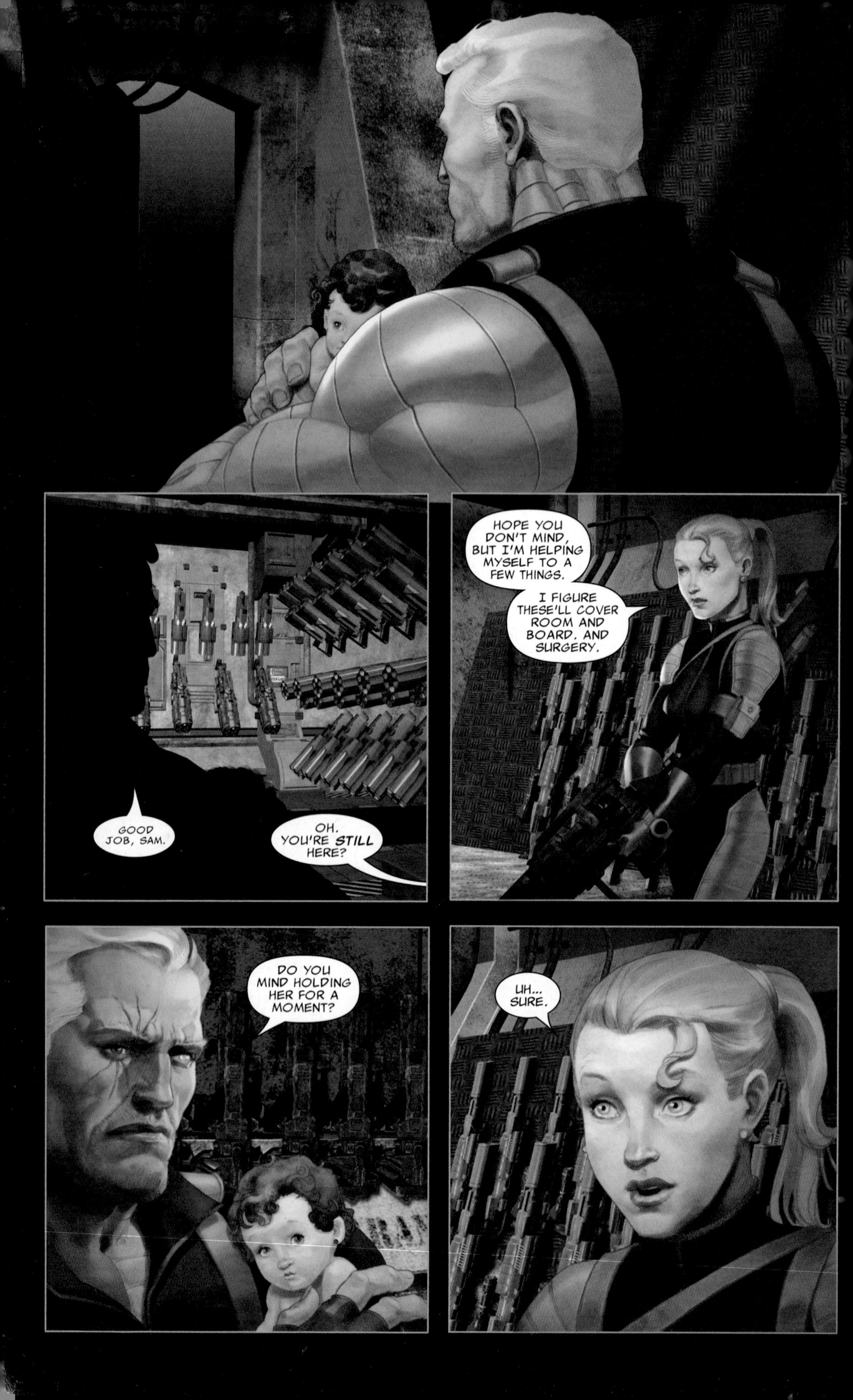
GOOD JOB, SAM.
OH. YOU'RE STILL HERE?
HOPE YOU DON'T MIND, BUT I'M HELPING MYSELF TO A FEW THINGS.
I FIGURE THESE'LL COVER ROOM AND BOARD. AND SURGERY.
DO YOU MIND HOLDING HER FOR A MOMENT?
UH... SURE.

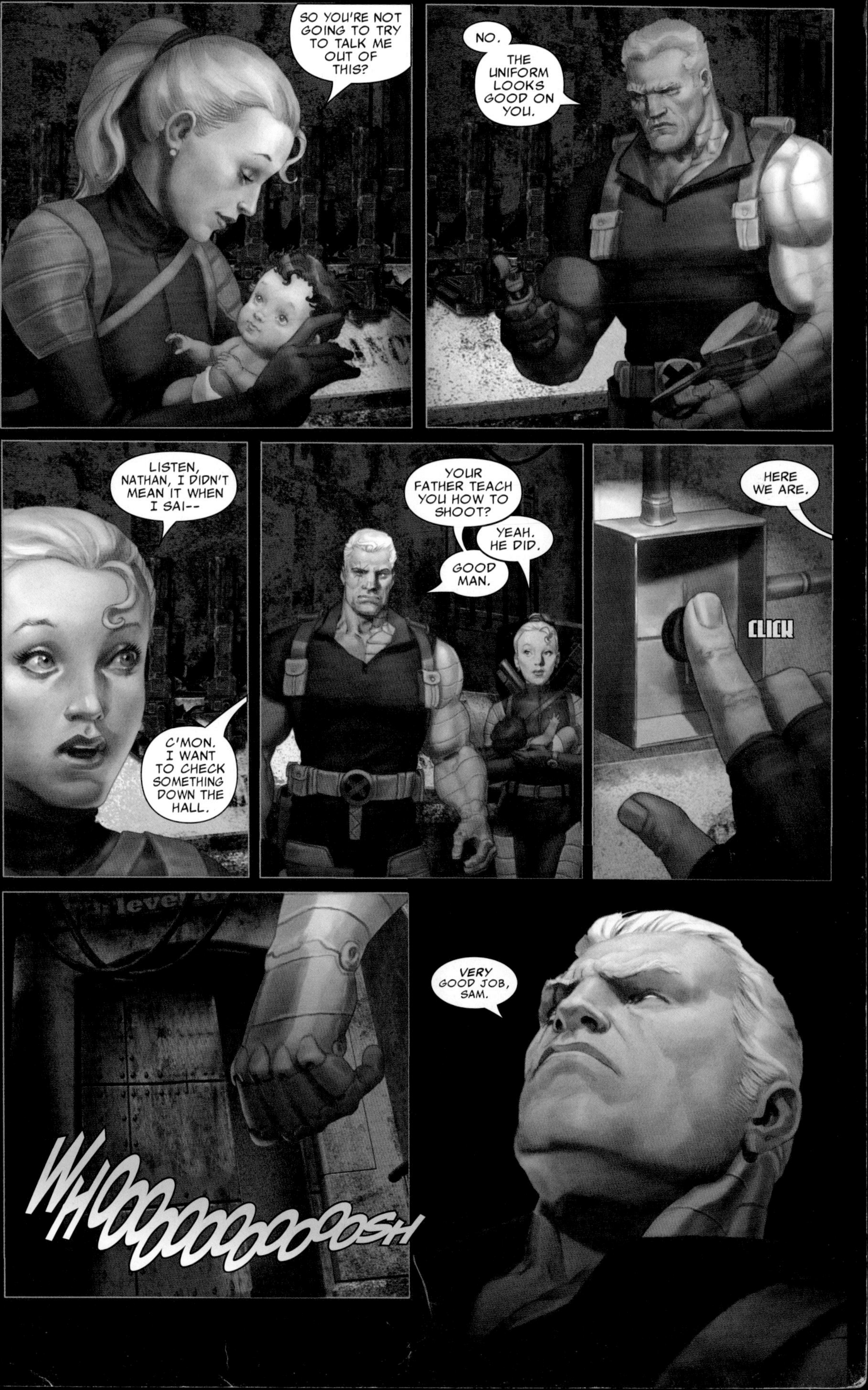
SO YOU'RE NOT GOING TO TRY TO TALK ME OUT OF THIS?
NO.
THE UNIFORM LOOKS GOOD ON YOU.
LISTEN, NATHAN, I DIDN'T MEAN IT WHEN I SAI--
C'MON. I WANT TO CHECK SOMETHING DOWN THE HALL.
YOUR FATHER TEACH YOU HOW TO SHOOT?
YEAH. HE DID.
GOOD MAN.
HERE WE ARE.
CLICK
WHOOOOOOOOOOOSH
VERY GOOD JOB, SAM.

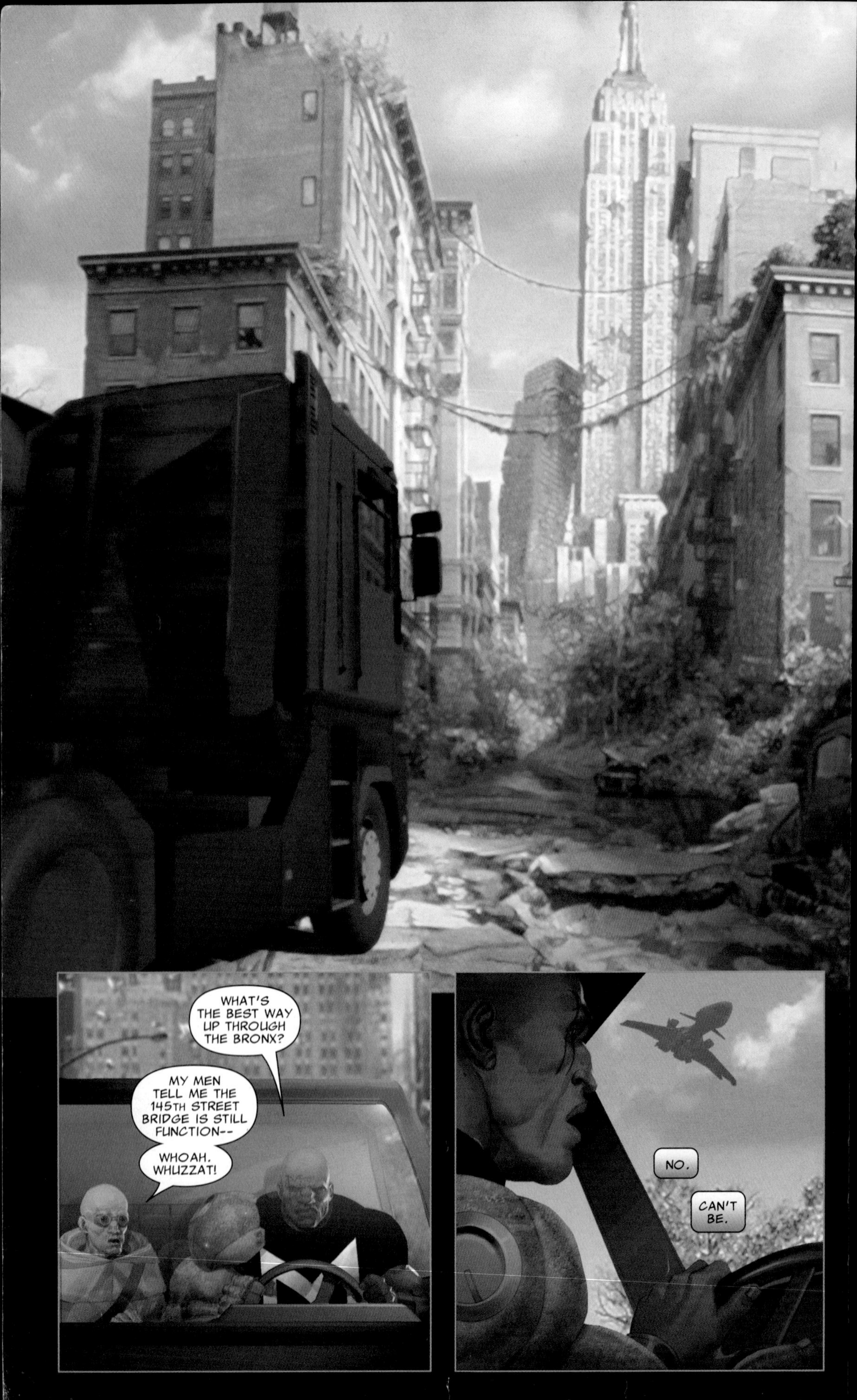
WHAT'S THE BEST WAY UP THROUGH THE BRONX?
MY MEN TELL ME THE 145TH STREET BRIDGE IS STILL FUNCTION--
WHOAH. WHUZZAT!
NO.
CAN'T BE.

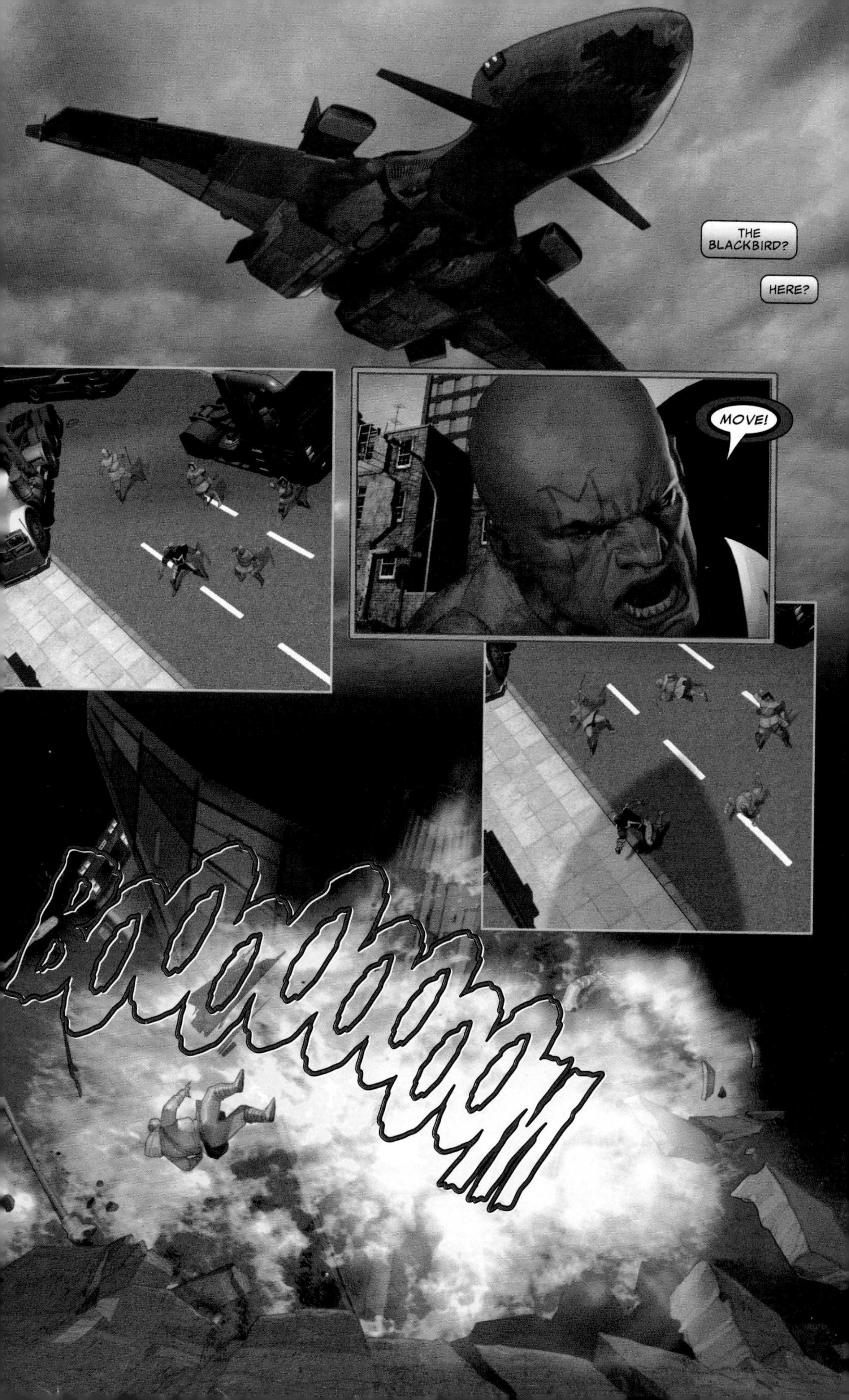
THE BLACKBIRD?
HERE?
MOVE!
BOOOOOOOOM

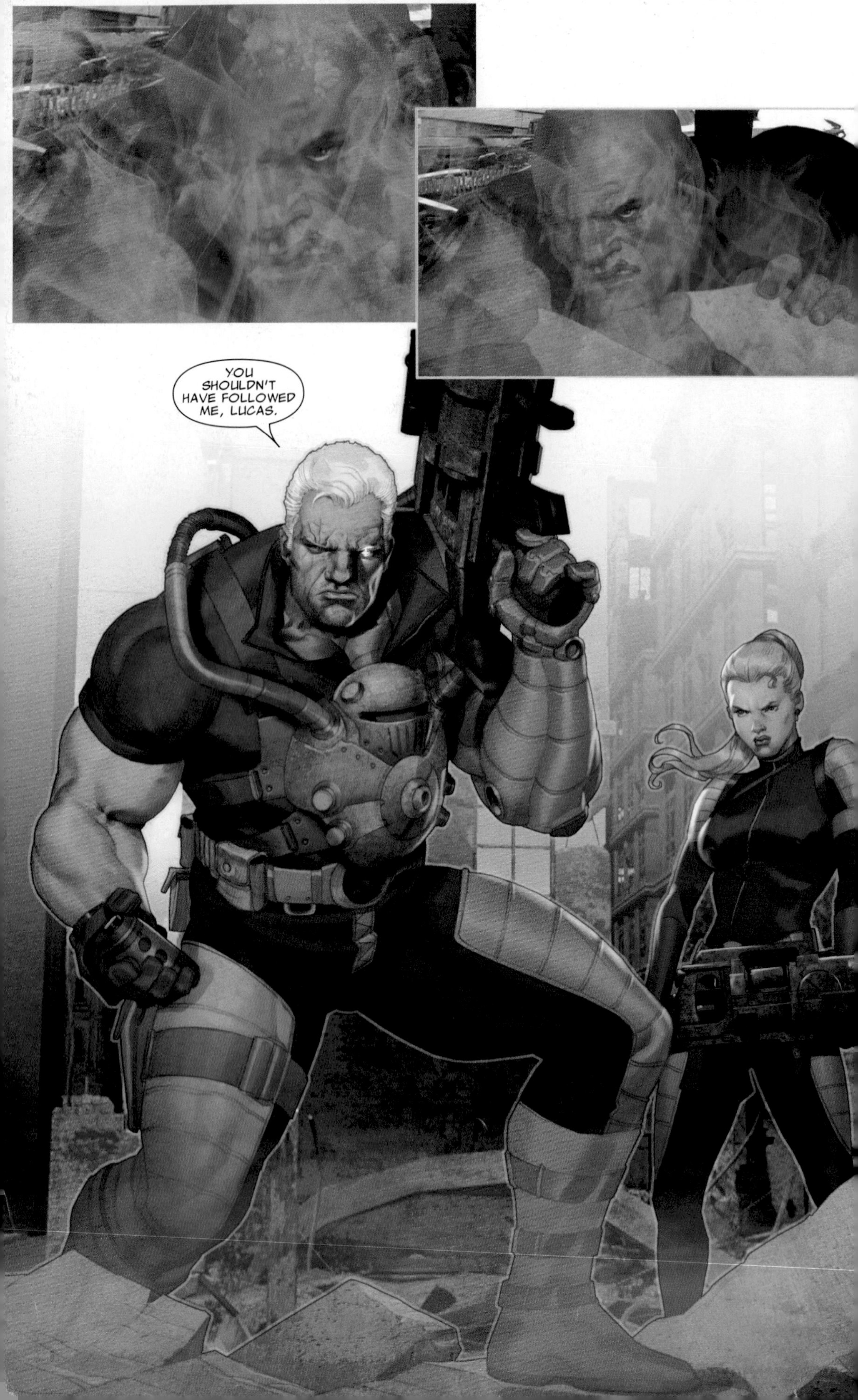
YOU SHOULDN'T HAVE FOLLOWED ME, LUCAS.

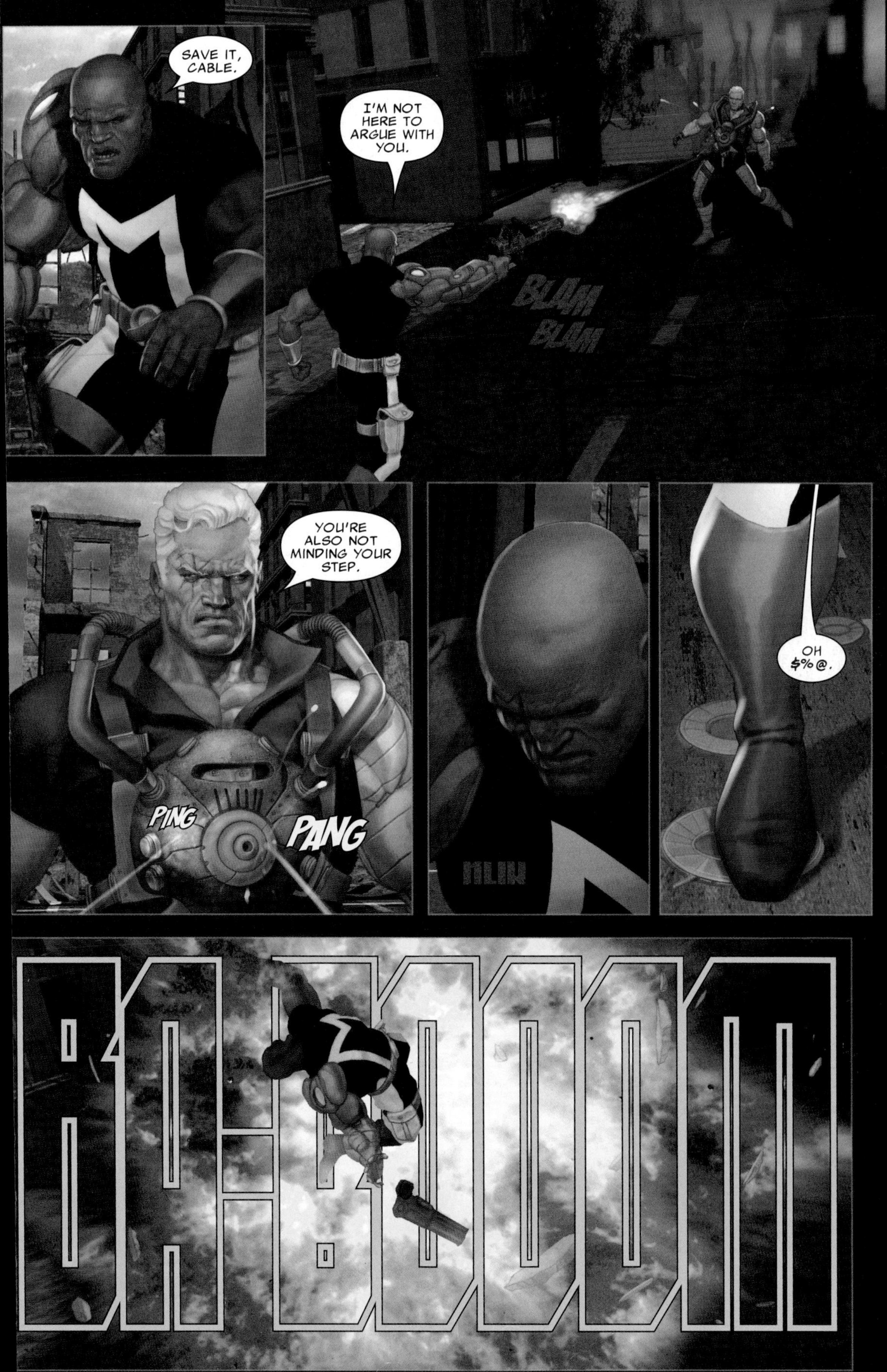
SAVE IT, CABLE.
I'M NOT HERE TO ARGUE WITH YOU.
BLAM
BLAM
YOU'RE ALSO NOT MINDING YOUR STEP.
PING
PANG
OH $%@.
BA-BOOOM

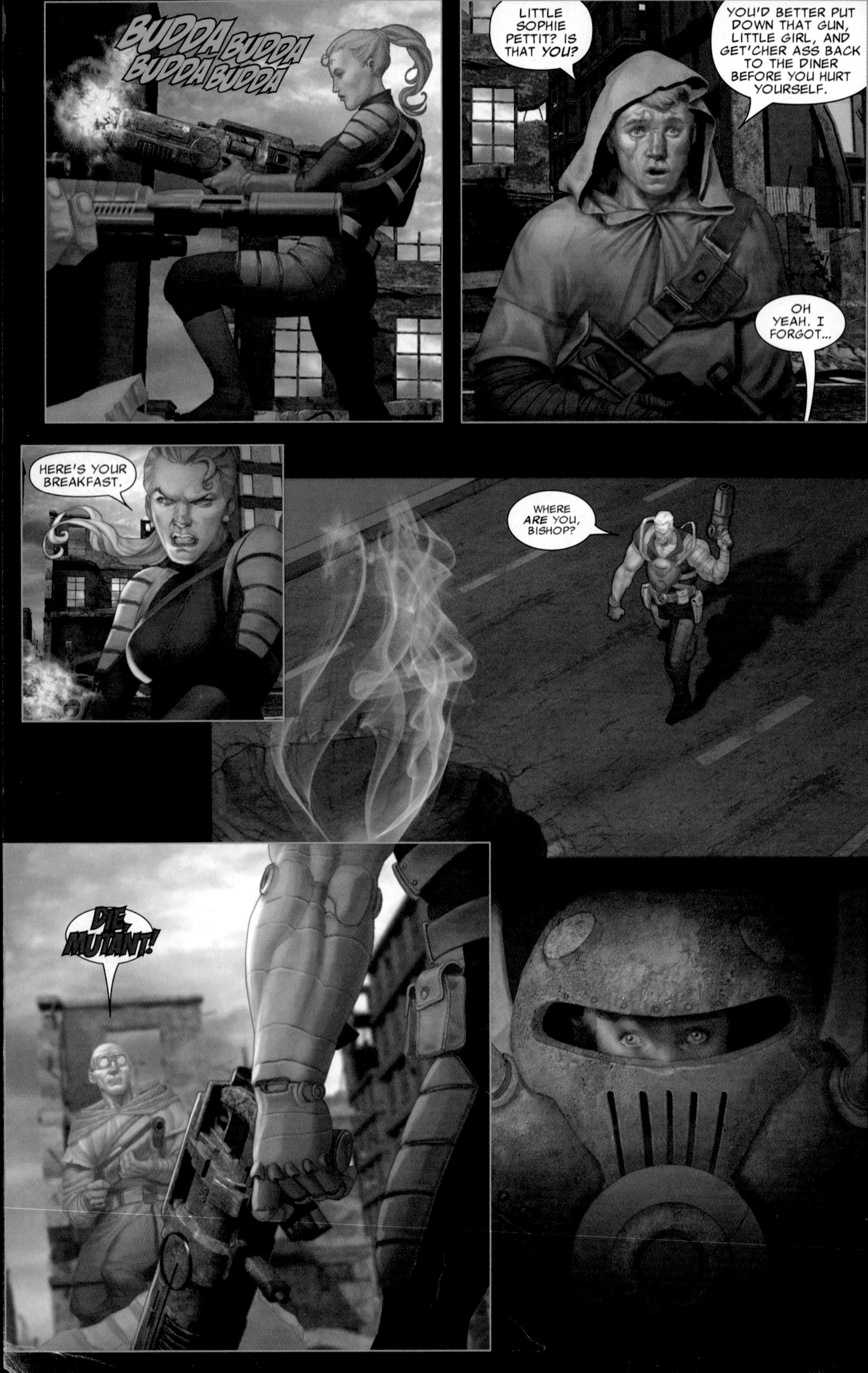
BUDDA BUDDA
BUDDA BUDDA
LITTLE SOPHIE PETTIT? IS THAT YOU?
YOU'D BETTER PUT DOWN THAT GUN, LITTLE GIRL, AND GET'CHER ASS BACK TO THE DINER BEFORE YOU HURT YOURSELF.
OH YEAH. I FORGOT...
HERE'S YOUR BREAKFAST.
WHERE ARE YOU, BISHOP?
DIE, MUTANT!

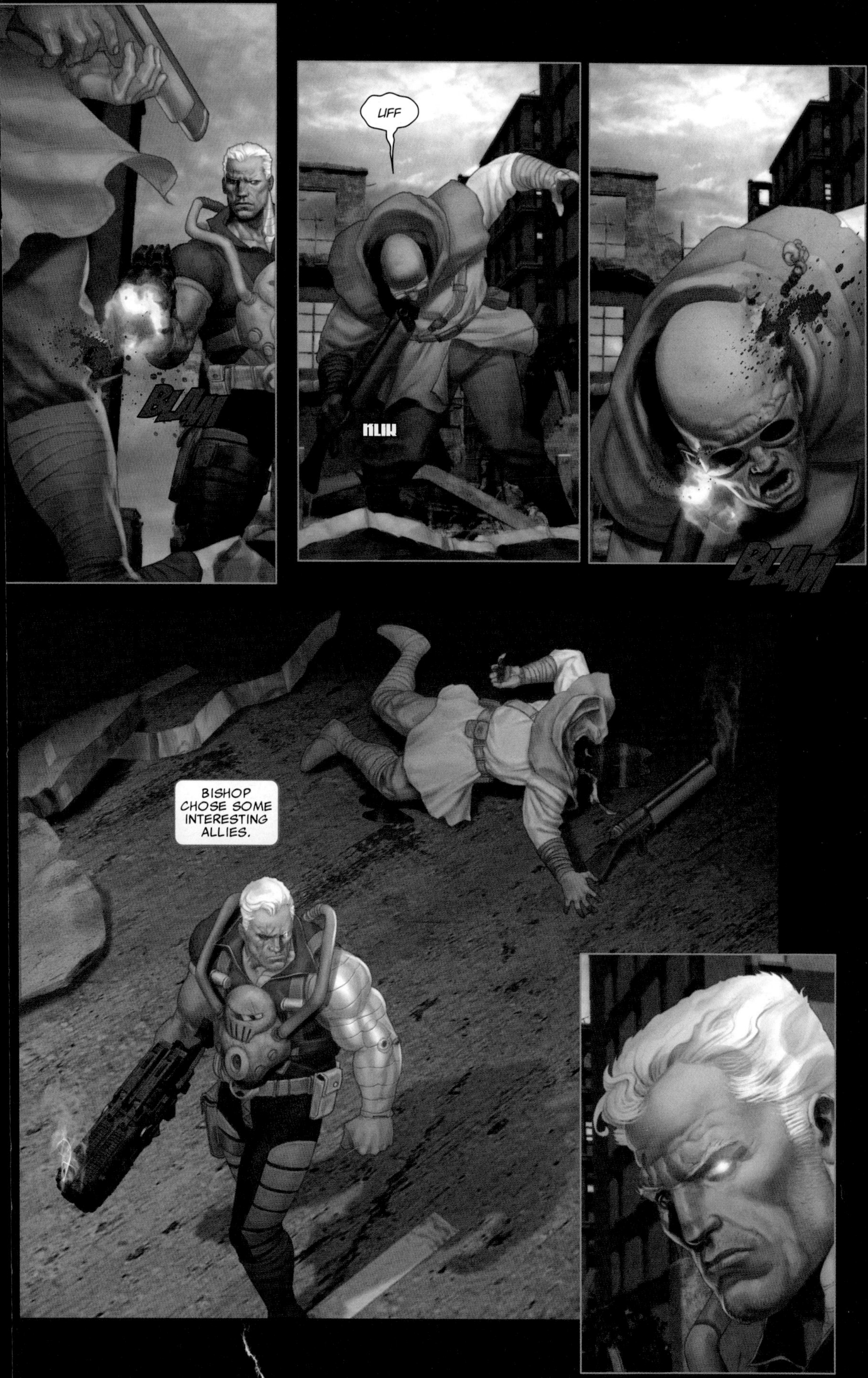
BLAM
UFF
KLIK
BLAM
BISHOP CHOSE SOME INTERESTING ALLIES.

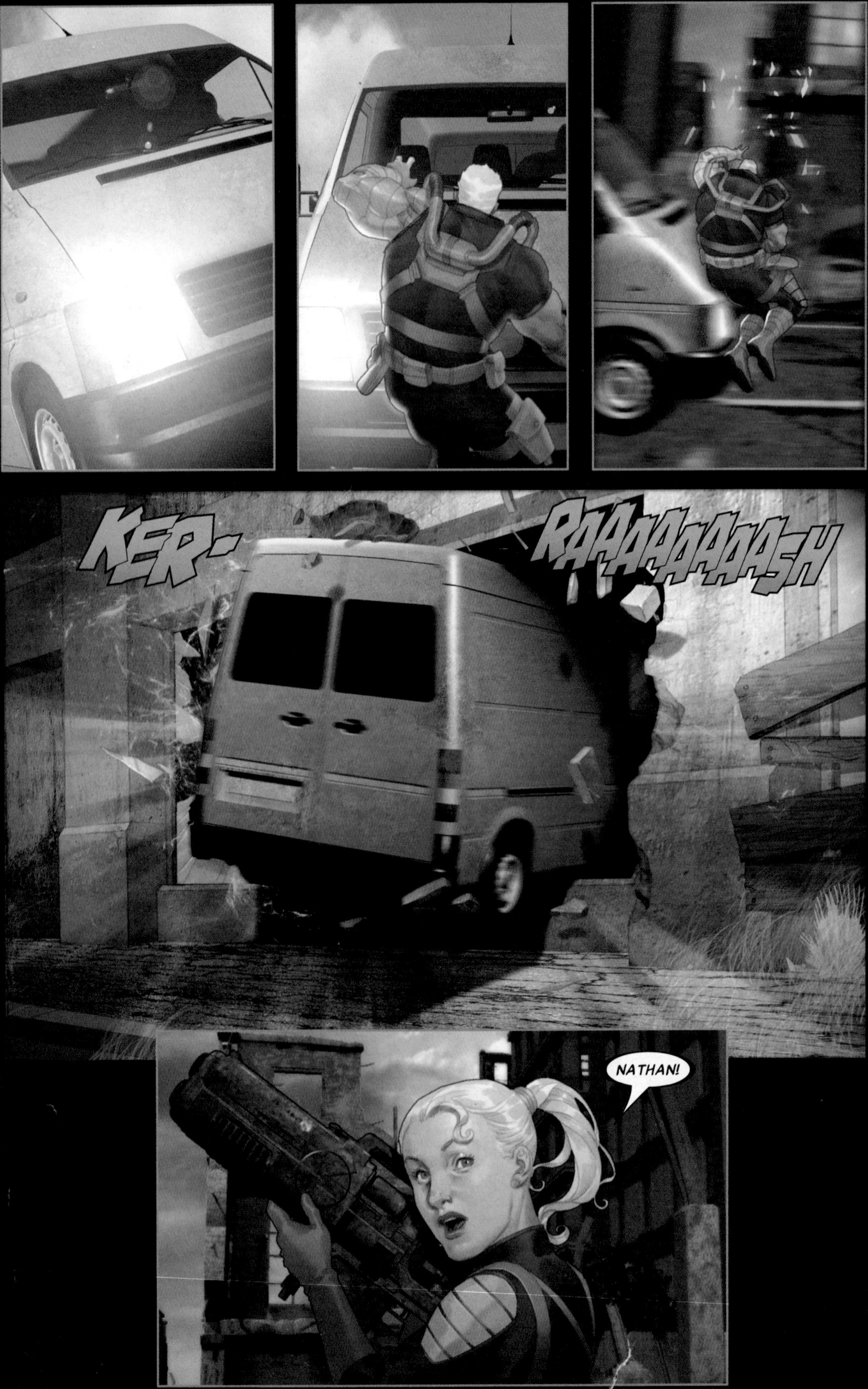
KER-
RAAAAAAAASH
NATHAN!

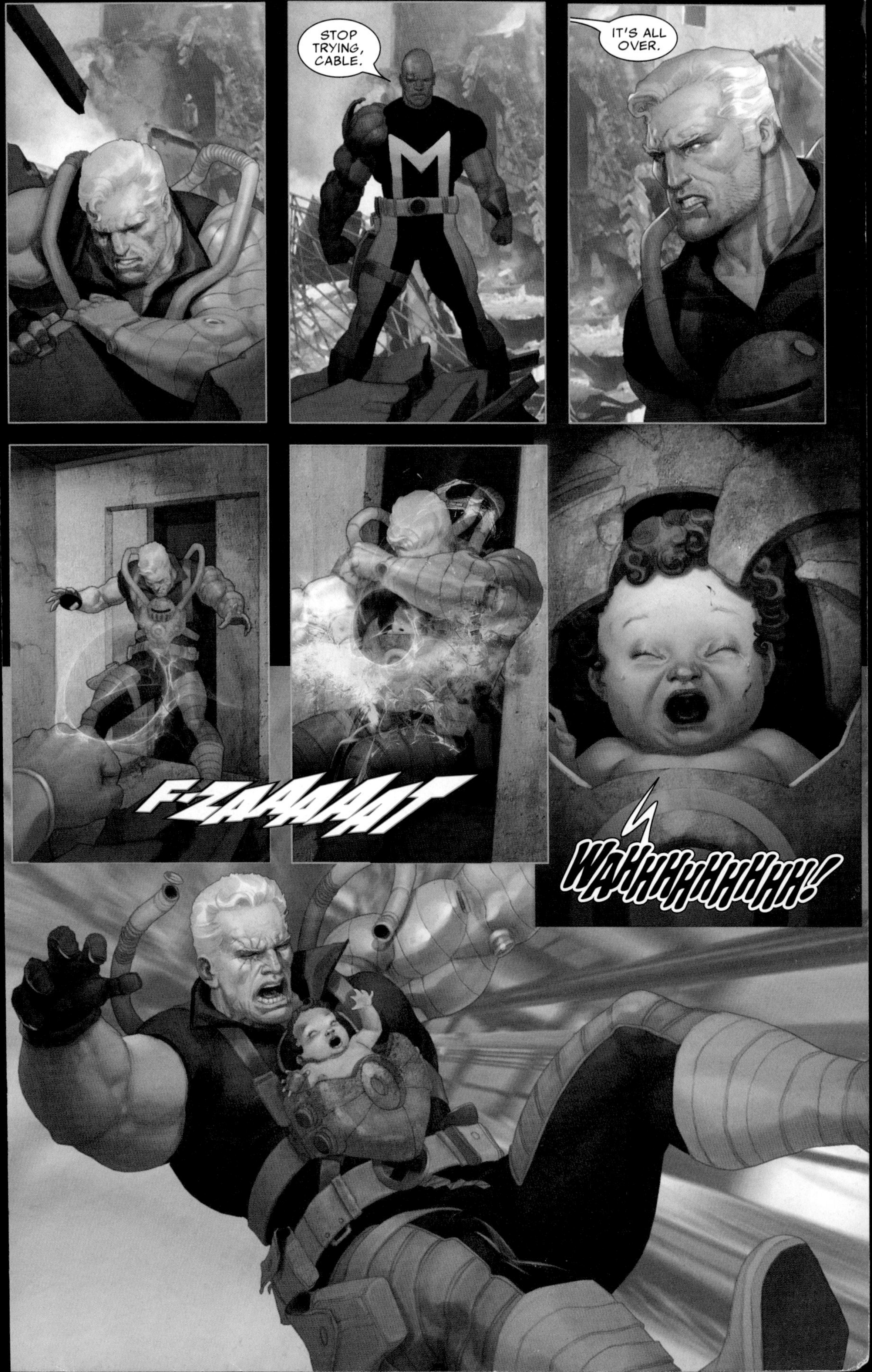
STOP TRYING, CABLE.
IT'S ALL OVER.
F-ZAAAAAT
WAHHHHHHHHH!

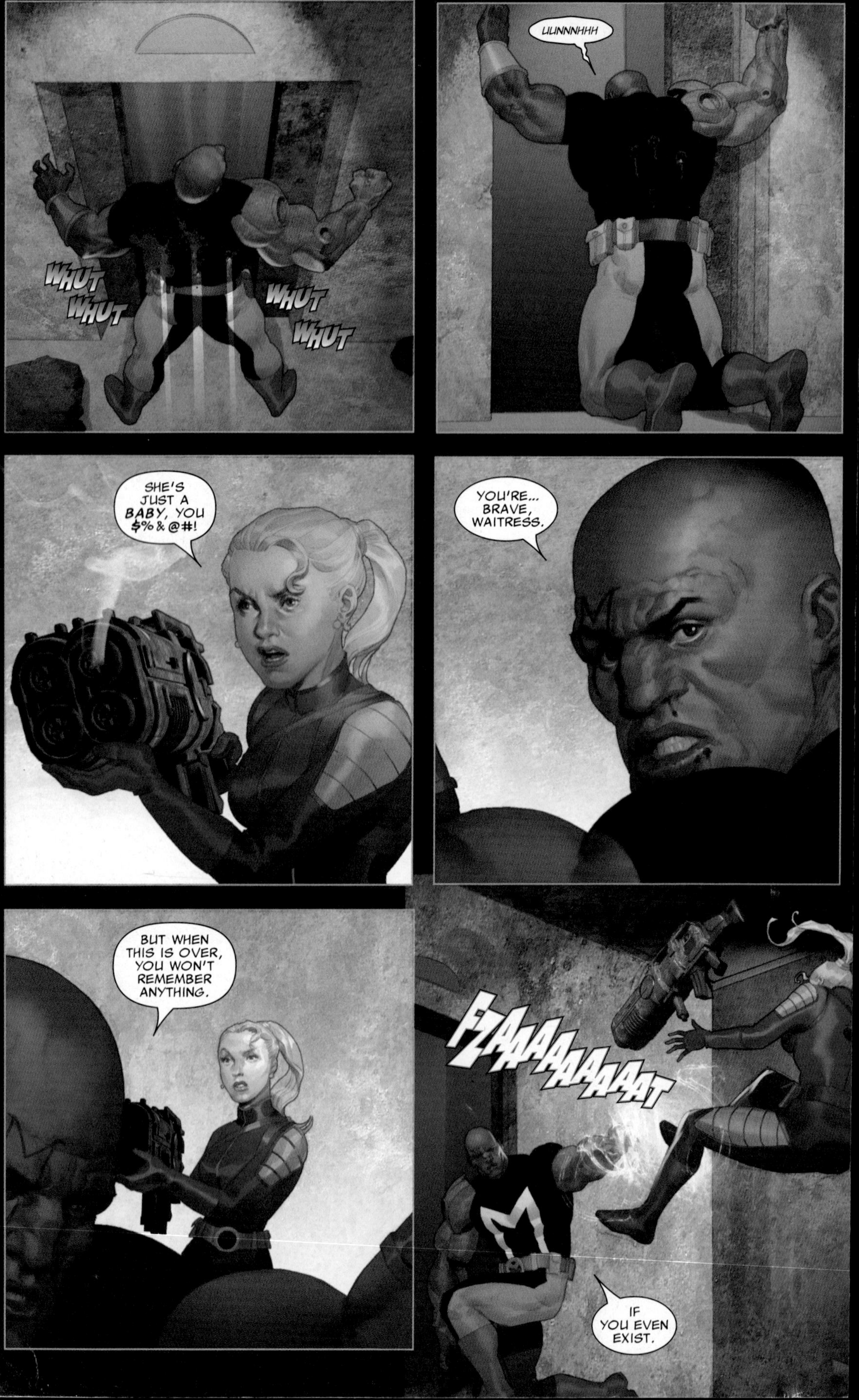
WHUT
WHUT
WHUT
WHUT
UUNNNHHH
SHE'S JUST A BABY, YOU $%&@#!
YOU'RE... BRAVE, WAITRESS.
BUT WHEN THIS IS OVER, YOU WON'T REMEMBER ANYTHING.
FZAAAAAAAAAAT
IF YOU EVEN EXIST.

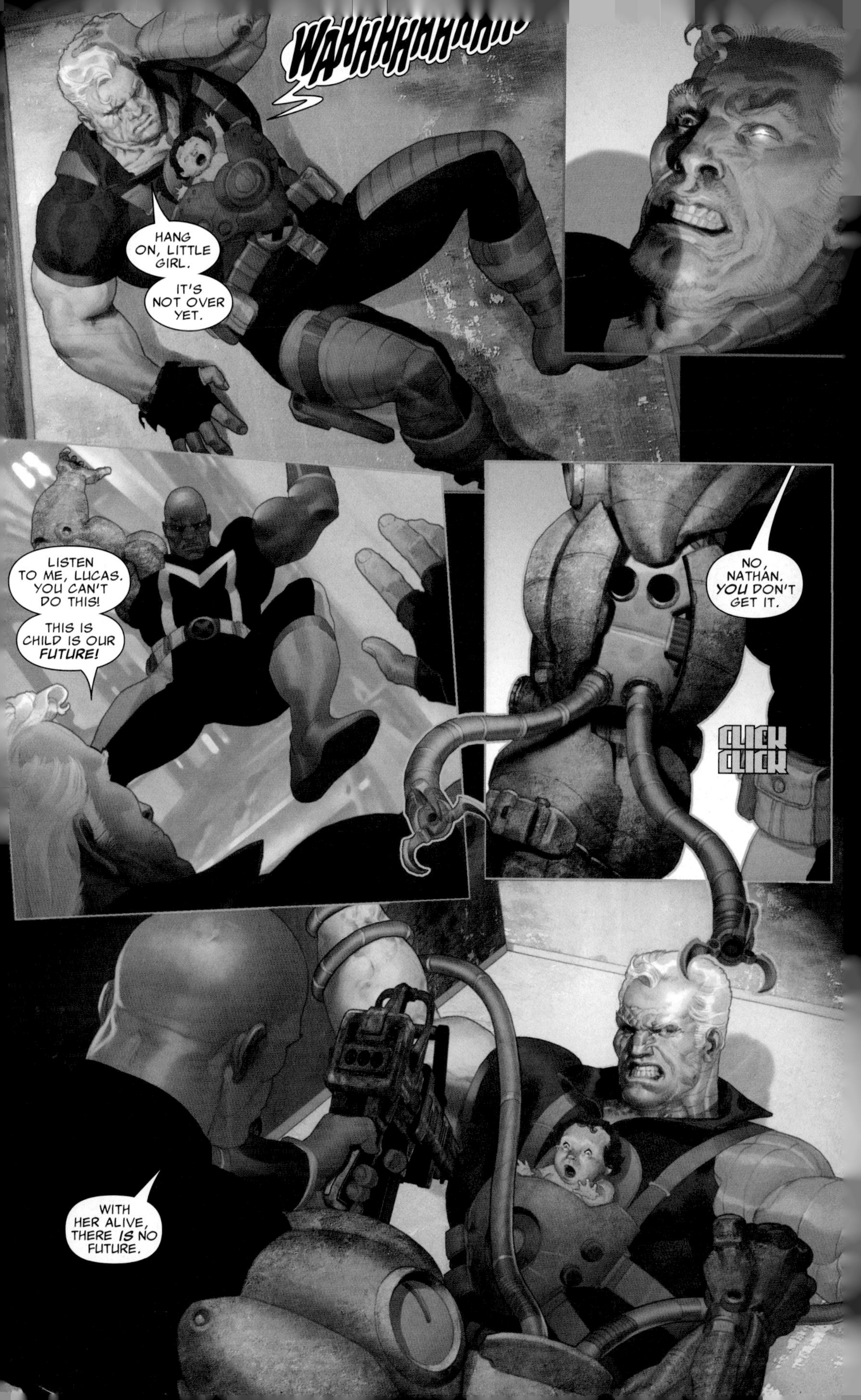
WAHHHHHHHH
HANG ON, LITTLE GIRL.
IT'S NOT OVER YET.
LISTEN TO ME, LUCAS. YOU CAN'T DO THIS!
THIS IS CHILD IS OUR *FUTURE!*
NO, NATHAN. *YOU* DON'T GET IT.
CLICK CLICK
WITH HER ALIVE, THERE *IS* NO FUTURE.

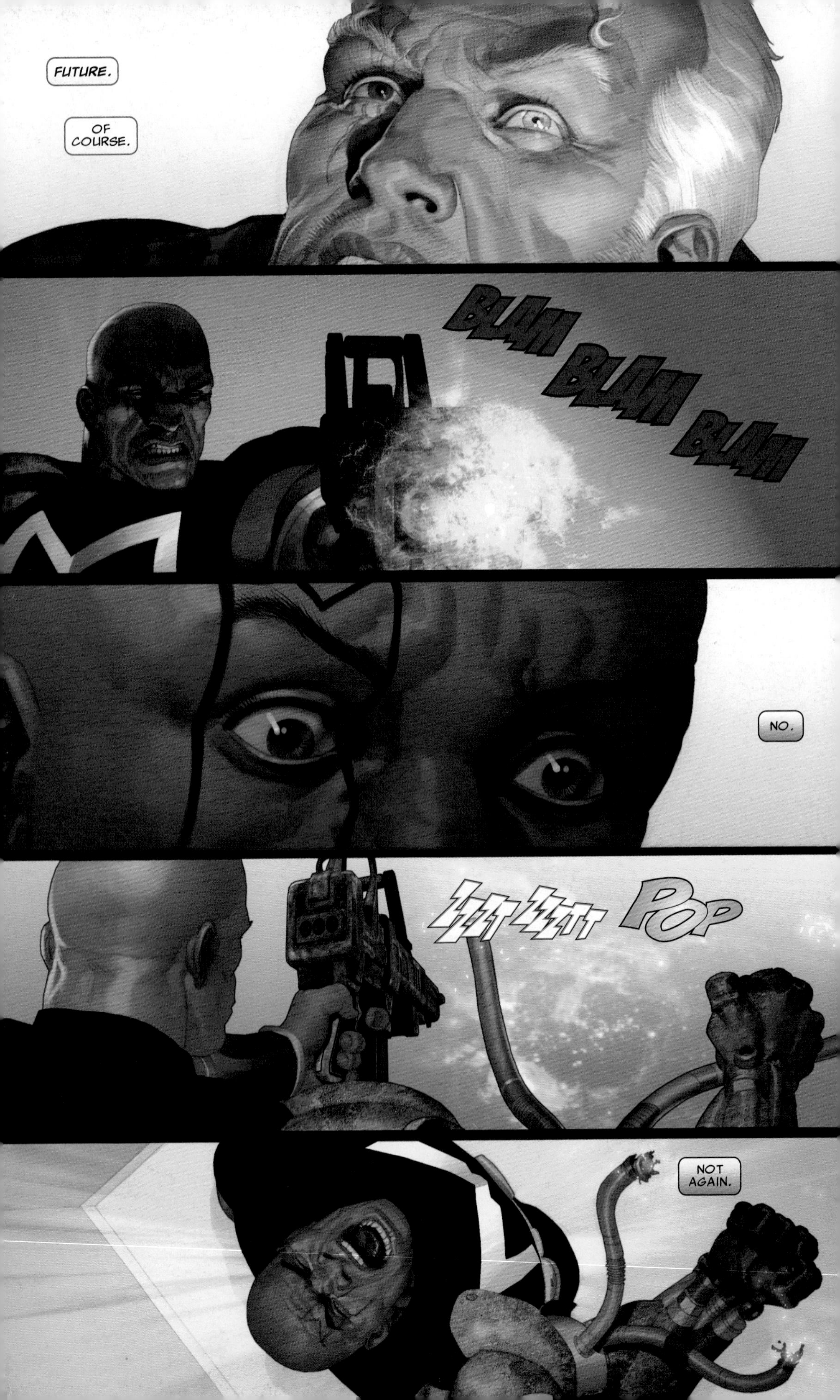
FUTURE.
OF COURSE.
BLAM BLAM BLAM
NO.
ZZZT ZZZTT POP
NOT AGAIN.

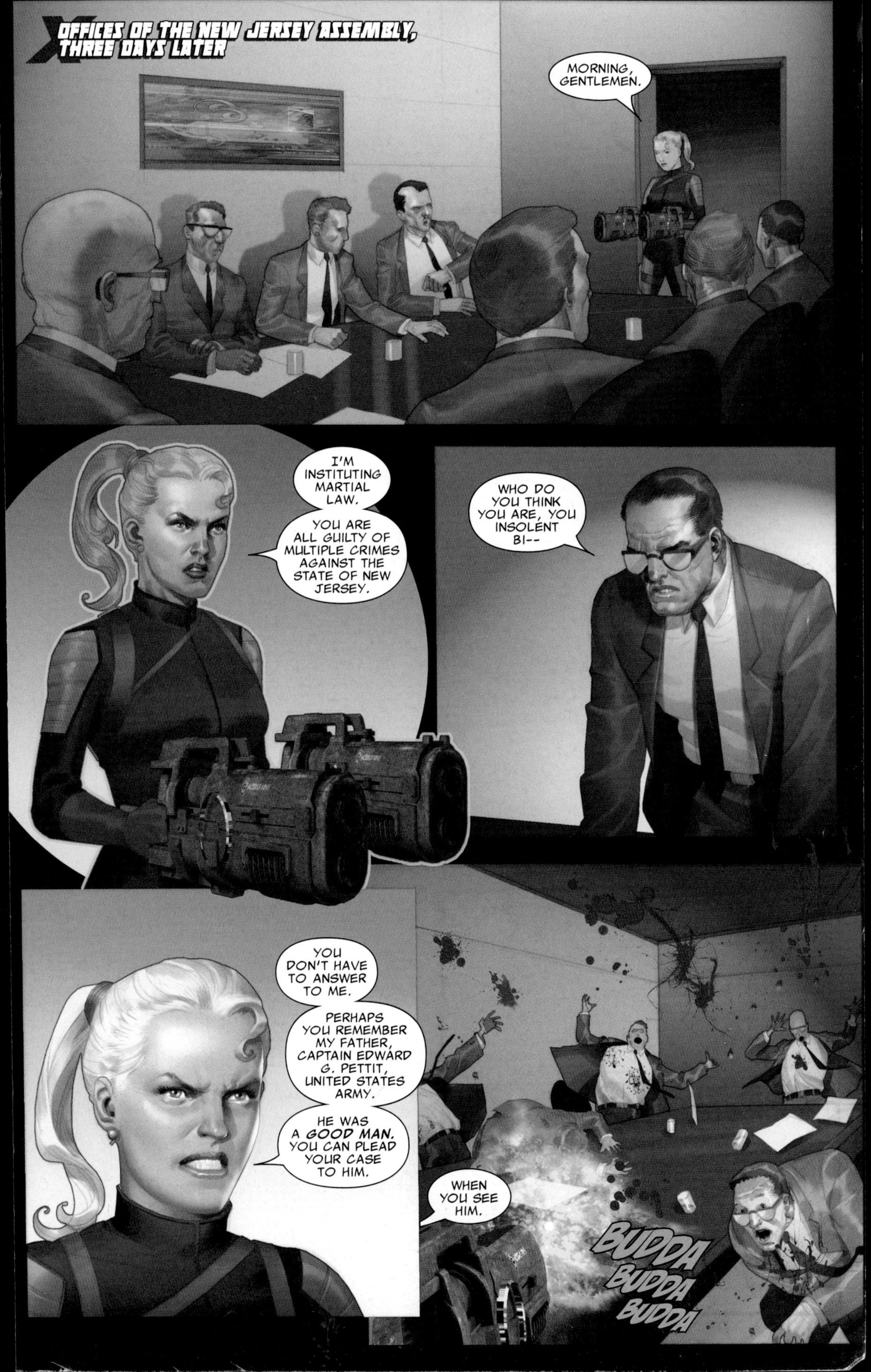
OFFICES OF THE NEW JERSEY ASSEMBLY, THREE DAYS LATER
MORNING, GENTLEMEN.
I'M INSTITUTING MARTIAL LAW.
YOU ARE ALL GUILTY OF MULTIPLE CRIMES AGAINST THE STATE OF NEW JERSEY.
WHO DO YOU THINK YOU ARE, YOU INSOLENT BI--
YOU DON'T HAVE TO ANSWER TO ME.
PERHAPS YOU REMEMBER MY FATHER, CAPTAIN EDWARD G. PETTIT, UNITED STATES ARMY.
HE WAS A ***GOOD MAN.*** YOU CAN PLEAD YOUR CASE TO HIM.
WHEN YOU SEE HIM.
BUDDA BUDDA BUDDA

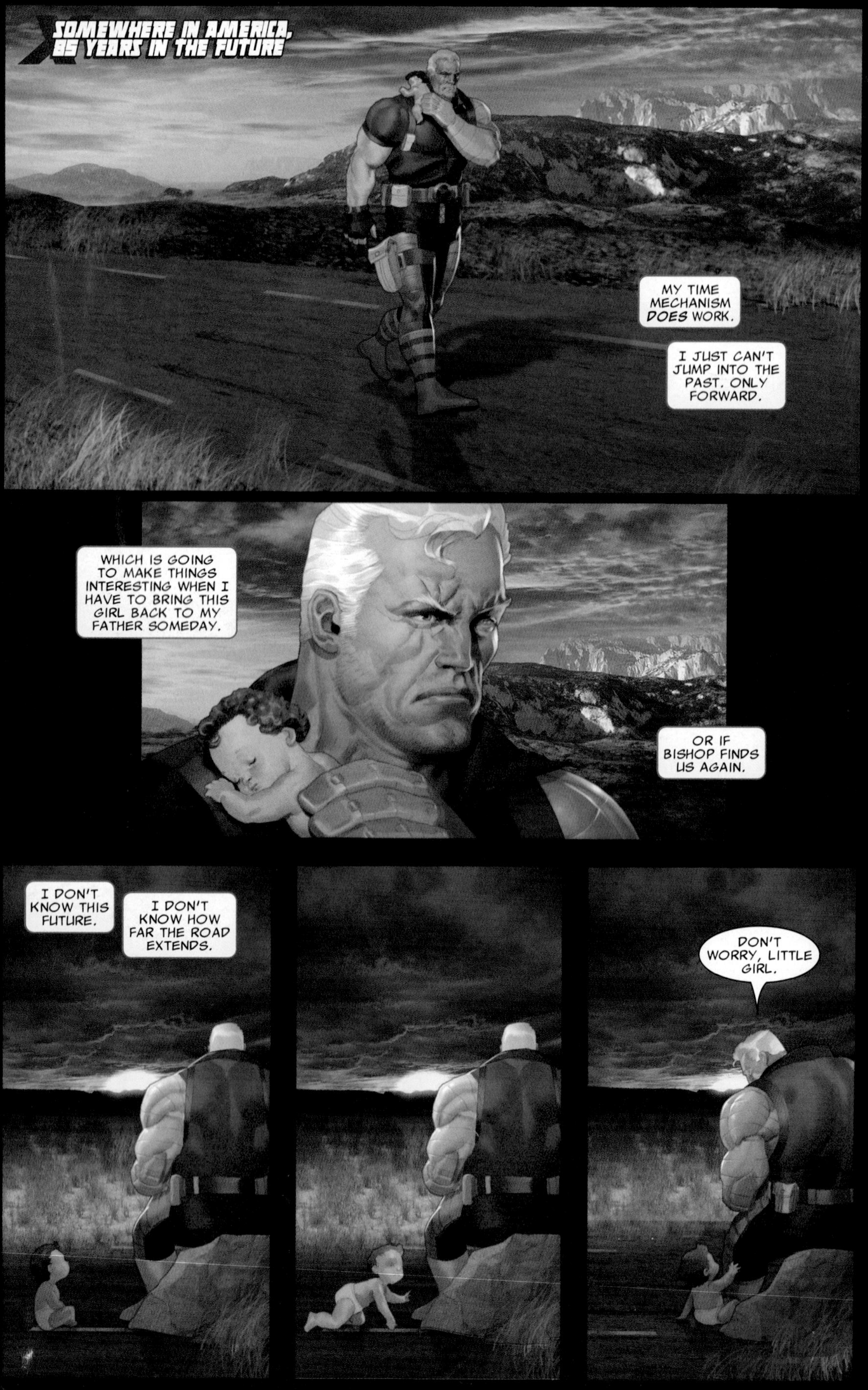
SOMEWHERE IN AMERICA, 85 YEARS IN THE FUTURE
MY TIME MECHANISM DOES WORK.
I JUST CAN'T JUMP INTO THE PAST. ONLY FORWARD.
WHICH IS GOING TO MAKE THINGS INTERESTING WHEN I HAVE TO BRING THIS GIRL BACK TO MY FATHER SOMEDAY.
OR IF BISHOP FINDS US AGAIN.
I DON'T KNOW THIS FUTURE.
I DON'T KNOW HOW FAR THE ROAD EXTENDS.
DON'T WORRY, LITTLE GIRL.

I'M A SOLDIER.
I'M TRAINED FOR EVERYTHING.
MAYBE EVEN THIS.
ARIEL OLIVETTI
NEXT: HOMEFRONT

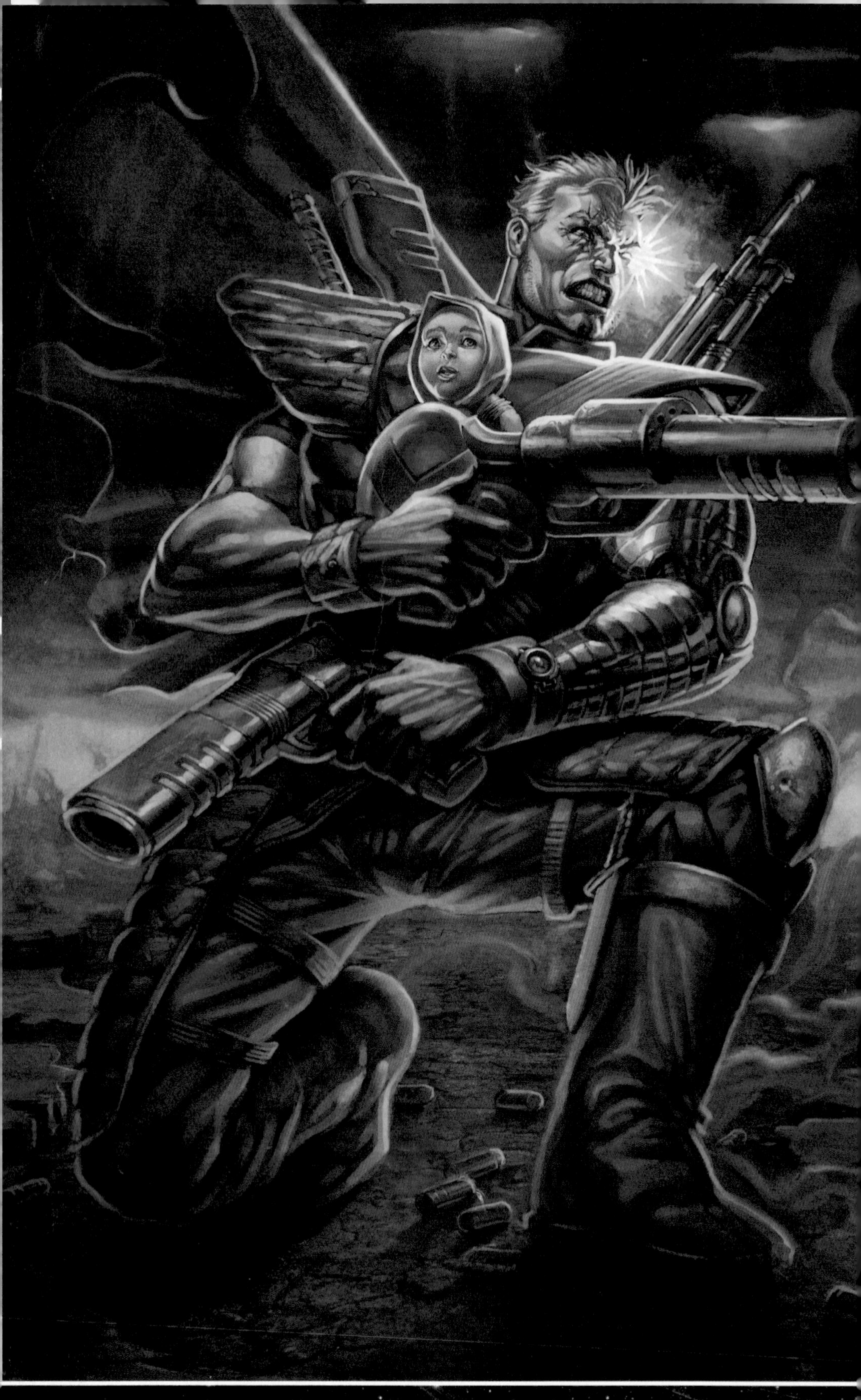

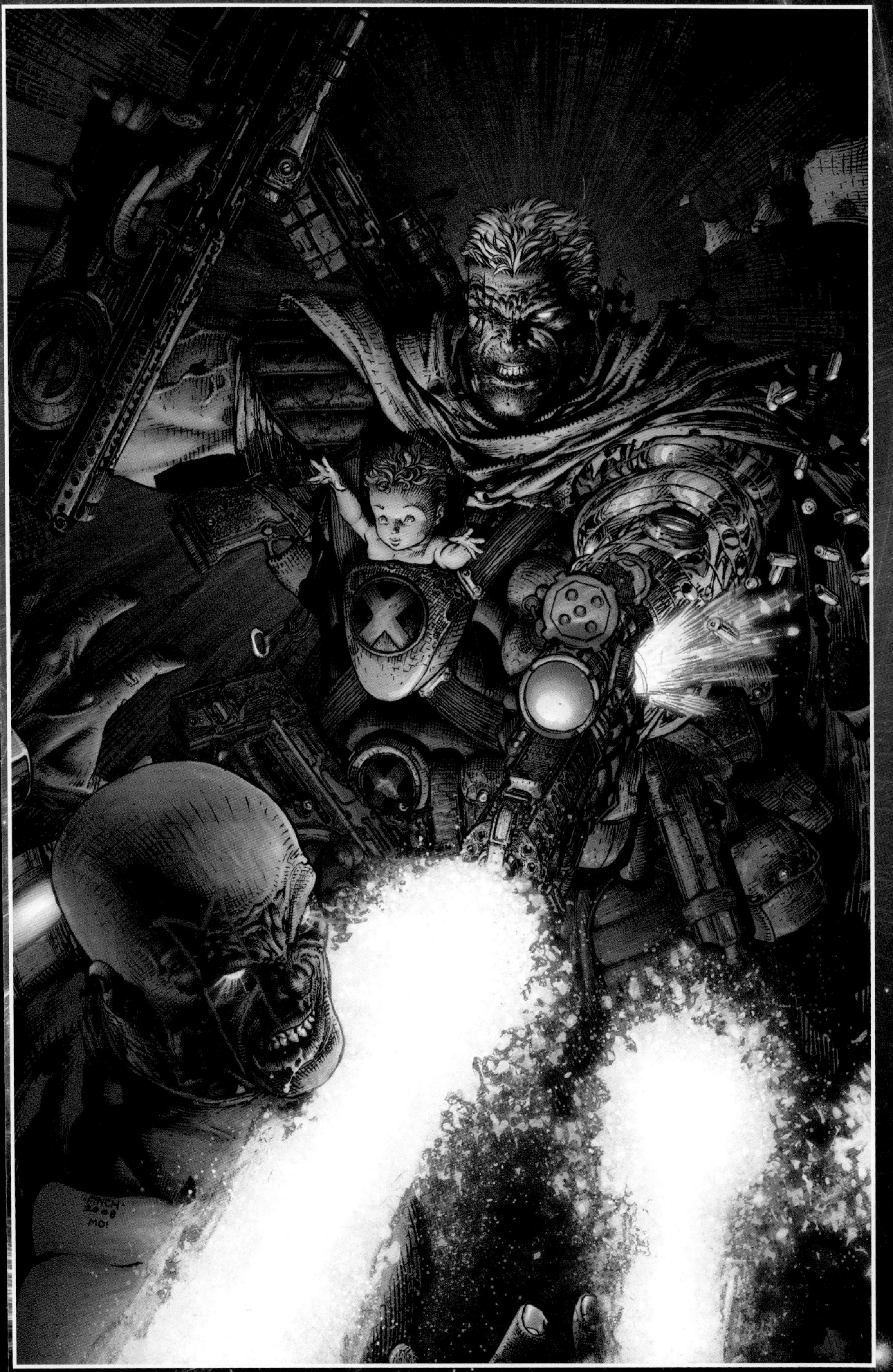
FINCH
2008
MO!

#2 VARIANT BY DAVID FINCH AND MORRY HOLLOWELL

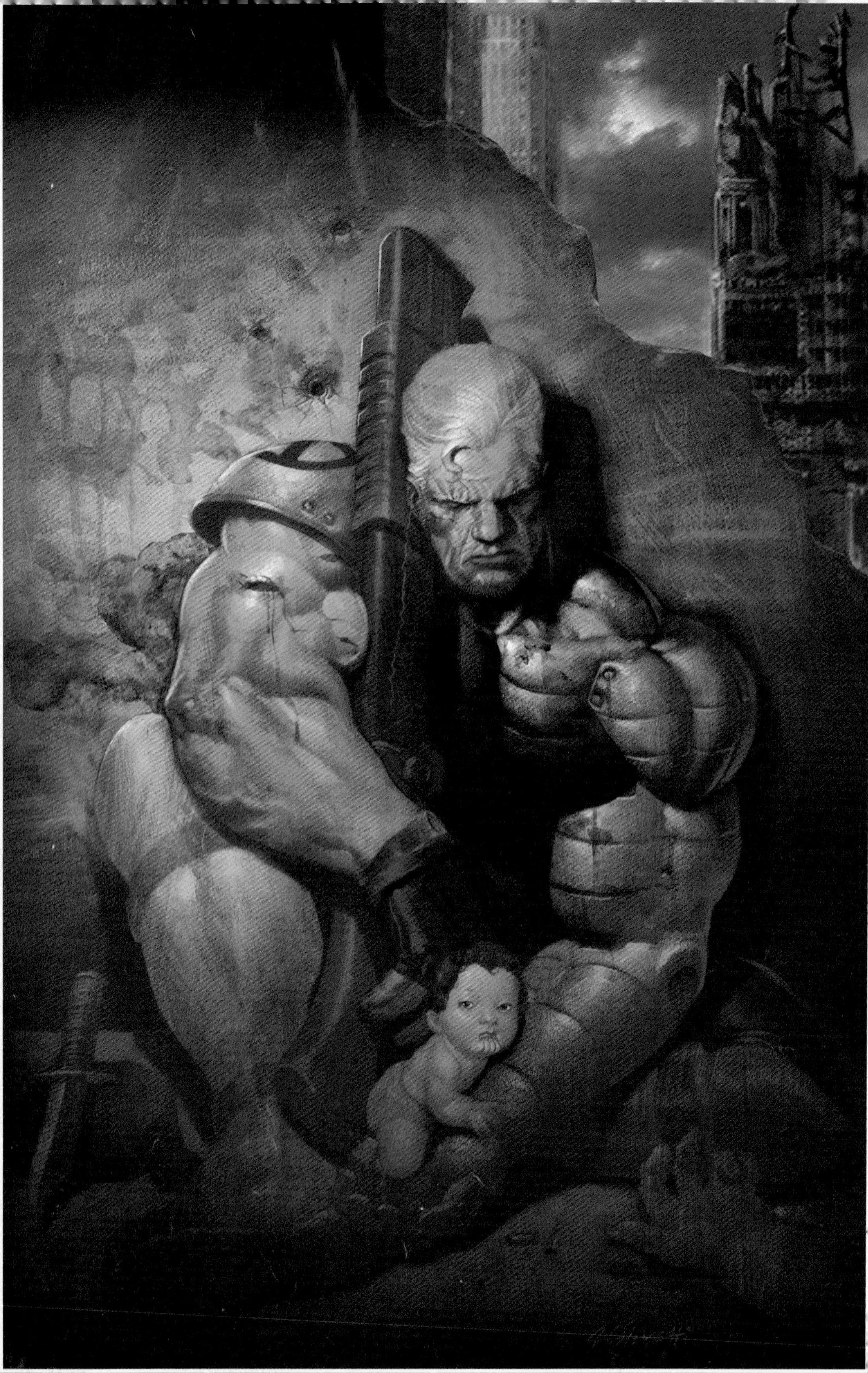

#3 SKRULLY VARIANT BY ARIEL OLIVETTI

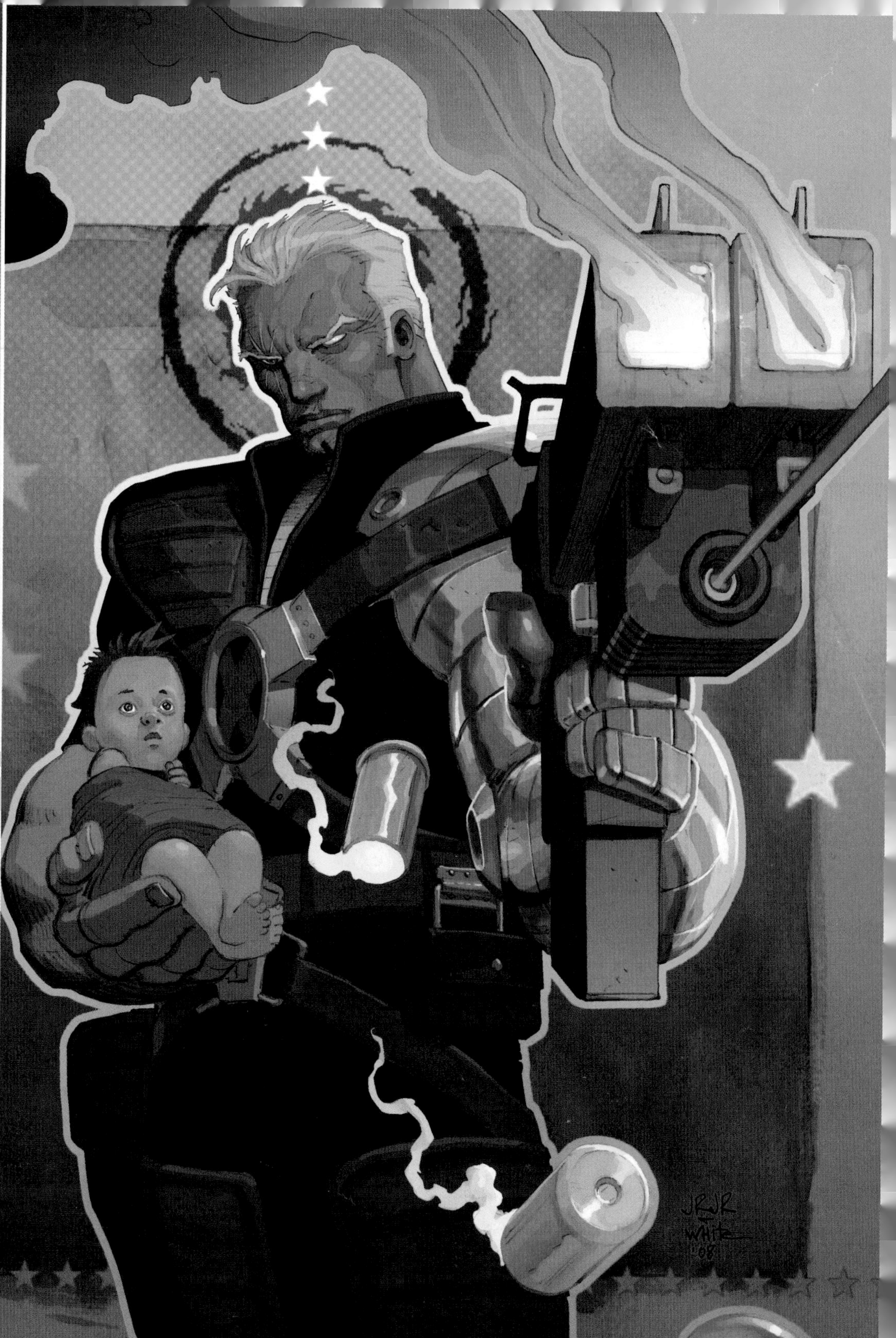
JRJR
WHITE
'08

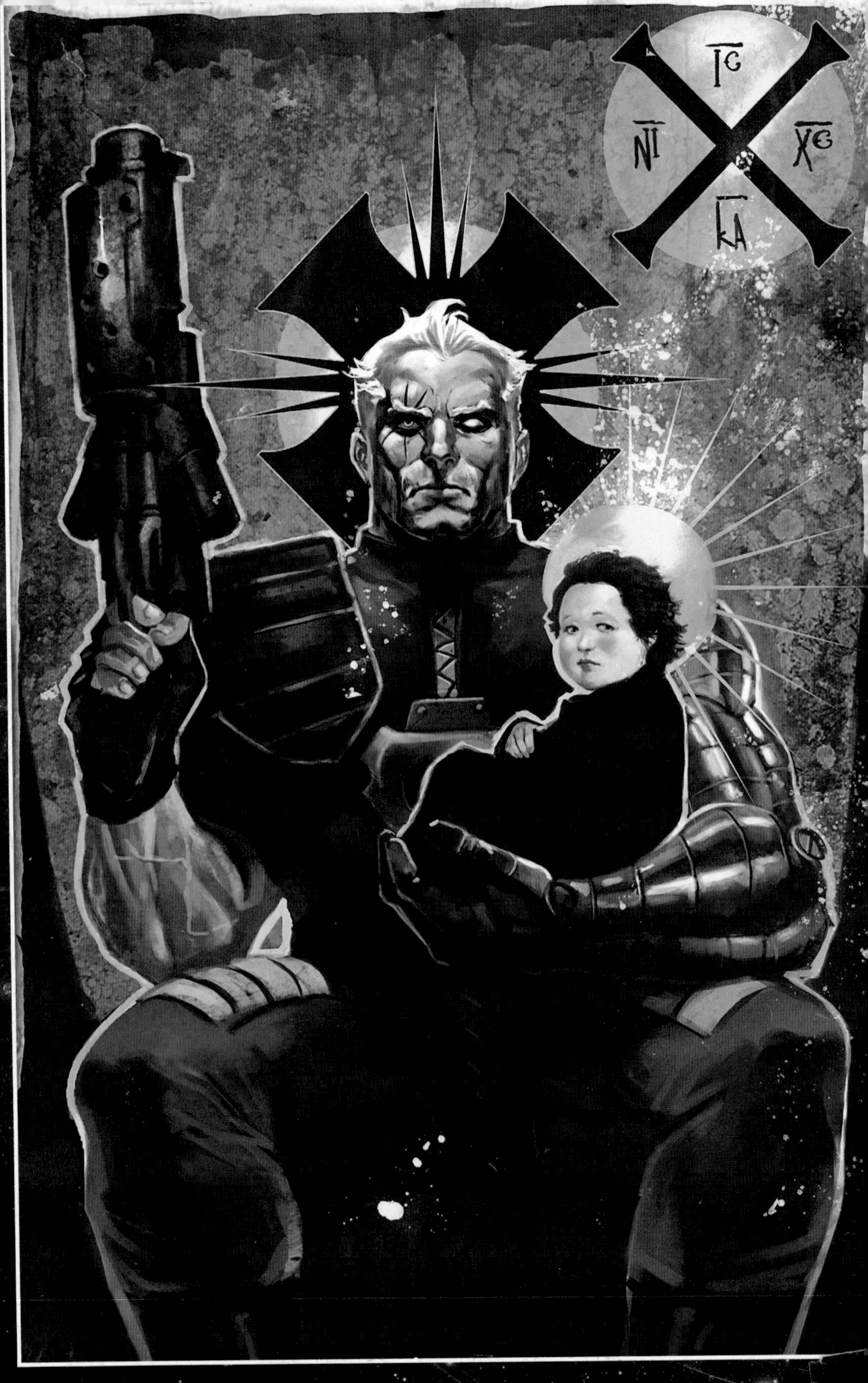
IC
NI
XC
KA

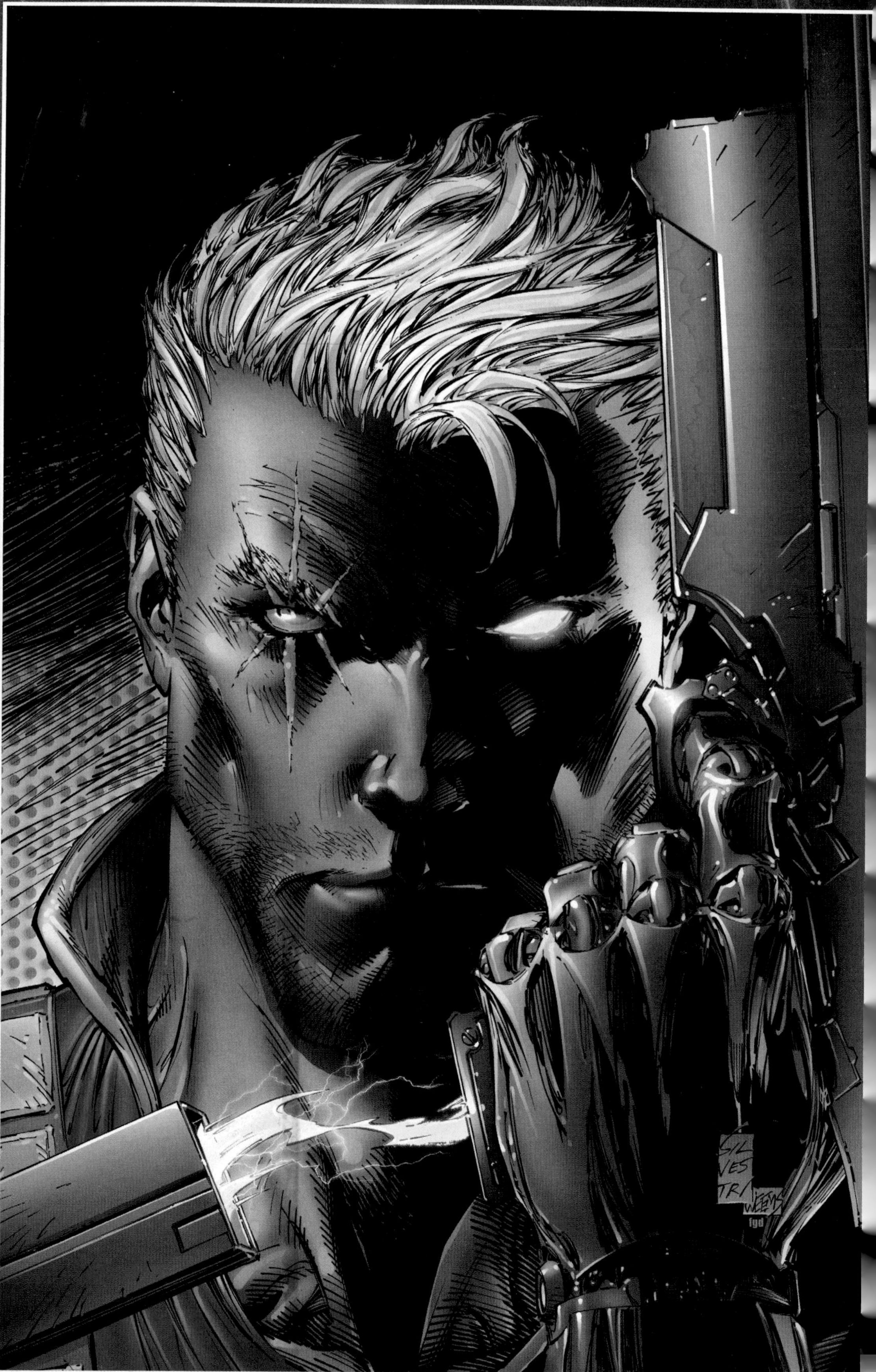
SILVESTRI
WEEMS
fgd

#5 VARIANT BY MARC SILVESTRI AND FRANK D'ARMATA

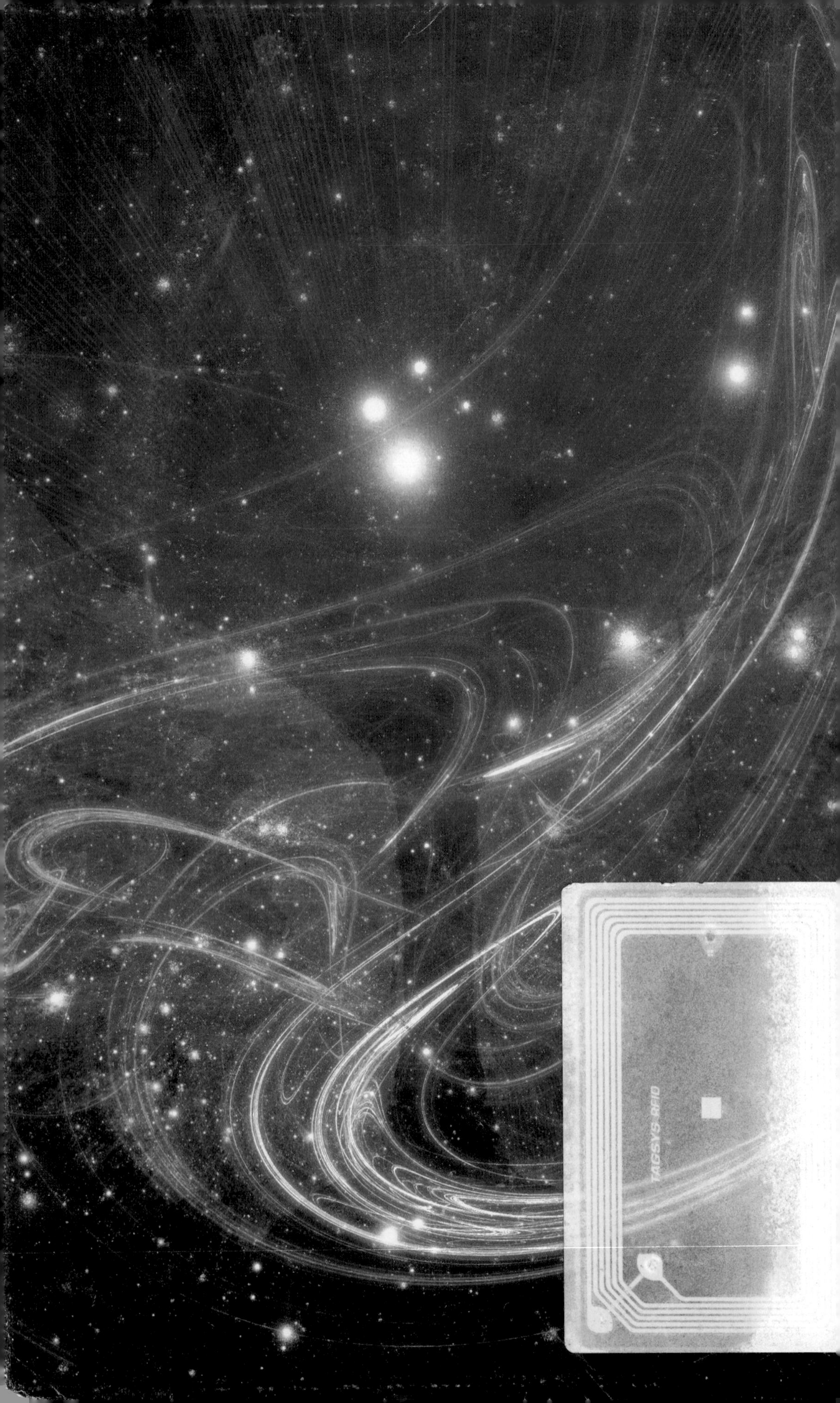